The Ashio Riot of 1907

A BOOK IN THE SERIES

Comparative and International

Working-Class History

General Editors:

Andrew Gordon / Harvard University

Daniel James / Duke University

Alexander Keyssar / Duke University

The Ashio Riot of 1907

A Social History of Mining in Japan

Nimura Kazuo

Edited by Andrew Gordon

Translated by Terry Boardman and Andrew Gordon

Duke University Press   Durham & London

1997

Designed by Cherie Westmoreland Typeset in Plantin Light
with Optima display by Keystone Typesetting, Inc.
Library of Congress Cataloging-in-Publication Data
appear on the last printed page of this book.

The costs of the publication of this book have been
supported in part by a 1994 Hiromi Arisawa Award, given
to Duke University Press for publication of an
outstanding work on Japan.

The translation costs of this book were subsidized
by a 1996 grant-in-aid for Publication of Scientific Research
Results, under the grant-in-aid program for scientific
research of the Ministry of Education, Science,
Sports and Culture of Japan.

FOR MISAKO, YOKO, KOICHI

Contents

List of Figures and Tables

Editor's Preface

This book is at once a study of a riot at a copper mine in 1907 and a powerful critique of the way labor economics and social history have been practiced in postwar Japan. As I read him, Nimura Kazuo pursues three fundamental goals in these pages.[1] The first is to explain why the workers at the Ashio copper mine, Japan's largest and one of the largest in the world, joined together in three days of unprecedented riot in February 1907. The second is to frame the events of these several days as a window through which to analyze the social, economic, and political structure of early industrial Japan. Third, and perhaps most important to the author, the study of the Ashio riot is used to launch a sharp critique of the dominant models of social scientific analysis in the postwar academic world in Japan. The book thus works on several different levels, implicitly and at times explicitly offering comparative insights and arguments. This gives it a claim on the attention of an audience outside the Japanese-speaking world and leads us to include it in this series.

In his introduction, Nimura discusses these goals at some length. To clarify his intentions and the significance of his argument for English-speaking readers with little background in Japanese history or familiarity with social science in Japan, he has revised the introduction and the prologue substantially for this translation. He has also added an epilogue that develops his comparative analysis at greater length. In this preface, let me comment briefly on the significance of this book from the perspective of a long-time student of Nimura's work and those whom he criticizes.

In his study of the Ashio riot, Nimura is setting himself against patterns of historical understanding that dominated Japanese intellectual life from the 1930s through the 1960s and remain significant to this day. Throughout the book, he attacks simplistic but deeply rooted views of the preindustrial past and its relevance to the rise of industrial capitalism. This clash plays out differently in the two major sections of the book. In his critique of the "atomized worker thesis" in chapter 1, he challenges improperly dismissive views of the preindustrial past. In taking on the "migrant labor thesis" in chapter 2, he attacks a theoretical framework that was excessively attentive to this past and excessively negative in assessing it.

By improperly dismissive, I mean a view of capitalism (or its elusive sibling, modernization) that exaggerates its power to obliterate all that came before and thus dismisses the possibility that industrial workers could draw on social or cultural resources rooted in past experience. Maruyama Masao described mine workers, and more generally the masses in the industrial revolution, as "atomized," as individuals whose older communities had been destroyed by what he and others called modernization. Nimura takes issue with this understanding. While Maruyama's analysis runs parallel to a Marxian approach that sees capitalism as a revolutionary force dissolving all previous social forms, Maruyama himself was not a Marxist scholar. Nimura is thus critiquing a dismissive approach common to a wide range of postwar scholars.

By excessively attentive and negative, I mean the even more numerous Japanese analyses that do find continuity with the preindustrial past, but locate this in "feudal" structures that purportedly survived to define a peculiar and distorted Japanese brand of capitalism. This negative view was essential to Yamada Moritarō's analysis of Japanese capitalism before World War II, described in Nimura's introduction as the fundamental target of his critique. It was likewise at the heart of Ōkōchi Kazuo's "migrant worker theory." Ōkōchi's elegant and long-dominant analysis explains the behavior of workers and of labor unions in terms of unchanging, premodern structural features of the labor market in twentieth-century Japan.

In contrast to dismissive or negative analyses of the early industrial era and its own historical antecedents, Nimura's study first of all demolishes the notion that the mine workers at Ashio (and by implication those elsewhere) were anomic or atomized men, possessing no community or coherent social order, acting in desperation, and exploding "spontaneously" without goals or understanding. He then offers an alternative view by describing continuity in social institutions and values that were "positive," in the sense that they enabled action rather than impeded it.

A third contribution of this history of the Ashio mine is a product of Nimura's method of dispute-centered analysis that investigates nearly every dimension of the riot. This book offers unusually balanced attention to matters of technology, work process, managerial and state strategy, and labor organization and activism. In Japan and elsewhere, histories of business management, technology, and labor far too often pursue their inquiries along separate tracks with inadequate attention to each other. This study is a model of a work that covers all three of these areas and clarifies the connections among them.

I expect that the first two of these three contributions will seem unexceptional, if not by now outdated, to many English-language readers familiar with what is now the rather old "new social history" reaching back to the 1960s. The fact that Nimura's contributions stand out in Japan shows the extent to which the Japanese intellectual world did not participate in this same turn. Because Nimura's work appeared in book form only in 1988, it is tempting to see it as an effort finally to introduce the methods and perspectives of the "new labor history" of E. P. Thompson, Herbert Gutman, David Brody, David Montgomery, and others to the Japanese academic world. And it is certain that Nimura read these works and was influenced by them as he undertook his own research and writing.

But it would be wrong to characterize this book as primarily a follower of Western scholarly trends. Nimura's study should be placed chronologically and conceptually parallel to these others. The study of the migrant labor thesis (chapter 2 of this book) was conceived and written in the 1950s as a critique from a student working within the mainstream of Japanese economic and historical studies. It was originally published in article form in 1959. Nimura's subsequent understanding of Ashio, as he expanded his focus and deepened his research, and then pulled it together into this book in the 1980s, was then informed in part by new trends in British and American historical studies.

The chief methodological innovation of the book, discussed at length in the author's introduction, is the idea of a dispute-centered study. This approach also might appear to be a response to the popularity among Euro-American scholars of microstudies of workers and strikes in particular communities. But again, Nimura's call for such an approach came out of his 1950s experience in studying Ashio. He anticipated the trend that emerged in the late 1960s and after in the United States in which young scholars look at the "workers of wherever" centered on a famous dispute in "wherever."

The value of a microstudy of a dispute such as the Ashio riot should become clear in the pages that follow. In addition, many younger scholars in Japan took Nimura's advice and focused their research on disputes at particular factories. In the 1970s, this work focused mainly on labor in the early twentieth century.[2] More recent work has examined the many fierce disputes of the early postwar era.[3]

This translation contains chapters 1 and 2 of the Japanese-language study of the Ashio riot, plus the conclusion. It also includes a revised introduction and prologue, and a new epilogue offering some comparative observations.

It does not include chapter 3. As the author notes in his introduction, that chapter tries to answer two riddles: Why were the highest paid workers at Ashio—the ore diggers—central figures in the riot? and Why were the copper refinery workers, whose earnings had fallen drastically in the years previous to the riot, not involved?

We decided to omit this chapter for several reasons. To explain the non-participation of the smelters, in particular, Nimura discovered he needed to undertake a detailed investigation of the changing refining technology, as well as the company's wage and personnel management policies. The discussion is necessarily quite detailed and technical and makes difficult going. Also, it is not framed as an argument against a prevailing interpretation, as are the other chapters. Rather, the author retraces his somewhat circuitous journey of questioning and discovery as he tries to figure out why the smelters had not played a more significant role in the 1907 riots. While this has the appeal of re-creating for the reader the historian's own intellectual journey, and is for this reason actually the author's favorite section of the book, it also makes the gist of the chapter a good bit harder to grasp than the others. Nimura and I agreed that the first two chapters stood on their own and reinforced each other, and that without substantial reorganizing, the third chapter would not have the same clarity or impact. We thus reluctantly decided to omit it.

Here let me summarize its argument. Nimura first shows that the smelters were relatively highly paid at Ashio in the 1870s and 1880s. Indeed, their wages were far higher than those of the ore diggers. But with their defeat in a strike in 1888, launched in opposition to the introduction of new furnace equipment, their wages fell dramatically, for the new furnace equipment required less-skilled labor. One reason the company could prevail in this strike was that it had already begun to cultivate a group of semiskilled, company-trained refinery workers to replace the skilled smelters who went on strike. Thus, in 1907 the wages of the new, less-skilled smelters were considerably lower than other mine workers. At the same time, they were more dependent on the company than the better paid ore diggers, which inhibited them from joining the riot. Ashio's competitors had not yet introduced this new equipment to the same extent, so the Ashio smelters could not hope to find jobs at other refineries.

In this fashion, chapter 3 sheds light on a complex process in which traditional artisanal skills were destroyed, and it explains the different behavior of two groups of miners as a result of this change. In addition, the chapter addresses the changing management style of the mine, comparing the approach of the mine's founder, Furukawa Ichibei, to that of his son, Junkichi. Nimura argues that the riot would not have taken place without the change from a relatively loose management style, in an era of high profits that enabled payment of relatively generous wages, to a much leaner style by the early twentieth century.

If we have omitted this chapter in part because it is extremely detailed and technical, readers should not expect the chapters that do follow to be mainly abstract sketches devoid of specifics. To the contrary, one further goal of the author in both remaining chapters of the book is to show readers that it is indeed possible for historians of Japan to re-create in vivid detail the world of people often called "nameless" and lumped together as a mass. His intent first became clear to me when I suggested we omit many personal names from the narrative in the interest of greater readability. I argued that the many names would be hard for non-Japanese speakers to keep straight, and that many of the individuals make only brief appearances in any case (some of these have, indeed, been omitted). But the author responded, "I put in names wherever I could find them for a reason. I thought this would help show that the managers and lodge bosses, and especially the rioters or miners, were people with names, life histories, and personalities, not an atomized mass."

I know of few works in any language that have excavated an elusive set of documents so thoroughly and succeeded in this goal so fully.

I wish to thank Terry Boardman for his excellent work in translating the first draft of this book. His painstaking efforts made my job as translator and editor quite painless. Nimura Kazuo offered patient and careful advice throughout the long process of preparing this translation for publication. I have learned much from observing his uncompromising determination to understand every relevant aspect of the Ashio story before proceeding to publish either the original Japanese version or this translation. I am also deeply grateful for his support, guidance, and friendship over the twenty years of our acquaintance.

Acknowledgments

I must first offer my heartfelt thanks to Terry Boardman and Andrew Gordon for making this book available to readers in the English-speaking world. Although my own Japanese style may be relatively clear, the numerous lengthy citations in this book include obscure slang expressions peculiar to the Japanese mining industry of a century ago, the technical mining vocabulary of another era, and the specialized terminology of prewar police and trial proceedings. I can scarcely imagine how difficult it must have been to render this into English. In particular, when one writes Japanese names in nonphonetic Japanese characters, one does not have to determine the correct pronunciation; however, to render these names in a phonetic alphabet such as English, one must know the pronunciation. It may be difficult for readers to believe this, but the English edition of this book is far easier to read than the Japanese version. This book is certainly not the sole creation of the author. It is the fruit of a joint effort with these two friends, whom I have known for twenty years.

In writing the Japanese edition I also had the generous support of many people. I owe a particular debt to the eminent historian of ancient Japan, Ishimoda Sho. Ishimoda not only awakened my interest in historical studies, he also helped me resolve to become a professional historian. In addition, I have benefited from many years of support from my teachers and colleagues in Hosei University, in particular at the Ohara Institute of Social Research. I am especially grateful for the six-month research leave they granted me in order to complete the first chapter of this book. The Center for Japanese Studies of the Institute of East Asian Studies, at the University of California, Berkeley, provided the perfect environment in which to spend this period of leave. I wish to thank Robert Scalapino, then the director of the Institute of East Asian Studies, Irwin Scheiner, director of the Center for Japanese Studies, and Eugenie T. Bruck, also at the Center for Japanese Studies. For helping to arrange my affiliation at the center, I am deeply grateful as well to Thomas C. Smith and his wife, Jeanne. During my stay I was fortunate to have numerous chances to exchange opinions with Thomas Smith, and he taught me a tremendous amount.

In pulling together the arguments in this book, I was greatly helped by the critiques and encouragement offered by members of the Association for Labor History Research, the Labor Issues Research Association, the Metal Mining Research Association, and the Japan Mining History Research Association. The former Ashio Mine technician and historian of Japanese mining, Murakami Yasumasa, played a special role from the time I was a student, guiding me expertly through the Ashio mine's tunnels and patiently explaining the details of mining technology. I will never forget the times he led me crawling through the narrow mine tunnels dating back to the eighteenth century, or the time I desperately followed him as we clambered up a straight vertical ladder deep in the mine, his dim lantern swaying in his hand.

Finally, I offer grateful appreciation to the numerous librarians and archivists at the following institutions, whose knowledge and kindness gave me access to so many books and documents as I pursued this research: the Meiji Period Newspaper Archive of the Tokyo University Law Faculty, the library of the Tokyo University Engineering Faculty's Metal Engineering and Resource Development divisions, the National Diet Library, the Tochigi Prefectural Library, the Hosei Univeristy Library. I am particularly indebted to Nishida Taketoshi of the Meiji Period Newspaper Archive for his help nearly forty years ago. In later years, when I undertook the work of cataloging and reprinting the materials held by the Ohara Institute for Social Research, I was inspired by his steady, quiet, and powerful efforts. The Japanese scholarly world has an international reputation for undervaluing archivists and librarians, but we must never forget the contributions of Nishida Taketoshi and the Meiji Period Newspaper Archive to research in modern Japanese history.

NIMURA KAZUO

Author's Introduction to the English Edition

This book is a case study of the uprising that occurred in February 1907 at Japan's largest copper mine, the Ashio copper mine. The Japanese edition consisted of three chapters and included the introduction and conclusion. For the English-language edition, however, for space and other considerations, chapter 3 has been eliminated.

When I wrote the Japanese edition, I did not anticipate an audience of readers outside Japan, or indeed outside the realm of Japanese specialists in modern Japanese history. As a result, the explanations in an unamended English translation would have been insufficient in many places. Further, I discussed debates within the Japanese scholarly world that would probably be of little interest to general readers. To address the former problem, I have supplemented the text or the notes where it seemed necessary, and I have rewritten this introduction and the prologue with non-Japanese readers in mind. Addressing the latter issue, I have asked the translators to eliminate passages that they judge to be of little interest to those who are not specialists on Japanese labor history. In addition, I have added an epilogue that reflects on the comparative study of mine labor and examines the history of Japanese labor in comparative perspective, drawing on the Ashio story but going beyond it as well.

The chapters are based on papers published at different times. Chapter 1 is actually the more recent, published in 1985. It speaks of the movements of the laborers before the riots and the development of the riots themselves, and as my latest writing it contains the broadest view of the research, so it seems appropriate to place it first. Its primary theme is a critique of the "spontaneous resistance" theory that had long dominated study of mining riots and Japanese social history more generally. I particularly take issue with the idea that the riots were "explosions of accumulated discontent from hopeless and atomized laborers," as articulated by the distinguished intellectual historian Maruyama Masao in his version of the "spontaneous resistance" theory. I do this by clarifying the active role played by the *tomoko dōmei,* here translated as "brotherhood," an autonomous trade organization that emerged among metal mining workers in the Tokugawa era (1603–1867).

To be honest, I had second thoughts about making Maruyama the target of criticism here. Unlike Ōkōchi Kazuo, with whom I take issue in the following chapter, Maruyama is a historian of political thought, not a labor historian. The argument I criticize is not based on any in-depth study of the Ashio incident. He was trying "to examine the influence modernization has on the members of a society with a view to showing the forms of reaction possible on the level of the attitude of the individual, rather than on the level of the socio-political system or ideas proper."[1] He presents Ashio only as one example. But Maruyama's conceptual framework constitutes a very interesting attempt to categorize individual attitudes in the process of social modernization with an eye toward enabling international comparisons. Also, he presents a crystal-clear interpretation of the Ashio incident, however brief it may be. Many other historians and social scientists have mentioned the Ashio riot as part of a broader argument about modern Japanese social or political history, with a perspective similar to Maruyama's, but none of these arguments are as clearly or elegantly conceived. For these reasons it is meaningful to examine how closely the facts of the case correspond to Maruyama's understanding, especially when considering whether it is possible to use a concept such as modernization in international comparison. The intent of this book is not simply to dissect the Ashio incident, but, through the analysis of the conflict to comprehend the character of Japanese society and especially of Japanese labor relations. In that sense, I hope the critique of Maruyama in chapter 1 has a positive meaning.

In chapter 2 I take up the *dekasegi-gata* (migrant labor pattern) theory of Ōkōchi Kazuo. First articulated in 1950, the theory was very influential in the decade that followed. I originally published the essay that is the basis for this chapter in 1959, calling it "The Fundamental Process of the Ashio Uprising: A Critique of the Migrant Labor Theory." The chief goal of chapter 2 is thus to critique Ōkōchi's theory, which exerted such a profound impact on Japanese labor studies. The core is a discussion of the history of the *hanba* (lodge) system run by mine labor bosses. I will not introduce the details here, except to note that the chapter makes it clear that technological development willy-nilly transformed various social relationships, especially labor-management relations, and that the logic of Ōkōchi's migrant labor theory, which assumed the stubborn continuity of premodern social relations, left no room to acknowledge these changes.

Chapter 3, omitted from this translation, was originally published as a series of journal articles between 1981 and 1984. It touches on myriad problems, but chiefly examines the following two mysteries. First, the ore diggers were the most skilled group at Ashio, and they worked shorter hours and received higher wages compared to other categories of Ashio workers, and compared to miners at other sites and to workers in other industries. Why were they the central participants in the riots? Second, the copper mine's refinery workers had received relatively high wages compared to the miners in the 1880s, but had suffered a sharp relative decline since then. Why did they not join the protests? To unravel these riddles, I put much effort into examining long-term changes in wage levels at the Ashio copper mine for those two categories of labor in particular, and I sought to explain the changes that occurred between the 1880s and the early 1900s. I discovered that changes in the labor supply-and-demand relationship basically accounted for the shift in wage levels, and I found it necessary to analyze the quantitative and qualitative shifts in the labor force. A discussion of the development of mining technology was indispensable in this effort, so the chapter included a rather extensive history of mining and refining technology.

While writing this book, my one constant goal was to examine and critique the premises of the "lecture school" (kōza-ha) of Japanese Marxism.[2] In the early postwar era, the lecture school analysis exerted an overwhelming influence on research in Japanese social science, in particular modern Japanese history. One of the most important and representative works of this school was Yamada Moritarō's *Analysis of Japanese Capitalism,* written in the 1930s.[3] Yamada's work emphasizes the premodern character of Japanese society, particularly the stubborn persistence of a "semifeudal system." He stresses the continued existence of premodern systems of land ownership and boss systems in factories and mines, pointing to these as strong evidence of the premodern character of Japanese society and economy. He therefore emphasizes that the Meiji Restoration (1868), conceived as a potential bourgeois democratic revolution, was a very incomplete one.

The kōza-school Marxism took it as a basic premise that Japanese workers received "structurally low wages," a belief that maintained an overwhelming influence in the study of Japanese labor problems through the 1960s. To quote directly from the slightly stiff and opaque language of Yamada's *Analysis,* "an absolute condition for the prosperity of Japanese capitalism" was "the mutually regulating relationship between semi-serf tenant rents and semi-slave wages." That is, the high rents demanded of tenant farmers by the "parasitic landowner system" required that families send out their sons and daughters as low-wage laborers to maintain the family. For this reason a relationship developed whereby "higher tenant rents became possible as supplemental wages became available, and, conversely, since the wages were supplemental to farming income, they could be kept at a low level," and this became the "foundation for the existence of Japanese capitalism." This interpretation presented a remarkably clear explanation of the rapid development of pre–World War II Japanese capitalism on the one hand, and the simultaneous poverty of the common people on the other, and many people found it convincing. I myself was greatly influenced by Yamada's *Analysis* during my apprenticeship as a student. I chose mine labor as a research topic in part because I believed that mines, with their restrictive lodge system and use of prison labor, were both sources of the "supplemental family income" that reinforced the landlord system and classic sites of the "semifeudal" relations that sustained the system of low wages for Japanese laborers. However, when I actually began to study the labor history of mines, I came to feel that the rigid structural framework of Yamada's *Analysis* overlooked historical change and was of no use in understanding historical realities. In a general sense, then, a critique of Yamada's premises informs the entire book.

It remains to address a methodological issue: Why use a case study of one three-day riot as the means to mount a critique of conventional wisdom concerning the entire sweep and basic processes of modern Japanese history? While the reasons may seem obvious, my personal appraisal of the state of research into Japanese labor history was involved, and it may be of interest to elaborate on this.

In the Japanese scholarly world of the 1950s, when I began to research labor history, historical studies of *labor-management relations* had not yet begun; the vast majority of labor history research focused on *labor movement* history. It sought to elucidate the successes and failures of the labor movements of the past, mainly by examining movement strategies and tactics. As a neophyte researcher I felt discomfort with this mode of study. Most research themes were chosen not because they posed important problems of historical understanding, but because they raised issues of practical interest to labor activists. This research tended to evaluate labor movements of the past from the political stance of the author, and the conclusions seemed to have been arrived at in advance. Conflicts within the labor movement were carried directly into academic debates that were dominated by a "good guys versus bad guys" historical consciousness. Writers typically pointed out tactical and strategic mistakes in the past to justify their present political positions.

Further, works that examined movement strategy and tactics were not even concerned to clarify the historical reality of labor movements; rather, debate centered on the explication of Marxist literature. One would think that a debate over tactics and strategy would be concerned with how, and whether, activists and rank-and-file laborers understood the leaders' policies, or be concerned with how these policies were (or were not) put into practice, but in fact this was rarely the case. In this context, I decided that historical studies of the Japanese labor movement needed to examine the characteristics of the laborers who were the putative supporters of the movement. I began to search for a method that would allow me to understand the particular character of the workers.

At that time, Ōkōchi Kazuo was the leading figure engaged in studies of labor movement history with a relatively similar problem consciousness. Ōkōchi asked what the distinctive characteristics of the Japanese labor movement were, and he answered that they all derived from the particular character of the labor force, namely, the dominant role played by migrant workers. Although I agreed that Ōkōchi was asking the most important question, I came to disagree with his answer. I was particularly troubled by the way his theory slighted the importance of historical change. But how could I articulate an effective critique? Ōkōchi's work had in fact already been faced with many abstract or theoretical criticisms, but it struck me that to simply repeat or deepen these critiques was not sufficient to refute his theory. So I settled on the method of addressing problems in his theory through empirical historical analysis.

Having made this decision, I chose the Ashio copper mine riot primarily for two reasons. First, I expected there to be no problem with the survival of the necessary records, because the Ashio riot was an extraordinarily large event. The government sent in the army and many court cases were prosecuted, so newspaper and court records should have been plentiful. Moreover, the Ashio mine was Japan's largest. It had expanded dramatically in the late nineteenth century, and was already well known even before the riot. Also, I expected that the famous Ashio copper mine pollution incident, often called Japan's first industrial pollution disaster, would have generated extensive records of that concurrent experience of social unrest.[4]

These expectations proved correct. All of the major newspapers of the day sent investigative reporters to the uprising and reported extensively on the course and the origins of the violence. Local newspapers published extensive day-by-day accounts of the subsequent court cases. Moreover, in a stroke of good fortune, I happened to discover secret documents of the prosecuting authorities relating to the case.

As I sought to develop a picture of the context of mining technology and the management of the Ashio mine, I found many articles in economic magazines and the like describing visits to the mine, and I found valuable material in publications of mining technology organizations, such as the *Nihon kōgyō kai shi* (Journal of the Japanese Mining Association). Well after I started doing this research I discovered a precious collection of records: survey reports written by graduate students of the Tokyo Imperial University, Engineering Division, Mining Department. Ashio was Japan's number one copper mine, a technologically progressive enterprise and much closer to Tokyo than most other mines, so every year pregraduation mining engineers would visit Ashio and record in great detail the technological changes from a specialist's perspective. Since technological changes can be a major cause of changes in labor-management relationships, these reports were extremely valuable in my study of the uprising.

For twenty years after publication of the essay that forms the basis of chapter 2, I stopped work on the history of Ashio. One reason lay in my frustration at discovering that valuable documents concerning the Furukawa enterprise existed, but were not available to scholars. In addition, I was prevented from resuming my research by my responsibilities as a member of the Ōhara Institute for Social Research at Hōsei University. Fortunately, various long-term projects to document, reorganize, and publish the institute's unique holdings of materials in Japanese and Western labor and social history had reached a point by 1981 that enabled me to seriously take up the subject of the Ashio riot once more.[5] I was also fortunate that in the interim a number of important new source materials had been made available with the publication of the *Tochigi Prefectural History* and the *History of the Furukawa Mining Company*. I now felt that I had sufficient resources to address the main questions of my research.

I decided to revisit the Ashio riot after more than twenty years for one further reason. In 1971 I had written a summary of the state of the field of Japanese labor movement history, and I had emphasized the importance of studying labor disputes. As this call for dispute-centered research also inspired the present volume, I would like to quote at some length from that 1971 publication:

> In the last ten years one of the main projects of historians of Japanese labor has been the study of the structure and history of labor unions in Japan. . . . Such research has mainly inquired into the reasons for the growth of enterprise unions. The scholar who first drew attention to this problem and who went on to establish the framework for its discussion was Ōkōchi Kazuo. Ōkōchi's thesis rested on the following historical analysis:

> > A great number of materials relating both to the history of the Japanese labor movement and to that of various other social movements have appeared since the end of the war, and indeed a few had also appeared before the war, but when these are examined from the point of view of the history of the labor union movement, they are seen to be exceedingly crude or dull. For the most part they are histories of the proletarian political parties or of various socialist factions masquerading as histories of the labor movement. As faithful historical records of the labor union movement in the strict sense of the term, such materials, we have all felt, leave a great deal to be desired. Of course, there have been some historical accounts of labor unions, but even these have mainly focused on industrial disputes and industrial relations problems of the more sensational sort that are normally featured in the daily press, and have hardly provided any record of normal labor union activity. In fact, there have hardly been any basic source materials which revealed anything of the rules, conference records or essential functions of labor unions.

> One can agree with Ōkōchi here to the extent that he was pointing out how out of date historical studies of labor unionism were. But the problem is that he considered industrial disputes to be "incidents" separate from normal labor union activity. In the prewar social and political context labor union activity was restricted, and government and capitalists consistently opposed any movement for independent labor unions. Workers were forced to resort to the weapon of strikes in order to defend and improve their working conditions. Strikes were indivisibly bound up with the organization and defense of independent labor unions. Without such disputes, there would not have been any of the "essential functions of labor unions" for historians to discuss.

> One can go further and say that in general, labor disputes reveal many contradictions not easily discovered in reading records of normal labor union activity. In fact,

studies of such disputes allow a more dynamic analysis of normal union activity. Further, the only way to know anything of the mentality and attitudes of workers who do not belong to any union, or of activists and ordinary union members who rarely left written records, is to examine their actions. Since the available written records tell us a great deal about industrial disputes, to ignore them would make labor studies impossible. In the extant accounts of labor disputes, we have before us the richest mine of information to illuminate the history of the Japanese labor movement.

The main question is thus: How best to dig that mine? Histories of industrial disputes have tended to fall into two categories: those that amount to little more than morality tales, chronicling the brave struggles of undaunted workers in the midst of difficult conditions, and those that present statistical analyses of disputes and explain strike demands and their effects in terms of general political, economic, and social factors. The critiques of Matsuzawa Hiroaki and of Ōkōchi Kazuo were no doubt directed at such histories.[6]

In order to go beyond such approaches, we must focus intensively on particular disputes that are representative of different periods. For this, it is necessary to examine not only the general relationship between the labor movement and the changing conditions of work in a particular industry, but also to explain the specific ways in which labor relations within a particular company are affected by changes in that company's process of capital accumulation. This will facilitate an understanding of the character and distinctive qualities of the participants in labor disputes.

I emphasize the importance of researching representative disputes in various periods because comparative analysis of such disputes will help clarify the historical characteristics of the labor movement. . . .

Scholars have seen the mine riots of the early Meiji years, and the strikes and disputes that followed the Sino-Japanese and Russo-Japanese Wars, as "spontaneous struggles against appalling working conditions." The use of the word *spontaneous* may simply imply that there was no labor union involvement or leadership, but social phenomena such as industrial disputes and riots cannot be described as "spontaneous" occurrences. Through a concrete comparative analysis of disputes in particular periods and in particular industries and companies, one can trace the qualitative differences between, and the historical backgrounds to, events that are far too easily categorized as "spontaneous occurrences."[7]

In this 1971 essay I emphasized the importance of studying disputes "in particular companies" for several reasons. First, I did so because in modern Japanese society corporations have played a particularly significant role in organizing people's lives. Thus, to understand in detail how people have dealt with each other in the workplace, we must investigate matters at the level of the individual company. Further, Japanese economic historians have been most energetic in research at the level of industrial sectors, and they have tended to let their theories dictate the search for evidence, picking up data that supported their claims and ignoring or overlooking those that did not. If company-level studies uncover evidence that does not fit an original hypothesis, then either the hypothesis must be reassessed, or the new evidence must be scrutinized more critically, or both. At a time when the validity of existing Marxian theories themselves are being questioned, such an approach is the more necessary. In many studies of modern Japanese history, shallow scrutiny of sources leads to uncritical reliance on existing theories, or else uncritical adherence to existing theories prevents close scrutiny of the sources.

I was fortunate that a group of talented young researchers responded to my call for dispute-centered research and produced much important new work. But I felt quite guilty for not following my own advice and publishing a major work that took the approach I had so easily recommended to others. In this context, the following remarks by Nakanishi Yō hit close to home. Nakanishi published a major survey of the field titled "The Current State of Social Policy: Research on Labor Problems in Japan."[8] I was delighted at the undeserved compliment that he paid to my short paper on the lodge system (the basis of chapter 2 of the present volume): "A superb achievement that elucidates the definitive superiority of the historical approach in . . . post-war research on 'labor studies.'" But Nakanishi went on to add the following criticism:

> Nimura has not succeeded in clearly elucidating "the method of his historical analysis." . . . One cannot find in his approach any methodological unity in the analysis of the "Ashio riot" itself on the one hand and "the basic process underlying the Ashio riot" on the other. His work does not improve on the principle of reciprocity between superstructure and sub-structure which is at the basis of historical materialist formulations. . . .
>
> Although it may in general be justified to analyze "labor organization" as a function of the development of "production technology," various groupings of workers can by no means be considered uniform. Radical changes in production technology invariably influence and reflect a whole variety of conditions including the organization of the labor force. Unless one's methodology adequately deals with this point, any attempt to discuss "the basic course of events" in terms of "developments in

production technology" is likely to be no more than a version of the "technological determinism" that dominates current research with negative effect.[9]

Clearly the only way to respond to this criticism was to analyze both the "underlying process" of the Ashio riot and the "riot itself," and then present a clear combination of these two analyses. I had long realized that my 1959 paper was a partial effort that had not adequately investigated even the "underlying process" of the riot.

Not long after Nakanishi's critique, a regular meeting of the Labor Movement Historical Research Association took up the theme of "Methodologies of Research into Labor Disputes." In his summary of the discussion, Kurita Ken commented as follows:

Much recent research has transcended the "good guys versus bad guys" approach that has hitherto dominated research in labor movement history. The most important result of this new work has been to show how workers and employers have jointly created industrial relations. That is, workers with their own divided interests have developed their movements, and employers have responded sometimes with repression and other times by striking compromises while striving to set up new structures of control. But the problem remains that results of detailed research into industrial disputes (research which is crucial to elaborate this process of evolving industrial relations) remains inconclusive.[10]

Clearly the only response to this criticism as well was to produce a detailed study of a labor dispute, and this strengthened my resolve to return to my study of the Ashio riot.

Over the years since I began to advocate research into labor disputes, I received a great deal of support as well as some stiff criticism. The strongest critiques have insisted that research into the details of a single company did not aid our understanding of the Japanese labor movement as a whole. In other words, research into individual disputes showed us the trees but could not bring the forest into focus. While such arguments have some validity, I stood by my belief that at this particular point in the history of our research, study of disputes in individual companies was needed. To be sure, a study of a single dispute shows us just one tree, but I felt that conventional research at the time remained outside the forest entirely and could not teach us anything about its internal composition. We had to enter the forest and investigate representative trees and shrubs to comprehend the nature of the forest as a whole. Of course, one tree does not grow in isolation, so we must also examine the relationships between the tree and its environment: the climate and soil, the insects and birds that visit or live in the tree. I believed that thorough study of a dispute in a single company would deepen our understanding of the "whole forest" that is modern Japanese society. One could not hope to understand the whole by stubbornly looking only at the whole in general terms. Whether this approach has borne fruit or not, I leave to the readers to decide.

When I determined to pull together my various studies of Ashio into a single book, the ideal would have been to rewrite and restructure the whole to make it clearer and easier to read. I made such plans many times, and even made slight beginnings. But each time the work failed to come together, and finally I decided to publish it in the present form, with the original discrete essays more or less intact. Not only was my energy limited, but since each of these essays was written with different problems in mind and with independent arguments, restructuring was not a simple task. Moreover, a study that introduces detailed evidence from a single riot almost a century ago could easily degenerate into boring recitation of facts, so I thought it best to maintain a certain tension and interest by retaining the argumentative or polemical form of the original essays. Inevitably this leads to some repetition, and perhaps some contradictory arguments, but I nonetheless published the book in its present form.

In quite a few places I introduce long passages verbatim from primary sources. Even for Japanese readers this made the book difficult, and reviewers criticized my extensive use of long quotes. In fact, I originally included these citations even though I knew they made for heavy going at times, for the following reasons. First, many of the facts presented in this book are not widely recognized by Japanese scholars, so I felt it necessary to show clearly what sources I used and how I analyzed them. Different interpretations of some of these sources could have yielded completely different conclusions. The sources that I have cited at length are precisely those problematic places. In such cases I introduce related contradictory sources and advance my argument while examining the reliability of each. My goal was to show that my argument not only used sources that support my interpretation but stood up even in the face of contradictory sources. In this translation, however, we have eliminated or reduced in length many of these long citations in the interest of readability. Yet my original impulse behind using these sources remains strong, and we have not eliminated all of them.

Prologue:

The Ashio Copper Mine and

the Japanese Mining Industry

PREINDUSTRIAL JAPANESE MINING

Today we commonly think of Japan as a nation poor in natural resources. But as Marco Polo's introduction of "Jipang" as a "Golden Land" in the late thirteenth century suggests, medieval Japan was one of the world's most productive mining nations, and gold, silver, and copper were crucial exports. Metal refining in Japan can be traced back to the seventh century (C.E.) in written documents, and archaeologically back to the latter half of the sixth century. However, metal refining in ancient Japan primarily used gold and iron dust for raw materials, so mining development was limited to particular regions.[1]

Japan's metal mining industry advanced quickly in the sixteenth and seventeenth centuries. At that time, copper and silver were highly valued as Japanese exports, and gold, silver, and copper mines developed all over Japan. Silver mining boomed first, and by the early seventeenth century Japan was exporting two hundred tons of silver per year, an extraordinary one-third of world silver production. After that, gold and silver mines began to decline, and by the end of the seventeenth century copper had taken center stage.

In the Tokugawa era (1603–1867) all mines were the property of the feudal lords. They were, however, managed in many different ways, from direct government control to subcontracting by townsmen or master miners. Even in cases of direct official management, the metalworkers and diggers who carried out the actual mining and refining would not have received their pay directly from the lord. It was common practice for a master miner who specialized in mine management to contract for sole responsibility for a single mine or subset of operations, and to employ workers at each production stage: pit digging, mining, dressing, refining, and so forth.

The number of specialized mining workers in Tokugawa Japan is not clear. However, documents survive suggesting that, at their height, the major mining centers nationwide had populations ranging from 10,000 to 200,000.[2] Of course, not all of these people worked in the mines. Moreover, the ebb and flow of mine fortunes were drastic and quick, and periods of prosperity in any one place were quite temporary, so adding separate city populations together will not give an accurate total. But even in the latter half of the eighteenth century, when the decline in mining fortunes became widespread, close to thirty sites were producing copper sent to Nagasaki for export. Considering this data, mine technology and labor specialists must have numbered not in the thousands, but in the tens of thousands. As people with specialized skills, their labor market encompassed the entire country. Surviving documents show that in the early seventeenth century the towns of origin of those living around the Akita domain Innai mines in northeastern Japan covered the whole nation, including far-flung Kyushu and Shikoku. Sizable numbers of residents hailed from Echigo, site of the Sado gold mine, the Chūgoku region, site of the Ikuno and Iwami mines and a highly advanced mining industry, and the urban Kyoto and Osaka areas.

Thus, through several centuries of history, Japan's mining industry on the eve of the Meiji Restoration of 1868 had created a nationwide specialized labor force, and mines were in operation all over Japan (see Figure P.1). But in the late Tokugawa era, miners dug ever deeper into the earth, and problems of drainage, air circulation, and transportation costs became technologically and economically prohibitive. As a result, the mining industry in Japan began to decline.

JAPANESE MINING INDUSTRY SINCE INDUSTRIALIZATION

The advanced Western technology imported when Japan resumed large-scale trade with the rest of the world in the mid–nineteenth century revitalized Japanese mining and made rapid development possible. Blasting powder and dynamite enabled the drilling of tunnels to proceed much more quickly than before, and steam or electrically driven drainage pumps and hauling winches instantly solved long-standing problems. Of course, the only reason this technology could be absorbed in such a short time is that there existed a sufficient number of skilled mine workers and specialists, drawing on centuries of traditional practice. Also, coal and copper quickly

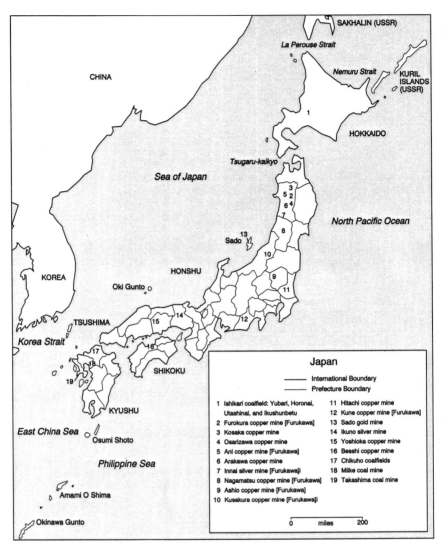

Figure P.1. Location of principal mines in Japan, ca. early twentieth century.

became exportable commodities on a par with silk, expanding the mining market by orders of magnitude. Because active searching for exploitable sites had been going on since about the sixteenth century, the locations of the potentially productive mines were well known, and rejuvenation based on new technology could commence immediately.

The use of coal in the Tokugawa period had been limited to a few manufacturing processes such as salt making. In the Meiji era it suddenly became an important export product. In addition, domestic demand grew rapidly as steam engines came to be used in factories, ships, and trains. The mining industry as a whole grew along with this demand. Without here offering a detailed analysis of the relative importance of this industry to the development of Japanese capitalism, we may simply note that highly profitable mining operations provided the foundation for Japan's chief *zaibatsu*—the huge industrial, financial, and trading monopolies—as they developed into vast economic empires.[3]

MINING LABORERS IN EARLY LABOR MOVEMENTS

As these mines became the "cash cows" of the *zaibatsu,* the industry mobilized a huge workforce. Records from before the 1880s are unfortunately too poor to allow reliable estimates of its size. The earliest date for which we have anything resembling a trustworthy figure is 1881. I have examined this question of labor force size in another work and concluded that mine labor was far more numerous than the conventional wisdom allowed.[4] I believe the mine labor force in Japan in 1881 included 32,000 metal mine workers and 19,000 nonmetal mine workers (chiefly coal mine workers), for a total of 51,000. After 1893, the statistics are consistent and reliable, and Table P.1 illustrates the subsequent changes in the number of mine workers. Table P.2 shows labor force size for 1900 and 1909 broken down by industry and enterprise size. Table P.3 lists the large manufacturing and mine enterprises in Japan in 1909. The largest enterprises for the most part were either arsenals or mines, and male laborers accounted for a high proportion of the mining industry workers.

Mine workers played a large role in the history of the Japanese labor movement, especially in the early industrial era. But most union organizations were weak, and the labor "movement" consisted primarily of strikes and riots. In the early years of Japanese labor history, over half of the labor disputes took place in mines, and these incidents are distinguished by their scale and level of violence. In the ten years prior to 1887, ten strikes took place at the Takashima coal mine alone, as well as myriad riots and protest actions. Among other mines, we find records of three strikes at Miike, and one each at Ani, Osarizawa, Innai, and Sado. In the course of this book, I

Table P.1. Mining Labor Force, 1893–1910

year	Total[1]			Metal			Coal		
	total (women)	underground (women)	surface (women)	total (women)	underground (women)	surface (women)	total (women)	underground (women)	surface (women)
1893	83,819			53,474			30,345		
1894	98,579			55,703			42,876		
1895	114,459			60,368			54,091		
1896	113,357			59,606			53,751		
1897	154,517			71,988			82,529		
1898	127,537			51,706			75,831		
1899	112,105			51,141			60,964		
1900	125,313			54,805			70,508		
1901	139,210			63,980			75,230		
1902	139,233			60,339			78,894		
1903	149,800			64,859			84,941		
1904	157,463			69,133			88,330		
1905	148,366			68,861			79,505		
1906	152,117(32,429)	97,214(16,709)	46,408(15,720)	63,620(10,126)	32,278(1,376)	22,847(8,750)	88,497(22,303)	64,936(15,333)	23,561(6,970)
1907	170,400(36,243)	106,152(18,834)	56,934(17,409)	70,301(10,475)	34,704(1,576)	28,283(8,899)	100,099(25,768)	71,448(17,258)	28,651(8,510)
1908	196,432			69,433			126,999		
1909	183,415(39,434)	113,218(21,386)	62,389(18,048)	70,384(11,238)	31,832(1,496)	30,714(9,742)	113,031(28,196)	81,336(19,890)	31,675(8,306)
1910	185,019(40,826)	112,380(21,414)	64,206(19,412)	75,625(12,697)	33,533(1,548)	33,659(11,149)	109,394(28,129)	78,847(19,866)	30,547(8,263)

Note: 1. Full-time blue-collar workers only. Figures not in parentheses include men and women. Nonmetal (sulfur, gypsum, silica, limestone, etc.) miners are not included.

Source: Ministry of International Trade and Industry, Minister's Secretariat, Research and Statistics Division, *Honpo kōgyō no sūsei 50 nenshi* (History of the mining trends of Japan) (Tokyo: Ministry of International Trade and Industry, 1963; Tokyo: Ryūkei shoshu, 1980).

Table P.2. Labor Force, by Industry, 1900 and 1909

Industries	Number of factories & mines by size of workforce						Total workforce by industry			
	over 500		over 100		over 10		1900	1909		
	1900	1909	1900	1909	1900	1909		total	male	female
Mining	49	90	121	—	472	—	140,846	235,809	184,766	51,043
Metal mining	14	29	51	—	206	—	54,805	74,105	61,657	12,448
Coal mining	35	58	70	—	266	—	70,508	152,515	113,957	38,558
Other mining	0	3	0	—	0	—	15,533	9,189	9,152	37
Textiles	58	115	340	585	4,277	8301	237,132	442,169	60,896	381,273
Silk reeling	3	25	238	436	2,558	2945	118,804	184,397	9,611	174,786
Cotton spinning	43	67	44	23	149	124	62,856	102,986	21,347	81,639
Weaving	12	19	51	95	1,367	4245	49,229	127,441	17,648	109,793
Other textile	0	4	7	31	203	987	6,243	27,345	12,290	15,055
Food	3	3	25	96	835	2396	25,403	62,867	43,543	19,324
Chemical	1	4	81	146	810	1579	35,566	65,966	42,668	23,298
Machinery	9	11	40	73	413	1092	29,730	54,810	51,863	2,947
Other industries	3	6	34	78	630	2027	23,728	62,858	40,509	22,349
Government-run works	12	22	11	67	27	67	36,237	117,259	92,875	24,384
Total	135	251	652	—	7,464	—	528,642	1,041,738	517,111	524,627

Source: Ishii Kanji, *Nihon Keizaishi* (Economic history of Japan) (Tokyo: Tokyo University Press, 1976), 151, 169.

Table P.3. Thirty Major Factories and Mines, 1909

Rank	Factories and Mines[1]	Number of workers
1	Kure Naval Yard	20,917
2	Tokyo Army Arsenal	12,561
3	Yokosuka Naval Yard	11,569
4	**Mitsui Miike Coal Mine**	**11,225**
5	Osaka Army Arsenal	8,075
6	Yahata Ironworks	7,553
7	**Fujita Kosaka Copper Mine**	**7,128**
8	**Furukawa Ashio Copper Mine**	**7,010**
9	**Tanaka Kamaishi Iron Mine**	**6,287**
10	Sasebo Naval Yard	5,591
11	**Hokutan Yubari #1 Coal Mine**	**5,543**
12	Mitsubishi Nagasaki Shipyard	5,389
13	**Kaijima Ohnoura Coal Mine**	**5,328**
14	**Mitsubishi Sinnyu Coal Mine**	**5,218**
15	**Mitsui Tagawa Coal Mine**	**4,990**
16	Settubo Kizugawa Spinning Mill	3,984
17	**Kaijima Ohtsuji Coal Mine**	**3,921**
18	Maizuru Naval Yard	3,762
19	Osakabo Sangenya Spinning Mill	3,646
20	Fujigasubo Hodogaya Spinning Mill	3,611
21	**Sumitomo Besshi Copper Mine**	**3,528**
22	Miebo Tsu Spinning Mill	3,493
23	**Mitsui Hondo Coal Mine**	**3,474**
24	Tokyo Muslin Weaving Mill	3,355
25	Kanebo Tokyo Spinning Mill	3,327
26	**Futase Coal Mine** (government-run)	**3,305**
27	Kanebo Hyogo Spinning Mill	3,221
28	**Mitsubishi Ouchi Coal Mine**	**3,220**
29	Nisshinbo Spinning Company	3,133
30	**Furukawa Ani Copper Mine**	**3,024**

Note: 1. The unit is single plant, not a company.

Source: Ishii Kanji, *Nihon Keizaishi* (Economic history of Japan) (Tokyo: Tokyo University Press, 1976), 169.

hope to explain why it was that coal and metal mines experienced so many strikes in these years.

AN OVERVIEW OF THE ASHIO COPPER MINE

Ashio is nestled in the mountains roughly in the middle of the main Japanese island, Honshu, seventy-five miles north of Tokyo, separated from the famous tourist sites of Nikkō and Chūzenji Lake to the south by a single mountain (see Figure P.2). Official records claim that the copper vein at Ashio was discovered in 1610, but these deposits were in fact already known in the mid–sixteenth century. Immediately after 1610 Ashio came under direct management by the Tokugawa shogunate, and by 1684 it was producing 1500 tons annually. No other mine equaled this rate during the entire Tokugawa period. However, like most mines of this era, its prosperity was short-lived. By the early 1700s subterranean flooding and air circulation problems had reduced yields by 90 percent, to 150 tons per year.

This mine revived in 1877 when Furukawa Ichibei took it over. He introduced blasting powder and dynamite for tunnel excavation, and he solved long-standing problems of drainage and air circulation. In 1883 an extremely rich vein of ore was discovered, the Yokomabu deposit, and by 1885 Ashio was producing 4131 tons annually, or 39 percent of Japan's total copper output. In 1906, the year before the riot, Ashio produced 6787 tons, still 18 percent of Japan's total, and employed 11,000 men directly. It was indeed the greatest mine in the nation.

Ashio and the Mine Pollution Incident

The Ashio copper mine today, like virtually all of Japan's mines, is a place of the past. Centuries of digging exhausted the rich veins, cheap foreign ore created a harshly competitive market, and the mine's Excavation Department closed over two decades ago, in 1973. In 1996 only a few Furukawa company employees remain at Ashio, operating a refinery that processes imported ore. Yet the name of the Ashio copper mine is widely known by Japanese people. This is not because it once claimed the title of Asia's largest copper mine, or because the computer and robotics giants Fujitsu and

Figure P.2. View of the Ashio Honzan area, the main stage of the riot. Painted by Tashiro Kogai in June 1907, four months after the riot. Courtesy of Mrs. Inaba Seitarō and Murakami Yasumasa.

Fanac trace their roots to the huge corporation that grew out of Ashio's rich deposits. People remember Ashio as the infamous site of Japan's first major industrial pollution disaster.

In the late nineteenth century, the mine's refinery belched clouds containing sulfuric acid that withered the surrounding forests, and the waste water from extracting and ore-dressing processes ran off into the Watarase River, reducing rice yields of the farmers who irrigated fields with this water and threatening the health and livelihood of the people who worked tens of thousands of hectares across the 6 prefectures, 12 counties, and 136 towns of the river basin. Thousands of farming families from Gunma and Tochigi prefectures protested many times They petitioned the national authorities in Tokyo and clashed with police. Eventually their leader, Tanaka Shōzō, created a great stir by directly petitioning the emperor for relief. In fact, the government had three times ordered Furukawa to take antipollution measures at Ashio, which helped prevent further damage but did not clean up toxic wastes already permeating the rivers and fields of the region.[5]

Together with the Ashio riot of 1907, this so-called Ashio mine pollution incident constitutes one of Japan's greatest social problems of the late nine-

Figure P.3. The copper refinery plant. Painted by Yamamoto Shōkoku in 1901. From "Ashio-dōzan zue" (a pictorial magazine's special issue on the Ashio copper mine).

teenth and early twentieth centuries. While some cases of environmental damage from mines in Japan predate the Ashio pollution, it was at this time and place that a powerful opposition movement first emerged to clash with the central government. As environmental destruction reemerged in the 1960s as a major social issue, and popular concern with the impact of pollution intensified, so Ashio's legacy as "the birthplace of pollution in Japan" has endured. And the concurrent mine riot at the turn of the century is of course related to the pollution case. Ashio produced such massive environmental damage in the early days of Japan's industrialization precisely because Furukawa invested in advanced technology and mobilized thousands of workers to exploit the rich veins of the mine. At that time copper played a major role in the Japanese economy, ranking second to silk among Japan's exports.

Ashio Town

The Ashio copper mine officially sits in the town of Ashio in Kamitsuga county, Tochigi prefecture. In 1907, when the riot occurred, this town's

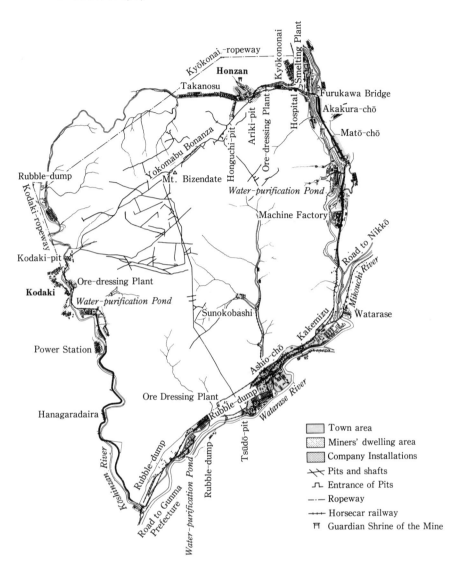

Figure P.4. Map of Ashio copper mine.

population numbered 34,827 people in 6133 households, roughly the size of the prefectural capital, Utsunomiya City. Ashio mine employees and their families accounted for approximately 23,000 of the total population, and many of the remaining 12,000 were construction and machinery subcontractors of the mine or shopkeepers who catered to mine personnel. Ashio was truly a company town.

A map of the Ashio mine area roughly resembles a picture of a person looking to the left, whose nose is mostly missing and whose head is somewhat flat on top and at the back (see Figure P.4). Located just above the ear is the peak of Mt. Bizendate. Under this 1273-meter-high peak lay some 1800 seams of ore of varying sizes extending from the northeast to the southwest, that is, from the back of Ashio-man's head to his eyes. Later came the discovery of the massive Kajika ore deposits, but these were unknown at the time of the 1907 riot. At the pithead entrances to the main tunnels dug to get at these veins were the ore-dressing stations and the miners' living quarters. In the north to northeastern area of the town of Ashio, toward the back of the top of Ashio-man's head, is the Honzan district, where work first began at the mine with the construction of the company offices. Here is where many of the earliest pits had been dug into outcrops. These early pits were redeveloped by Furukawa, who opened them up to reveal rich new lodes. The main pits here were the Honguchi and Ariki pits. Since the pitheads of these two lodes were also in the Honzan area, this meant that the miners' shacks, the ore-dressing and refining stations, the mine offices and warehouses—all the main facilities of the mining operation, in fact—were clustered around the northeast skirt of Mt. Bizendate. Fully one-third of the population of the town of Ashio, approximately 12,500 people, worked in this small area. Also located here at Honzan were the Furukawa Company's Ashio mine offices as well as the living quarters of the director and his officials, the site of the worst violence during the riot. Set 830 meters above sea level, Honzan was the highest point in the Ashio town district. It was mostly the property of the Furukawa Company; there were no townspeople's houses in the area.

In the west, looking from the eyes to the nose on the map, was the Kodaki district, home to over 5000 people. Here too, Furukawa successfully reopened old pits and located the pithead, 730 meters above sea level, of the Kodaki mine that extended from the southwestern end of the lodes back toward the Honzan area. Kodaki was the most isolated part of the mine complex. There was no direct route connecting Kodaki to the world beyond Ashio; the location was dangerous and transport difficult. There were few shops and hardly any places of entertainment. There were other reasons why the Kodaki pit was not involved in the riot, but certainly its isolated location was a factor.

In the southeast, looking from the chin to the throat, one finds the Tsūdō district with its Tsūdō pit, located at the lowest point (602 meters) of the Ashio mining operation on the Watarase River. Tsūdō was sunk to serve as the main transport and drainage tunnel. Whereas the Ariki and Kodaki pits followed the lodes and were known as extraction pits, the Tsūdō main tunnel was dug as an access pit, cutting across lodes and extending northwest toward a point directly underneath the peak of Mt. Bizendate. Tsūdō was the most recently developed part of the Ashio mine. Even so, it had a large mine-connected population and many shops because this area included the original Ashio postal relay stations along the highway route through the famous shrine of Nikkō, and because it was midway between Honzan and Kodaki. This was Ashio's "downtown" area, site of all the main public buildings: the town hall, the Ashio branch office of the Nikkō police department, the post office, and the municipal primary school. There were small theaters, inns, restaurants, brothels, and temples.

At the back of Ashio-man's head, across from the refining station in the easternmost sector of Honzan, is Akakuramachi. Just below this, along the banks of the Matsuki River which runs down to Tsūdō, is Matochō. Workshops for making and repairing the mine machinery were found in the most southerly area of the Matochō district. On the right-hand bank of the Matsuki River, facing the mine, were the primary school built and run by the Furukawa Company and also the settling reservoir installed to detoxify the mine waste water. Like Tsūdō, Akakuramachi and Matochō also had their shops, eating houses, small theaters, and inns, as well as company property and private houses. Finally, the confluence of the Matsuki and Mikouchi rivers between Tsūdō and Matochō form the Watarase River, and the district of Watarase was located on left bank where the two rivers meet. This was the entrance to Ashio from the Nikkō highway.

The Operators: The Furukawa Family

The operator of the Ashio mine, the man called "the Mining King of East Asia," had previously been the chief clerk of the powerful Ono merchant house. His name was Furukawa Ichibei (see Figure P.5). In late Tokugawa Japan, the Ono group was a house on a par with Mitsui, and although finance was its core operation, after the Meiji Restoration it moved into international trade and mining. In his days with Ono, Ichibei won renown for his tremendously profitable exporting of silk and silkworm eggs. In 1874 Ono went bankrupt and Ichibei was out of a job, but he had won the regard

Figure P.5. Furukawa Ichibei (1832–1903). Photo from *Furukawa Ichibei-o den* (Biography of the venerable Mr. Furukawa Ichibei), by Shigeno Kichinosuke and published as a private edition in 1926.

of the famous financier Shibusawa Eiichi, and with his strong backing, Ichibei tried his hand at running a mine. In the 1870s he hit a rich vein at the Kusakura mine, and subsequently his Ashio operation prospered. With these profits, he bought metal and coal mines one after another across Japan. By 1900 he possessed eighteen metal mines and four coal mines and controlled around 40 percent of Japanese copper production.

Ichibei died in 1903, four years before the riots, but actual control of the Furukawa family operations had already passed to his adopted son, Junkichi, in 1897 (see Figure P.6). Junkichi abandoned Ichibei's policy of aggressively pursuing market share by plowing profits into purchasing mines and expanding operations. He adopted a more conservative policy aimed more at stabilizing profits rather than expanding production. Under Junkichi's leadership the Furukawa family operations shifted from individual management to corporate organization (see Figure P.7). At the time of this transition, Junkichi was extremely ill, and he appointed Hara Kei (also pronounced Hara Takashi), the protégé of his birth father, Mutsu Munemitsu, as the corporate vice president.[6]

Figure P.6. Furukawa
Junkichi (1870–1905).
Photo from *Furukawa
Junkichi-kun den*
(Biography of Mr.
Furukawa Junkichi), by
Shigeno Kichinosuke and
published as a private
edition in 1926.

Soon after the Furukawa enterprises were incorporated in December
1905, Junkichi died, and Ichibei's birth son, Toranosuke, became the nominal company president. But Toranosuke was a youth studying in America at
the time, and Hara Kei was the de facto head of operations. Hara, however,
left the vice presidency after less than a year to assume the office of home
minister in the Saionji cabinet in January 1906. Therefore, at the time of the
riots, Kimura Chōshichi, Furukawa Ichibei's right-hand man and constant
companion since his days with Ono, was responsible for day-to-day operations, with the assistance of Kondo Rikusaburō.

Kondo was an 1880 graduate of the Mining Department of the School of
Engineering, predecessor to the Engineering Department of Tokyo Imperial
University, and he had been a technician at the government-operated Ani
copper mine. He joined the Furukawa operation when the Ani mine was sold
to Furukawa. He was in fact the company's first college-graduated technician, and was twice sent to study abroad by Furukawa, for a total of two
years, giving him a strong Western education.

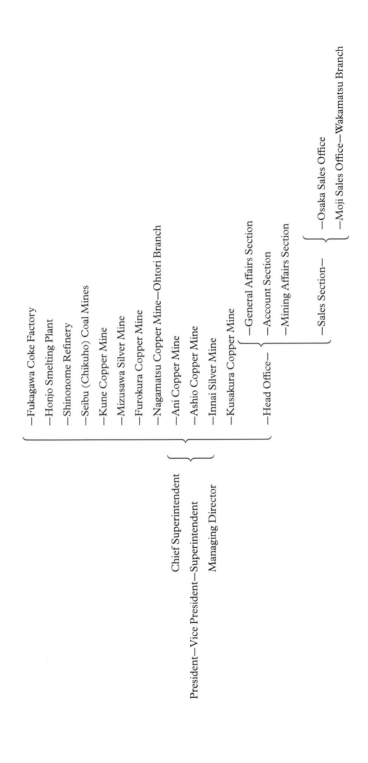

Figure P.7. Organization of Furukawa Company, April 1905.

The Ashio Mine Office and Its Management Staff

The Furukawa Corporation's Ashio mine office directly ran the Ashio copper mine. At the time of the riot the head of the office was Minami Teizō, former chief of the government's Tokyo Mine Inspectorate. The third anti-pollution edict, issued in 1897, was put forth in his name. Less than three years later, in January 1900, he entered the Furukawa organization, and in September 1903 he became head of the Ashio mining office. Although he had briefly served in the Mine Inspectorate, his chief previous experience had been as a Finance Ministry bureaucrat, and he was in fact a complete novice at mining technology.

Minami supervised six departments: general management, pits, refining, engineering, electrical, and supplies (see Figure P.8). The Pits Department, in charge of excavation, extraction, dressing, and other aspects of pit operation and ore selection, was separated into Honzan, Tsūdō, and Kodaki divisions, each with a pit chief. The Refining Department was entirely responsible for the refinery at Honzan. The Engineering Department handled the assembly, maintenance, and repair of mechanical equipment. The Electrical Department oversaw power generation and transmission and the maintenance of electrical equipment. Production materials and the daily needs of workers were purchased, transported, stored, and distributed by members of the Supplies Department. The General Management Department essentially handled everything else, including accounting, schools, hospitals, and even the patrols of the corporate security guards.

Ashio's department heads were all graduates of colleges or technical commercial high schools. The pits, refining, and engineering managers were bachelors of engineering from Tokyo Imperial University, and the general manager was from the law faculty. All four were young men in their thirties, less than ten years from graduation. In 1906 a total of 319 white-collar staff served in the six divisions, mostly graduates of college or higher. There were 97 people in general management, 86 in pits, 11 in refining, 36 in engineering, 21 in electrical, and 68 in supplies. Aside from these full-fledged managerial staff people (*yakuin*), the mine employed 387 "assistant staff" members (*junshokuin*) recruited from among the mining laborers. The regular staff were ranked from first through eighth class, and were paid monthly, while the assistant staff were ninth or tenth class and paid day wages.[7]

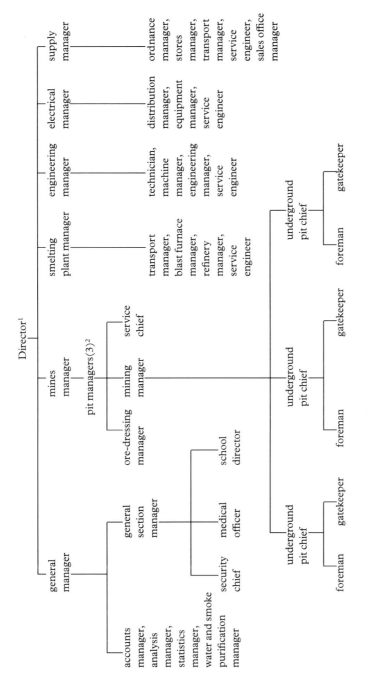

Notes: 1. The Ashio management structure in this period was frequently altered. This diagram is drawn from two surveys, "Ōkawara Saburō Observation Report," August 1906, p. 15, and "Hosotani Genshirō Observation Report," May 1905, p. 21. 2. Each of three pits (Honzan pit, Tsūdō pit, and Kodaki pit) had a manager.

Figure P.8. Management structure of Ashio copper mine.

The Workers

In June of 1906 Ashio employed 11,105 full-time workers. The 575 female employees made up just over 5 percent of the total, so the mine workplace was overwhelmingly a male society. Two-thirds of laborers worked in the pits, and half of these, or one-third of the total, were miners. The main work of the miners, called "hand-diggers," was to drill blasting holes with hammer and chisel, collect ore, and open new tunnels. There were 1150 to 1300 of these hand-diggers at each of the three sites, for a total of about 3600 men (of whom 300 were apprentices), and theirs was the core occupation at Ashio. In addition, the mine employed men who operated the machine drills used to open dynamite holes for blasting new tunnels, but these men numbered fewer than one hundred. The most numerous group of pit workers after the diggers was the transport workers. Almost two thousand of these people hauled ore and waste from the ore extraction face to the surface, while an additional 300 transport workers piled the rock into hand trucks and pushed it to the main tunnels, and others drove the electric trolleys or laid the track. The work of maintaining the tunnels fell to about one thousand shorers, a more skilled job than mine digging. At the time of the riot, shorers were considered to be in very short supply, and over half of them were apprentices. Similarly skilled were the stonecutters, also involved in tunnel maintenance and construction. Other pit workers included mechanics, who operated and maintained winches, trolleys, water pumps, and other machines, and slurrymen, who extracted copper sediment from the waste water, using scrap iron that attached itself to the copper ions.

The most numerous of the surface workers were an additional one thousand transport workers. The work of hauling ore, waste rock, and finished copper and supplying the refinery with coke and limestone required many laborers. In addition, Ashio's physical isolation required the import of daily goods, including food, and the maintenance of adequate reserves. Transport jobs were many and varied, including trolley pushers, cable car operators, electric train drivers, and drivers for the horse-drawn cars.

Following the transport workers in numbers were the dressers. Their job was to crush the ore brought out of the tunnel, and process it into high-quality ore powder. Some six hundred people did this at the three sites. About half of these workers were women, with the male workers primarily operating the dressing machinery while the women selected ore by eye and

(9a)   (9b)

Figure P.9a. A miner and an apprentice wearing a water-resistant coat. Painted by Tashiro Kogai in 1907. Courtesy of Mrs. Inaba Seitarō and Murakami Yasumasa.
Figure P.9b. Miners with portable cushions made of straw used to offer some comfort when miners rested on the hard surfaces in the pits. Painted by Tashiro Kogai in 1907. Courtesy of Mrs. Inaba Seitarō and Murakami Yasumasa.

hand. Although numbering just over two hundred, the refinery workers were another core group of mine laborers. In addition, the engineering and electrical departments employed several hundred workers; electricians ran the power plant and maintained electrical equipment, and mechanics did the same with various other machines. Finally, although the statistics of Ashio employees do not count them, the mine hired numerous temporary and day laborers (see Figures P.9a, P.9b).

Female Laborers

The total of 575 female laborers at Ashio in 1906 accounted for barely 5.2 percent of the workforce. All of them were surface workers. The situation in coal mining differed. At the Chikuhō coal fields in Kyūshū, for example,

Figure P.10. A company store. Painted by Yamamoto Shokoku in 1901. From "Ashio-dōzan zue" (a pictorial magazine's special issue on the Ashio copper mine).

husband and wife teams commonly worked in the pits as coal diggers, and women constituted approximately 30 percent of the pit workforce in the 1920s.[8] But in metal mines such as Ashio, a sort of taboo existed that forbade female pit workers. Legends held that the protective god of the mountain was female, and that she would become jealous and cause disaster if women entered the pits. Even at Ashio, when Furukawa first took over operations a labor shortage required that women be used as pit transportation workers, and records show that Ichibei gave them bonuses. It is testimony to the strength of the metal miners' belief in the taboo against women in the pit that the practice of employing women in the pits disappeared shortly thereafter.

At Ashio in 1906, most of the female laborers worked as hand-sorters in the ore-dressing process (see Figure P.11). Before ore dressing was greatly mechanized, this was a key area of employment for women in the mines, but their numbers were reduced with the influx of machinery. Women also

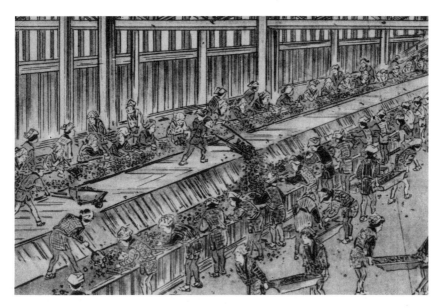

Figure P.11. The ore-dressing plant. Painted by Yamamoto Shokoku in 1901. From "Ashio-dōzan zue" (a pictorial magazine's special issue on the Ashio copper mine).

worked as switchboard operators, nurses, fuse makers, and at other miscellaneous tasks. Their wages were barely half those of male workers: in early 1900, when the daily wage of a male ore dresser averaged 40 sen, female dressers earned 17 to 18 sen.

Family members of employees totalled 11,987 people, of whom 8213 were women and 2773 were children of elementary school age and younger. Most of the supervisory staff employees were married men, but nearly half of the male laborers were single.

The Miners

The rioters were mostly pit workers, particularly mine diggers. For convenience, we will refer to the diggers simply as miners. In view of their central role in the riot, we must look more closely at their working conditions.

The job of the miners involved the drilling of holes for explosives with hammer and chisel. The size of the hole varied with the face, but was normally about 30 millimeters in diameter and 30 to 60 centimeters in depth. The miner held the chisel, shaped as in Figure P.12, in his left hand, while he

Figure P.12.
A hand-digger working
at a rock face. Painted by
Yamamoto Shokoku in
1901. Cover illustration of
the "Ashio-dōzan zue" (a
pictorial magazine's special
issue on the Ashio copper
mine).

wielded the 1.5-kilogram hammer in the right. He rotated the chisel with
each strike, so the shifting blade produced a round hole. Water was periodically used to flush chips and powder from the hole, and a large iron scoop
was used to draw out debris. As the drilling progressed, the miner would
switch to a longer, narrower chisel to continue.

When the work space allowed it, an assistant would hold the chisel while
the miner struck it with a two-handed, 4- to 5-kilogram hammer. This two-
person drilling was more effective and damage to the tools was rarer, but the
ore extraction face was normally too narrow for this method, which was
generally reserved for tunnel drilling.

When the hole was completed, the miner would pack it with black powder
using a wooden pestle, add a fuse, seal the hole with clay, light the fuse, and
blast the charge. Both black powder and dynamite were used. Dynamite has
more explosive force than powder, and could be used on harder rock and in
wetter conditions, but it was also much more expensive. The decision concerning which to use could make quite a difference in operating expenses.

These tasks were not only physically demanding, but they also required substantial experience and judgment. Awareness of different rock types was essential; the ability to spot cracks and the grain in stone, and judge the angle, depth, and number of holes to drill all made a difference in the speed and effectiveness of ore extraction.

The miners' skill at these tasks of course affected the pace of extraction and the operating costs, and Ashio paid the miners with wages linked to their output. (The method of setting pay is discussed in detail in chapter 1). In Japanese labor history, one finds little record of opposition to piece-rate pay systems, and I intend to reexamine the reasons for this at the end of this book. Here I will simply note that the piece-rate system caused miners to drive themselves to produce, creating a situation in which very few staff supervisors were required to maintain direct contact with the laborers.

Supervisors

The 1907 Ashio riots set miners against supervisors. As this was the fundamental axis of opposition in the riot, we must examine with care the people who directly supervised the miners.

The Pits Department had complete jurisdiction over miners and all other pit workers. The Pits Department itself was divided into four sections. Three of these were geographical divisions, namely, the pits at Honzan, Tsūdō, and Kodaki. The other was the Survey Section, a single office to compile production statistics and the like, responsible for all three sites. The head of each pit was essentially a section chief, and the Honzan and Tsūdō pit chiefs were graduates of the Mining and Metallurgical Department of the Engineering School of Tokyo Imperial University. The Kodaki chief was exceptional, having been promoted from the ranks of the mine workers.

Each of the pits was further divided into three subsections, with an extraction chief responsible for pit operations, a dressing chief who oversaw the above-ground dressing operation, and a general affairs section. Underground, each pit was divided into seven or eight districts, and guard posts were scattered throughout the pit, each in charge of one or two districts (see Figure P.13). District chiefs were selected from among the employees in each district. Each district chief was assisted by extraction supervisors and gatekeepers. In terms of status, these men stood between the workers and the administrative staff; they were the lowest level of supervisors, in direct con-

Figure P.13. A guard post in the mine. Painted by Yamamoto Shokoku in 1901. From "Ashio-dōzan zue" (a pictorial magazine's special issue on the Ashio copper mine).

tact with the blue-collar workers. They consisted of roughly equal numbers of graduates from technical vocational schools and workers promoted from the ranks. Although we have no statistics showing precisely what sort of workers were promoted to these positions, we can extrapolate from a number of individual cases to say that miners with well over ten years of experience and demonstrated leadership skills were the sort usually selected. Former shorers were more numerous than other sorts of workers.

It is very important to recognize how few supervisors served in each pit, considering they were responsible for round-the-clock management of over 7000 pit workers. On average, each supervisor had charge of fifty-five laborers (see Table P.4).

In addition, at the entrance to the Ashio Mining Company lands stood an inspection post, staffed by about forty patrolmen (see Figure P.13), all with police experience.

Table P.4. Pits Department Management Employees

	Honzan	Tsūdō	Kodaki	Total
Pit chief	1	1	1	3
Extraction supervisors	30	53	26	109
Gatekeepers	6	12	7	25
Total	37	66	34	137

They attended worker meetings, recorded speeches, and observed the activities and language of labor activists.[9]

THE LODGE SYSTEM

At the heart of the work and life of Japanese miners stood the lodge system. (The lodge system is the principal subject of chapter 2, but we must offer a simple overview at the outset). The literal meaning of the Japanese term *hanba*, here translated as "lodge," is "eating place." In fact, each *hanba* included both a mess hall where the miners ate and a dormitory where they slept. Even today the term is used to refer to simple, prefabricated housing provided for laborers at construction sites. But the lodge system was more than a matter of room and board. In Japan it was a mechanism of labor management peculiar to metal and coal mines. A man known as the lodge boss mediated between the mine's management and the mass of the workers. It was this boss, and not the mine's white-collar managers, who was responsible for recruiting and hiring workers, distributing their pay, overseeing their daily lives, and distributing work assignments. Each of these bosses housed and fed the men he had recruited and hired in a lodge (*hanba*), which he also managed.

Like most mines, Ashio was quite remote from other communities. Its manpower needs far exceeded the labor supply within commuting range of the mountain, and few applicants would make their own way to Ashio seeking work in the dark and dangerous pits. The system of lodges came into being as a subcontracting mechanism to gather the necessary workers, provide for and supervise their daily lives, and allocate both work assignments and wages.

Table P.5. Numbers of Lodge (*hanba*) Bosses

	Honzan	Tsūdō	Kodaki	Total
Tōyaku	21	25	21	67
Kumigashira	10	10	9	29
Futō	8	9	4	21
Total	39	44	34	117

Matsubara Iwagorō, a journalist justly famous for his investigative reporting on the poor, has left us the following account of the institution of the lodge system at Ashio at the close of the nineteenth century:

The lodges [*hanba*] are facilities for the care of the miners, and there are currently 28 sites [*kumi*]. Each lodge includes a kitchen and mess hall and a sleeping space and provides the miners with their breakfast and dinner. The lodges are intended solely to accommodate single men. . . . They resemble long barracks built of wooden planks. Most are situated in the vicinity of the refining stations, while one lodge consisting of several dozen shacks is sited halfway up the mountain in a separate district. The four walls of each building are put together with rough wooden planks, with their flimsy roofs weighted down by lines of stones of various sizes. Each building is about 10 ken in length (1 ken = 1.82 meters) and each such lodge accommodates 30 to 50 miners. Each lodge is supervised by a man called a *tōryō*, who has complete authority over all matters relating not only to the miners' pay, but also to their daily rations, bed and board, and every aspect of their lives. . . . Let me discuss the conditions of these accommodations. As noted, the buildings are constructed out of rough wooden planks. In their extreme filthiness they compare unfavorably to the worst of Tokyo slum dwellings. Most are only slightly superior to the worst rented accommodations. They have neither ceiling nor floor; crude straw mats are laid on the bare ground around open hearths. Only in the sleeping area are a few wooden boards laid down to guard against the damp. On top of these are placed wooden draining boards and over these in turn are laid thin straw mats, never *tatami*. No ceiling, no *tatami*, no furniture; a constant accumulation of rubbish, filthy eating utensils, and bedding that gives off a dull sheen, so covered is it with soot and dirt. A person who sets eyes on all this abundance of filth for the first time is rendered quite speechless.[10]

Table P.5 shows the numbers of various sorts of lodge bosses in each of the three main pit areas. The terms *kumigashira* or *tōyaku* indicate the lodge bosses in charge of underground work groups, while *futō* refers to gang bosses of miscellaneous surface workers. All those called *tōyaku* or *kumigashira* were in charge of a lodge, whereas men called *futō* did not necessarily have their own lodging house. Furthermore, although all miners had to work under a lodge boss, they did not necessarily have to live in a boss's quarters. Those with families lived in company-owned tenements (*nagaya*); some single miners lived in the tenements or else rented accommodations in the town.

MINING BROTHERHOODS (*TOMOKO DŌMEI*)

The organizations known as *tomoko dōmei,* here translated as mining brotherhoods, played a vital role in the history of Japan's mine workers. These brotherhoods were a form of craft guild of the miners, autonomous trade organizations with a history reaching back well into the Tokugawa era. Their functions can be roughly divided into three categories: training, mutual aid, and self-government.

To become a full-fledged member of the brotherhood, an applicant was required to apprentice to a designated member for a period of three years, three months, and ten days. During his apprenticeship the novice would learn not only the necessary technical skills, but also the manners and protocols of the brotherhood. This apprenticeship established a pseudofamilial relationship between the master and apprentice that implied a mutual lifetime commitment, and it conferred on the apprentice the responsibility to maintain the master's gravesite upon the latter's death.[11]

Mutual aid was a function of the brotherhood comparable in importance to that of training. Unemployed brotherhood members were known as *rōnin,* a term that originally described a masterless samurai. A *rōnin* miner could present himself to a brotherhood and prove his identity as such by making the necessary ritual greeting.[12] He would be entitled to one day's board and lodging from his "brothers" (*tomoko*). If he wished to work at the mine and there were openings, the local brothers would introduce him to the mine owner or manager, and he was taken on. If there was no work to be had, the brothers gave him a little money, and the *rōnin* continued on to another mine. In addition, if illness or injury prevented a brother from working, the brotherhood gave him a certificate that entitled him to request alms of brotherhoods elsewhere. One certificate certified a temporary injury, another was for permanent disabilities. With either of these, a brother was able to travel from mine to mine and receive assistance from the miners at each site.[13]

Although the brotherhoods were originally organized according to un-written custom, by the time of the riot the Ashio brotherhoods were governed by written bylaws, and they consisted of four distinct organizations at Honzan, Kodaki, Tsūdō, and Sunokobashi, although the last was considered part of the Tsūdō pit by the corporate office. Each brotherhood was an independent organization, but the internal structures of all four were essentially identical. The Kodaki pit brotherhood's "General Rules and Regulations for Ashio Miners," revised one year before the riot, is still extant, and through it we can sketch the outlines of the Ashio brotherhood organization.[14]

The basic unit of the brotherhood was the lodge (*hanba*), and two men from each lodge (*sanchū-iin,* here translated as "lodge representatives") were chosen to attend the meetings of the miners' assembly (*sanchū gikai*), where decisions were made regarding the direction of the brotherhood. The chairmen (*ōtōban*) played a central role in the operation of the brotherhood. They had the authority, for example, to call for a meeting of the assembly. It is not clear why the Kodaki rules include no stipulations for the election of these key officials, but other sources make it clear that the chairmen's positions were not permanent, but rotated monthly among the lodge representatives to the miners assembly. The lodge that provided the chairmen was known as the *hakomoto* (box keeper), and was responsible for the box (*hako*) containing the brotherhood ledger and other important documents.[15]

Among the various regulations in these bylaws, those articles regarding *hakuzoku,* or the theft of copper ore, were particularly important, judging from their detail and number. The term *hakuzoku* referred to the theft by one miner of the ore dug by another. As a miner dug his ore, he bagged it and attached to each bag a wooden tag branded with his number. The rules protecting the miner's ore are extremely strict and detailed. For example, if a bag broke, even moving the ore into another bag without the supervision of a lodge representative would be considered theft. In unclear cases, the miners' assembly would be convened to make a determination, and the expenses of the meeting would be borne by the lodge of the accused. A miner convicted of theft would be expelled from the brotherhood and his name and crime made known to brotherhoods at other mines. The training and mutual aid functions of the brotherhoods are well known among scholars, but these detailed rules of conduct and judicial procedure demonstrate a less-recognized point: the brotherhoods also functioned as self-governing institutions.

Chapter 1

The Subjective Conditions of the Ashio Riot:

A Critique of the Theory of "Atomized Laborers"

From the 1870s to the end of World War I, Japanese workers, mine workers in particular, frequently rioted. I believe that scholars in Japan have still not studied this form of workers' activity sufficiently. They have tended to simply dismiss "the riot" as an example of "violent disorder perpetrated by an ignorant mass or an unconscious workforce." Was this actually the case? What kind of workers started the riots or took part in them, and for what reasons? What kind of riots were they? In this book, I seek to examine such questions afresh through study of the Ashio riot of 1907.

We must begin by examining previous scholarly treatments of the Ashio riot. The first point to make is that no scholar has dealt with the subject in and of itself. Most have simply touched on it in passing in the course of their work on more general historical issues. Typically, they refer to it as "a spontaneous rebellion by unorganized, economically deprived workers," thus generating an image of the Ashio workforce as lacking any sense of independence or solidarity.[1]

THE THEORY OF ATOMIZED LABORERS

Among the most noteworthy of these treatments is that of Maruyama Masao. He conceived a diagrammatic scheme that portrayed stages of the modernization process in terms of types of individual attitudes. As part of this scheme, he analyzed the mine workers of the early 1900s as follows:

Those who may be regarded as typically representative of ATOMIZATION in the 1900s were the workers in such mining industries as coal, copper and silver, or in the shipbuilding and steel industries. The great increase in the productive power in those industries—due to military necessities unmatched in other areas of industry and agriculture—forced them almost constantly to recruit additional labor. Whereas the recruitment of female workers in the textile industries depended heavily upon connections with their native places, the male workers in the mining and heavy industries were either picked up "at random" from among the multitudes of idle labor in the agricultural areas by the "collectors" each company had dispatched throughout the nation, or were taken from the vagrant population "voluntarily" flowing into these industries. One of the characteristics of labor relations in the early days of the industrial revolution in Japan, as distinguished from the period since the middle of Taishō, (1912–1926) was that the employers, relying on the almost limitless number of available workers, were quite unprepared to maintain stable and continuous labor relations, and correspondingly, there was a high degree of migration of workers from one factory to another. This is not to be understood in terms of social mobility in the modern world, for the laborers had not yet constituted a social "class," but existed only as a great multitude of tramps or displaced persons. Moreover, labor conditions in these industries were unbelievably miserable; the *naya* institution of coal mining workers is one obvious example.

What made matters worse was the fact that the rapid expansion of industrial equipment just after the Russo-Japanese War resulted in the decrease of *oyabun*— workers who had hitherto kept personal, albeit patriarchal contact with the "inferior" laborers. Now a situation emerged in which the field officials, often representing the worst side of bureaucratic personality, came to supervise directly great numbers of workers who had already been deprived of every sort of protection. The strikes and riots that broke out frequently in large mines and armament factories soon after the war must be comprehended against such a background. Disturbances in an arsenal in Osaka and in a naval dockyard in Kure (both in 1906) and the famous riots in the Ashio and Besshi copper mines (both in 1907) were chain reaction explosions giving vent to the pent-up grievances of the workers. Their huge destructive power, revealed in such outrages as arson, bomb explosions in buildings, and the assault on the official residence of supervisors, shook the government and company authorities and led to the summoning of troops. True, the contemporary socialists and anarchists were not a little encouraged by the successive uprisings, but these were in fact nothing more than the spasmodic fits of desperately atomized workers and not in any sense part of an organized labor movement. It is no wonder, then, that all such events were squelched very shortly, with small likelihood that they would continue to develop or to spread.[2]

Many of the historical details that inform Maruyama's assumptions and analysis deserve comment in themselves,[3] but what needs above all to be discussed here is the picture of the workforce that he presents, the characteristics of which can be summed up in the word *atomization*. What does Maruyama himself mean by this term?

He argues that in the process of modernization, the individual who has grown up within "traditional" society "is freed" from the restraints of the collective, which has been ruled by fixed standards of traditional behavior. Maruyama calls this universal phenomenon "individuation." He writes:

> Now I should like to suggest that there are four possible patterns of such an individuation process which can be distinguished according to the attitude of the person experiencing various phases of modernization, and which determine his sense of relationship with his community. These four are INDIVIDUALIZATION, DEMOCRATIZATION, PRIVATIZATION, and ATOMIZATION.

The diagram below shows the interrelations and movements of each pattern in the simplest form possible.

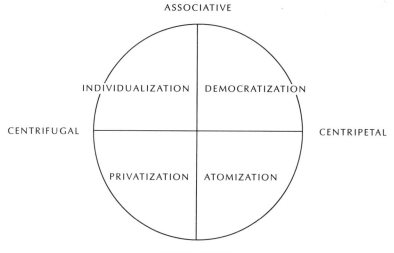

In this scheme, the horizontal axis represents the degree of the individual's distance from the focus of political authority, so that the further a person goes toward the left, the more the degree of centrifugality increases; i.e., the less he is interested in identifying himself with the center of decision-making. In this way, INDIVIDUALIZATION and PRIVATIZATION may be placed toward the left along the axis, in contrast to DEMOCRATIZATION and ATOMIZATION, both of which represent centripetal attitudes toward political authority. The vertical axis, on the other hand, may be made to represent the degree of association that individuals develop voluntarily with each other. Here as we go up the axis we get more associative individuals—those who are ready to associate themselves with their neighbours in order to attain various, not necessarily political, purposes. As we go down, we get *dis*SOCIATIVE individuals whose sense of solidarity with their fellow men is comparatively weak.

Maruyama goes on to characterize the "atomized" individual in the following way:

Diametrically opposed to this [INDIVIDUALIZED] individual is the ATOMIZED individual, who is centripetal and dissociative. He is other-directed. He is the person who bitterly suffers from the actual or imagined state of uprootedness and the loss of norms of conduct (anomie). The feeling of loneliness, anxiety, fear, and frustration brought about by the precipitous change of his environment characterizes his psychology. The atomized individual is usually apathetic to public affairs, but sometimes this very apathy will turn abruptly into fanatic participation in politics. Just because he is concerned with escaping from loneliness and insecurity, he is inclined to identify himself totally with authoritarian leadership or to submerge himself into the mystical "whole" expressed in such ideas as national community, eternal racial culture, and so on. The eruption of this pattern of "individuation" is usually a phenomenon of the stage of high modernization, as was typically the case in pre-Hitlerite Germany. But we can also apply the category to urbanized individuals in the early phase of modernization, for example, in many developing areas.[4]

Problems

Leaving aside the question of whether such a diagrammatic scheme is really an appropriate analytical tool, I will address here the validity of a view of Japanese mine workers in the early 1900s as "an intense example of the tendency to atomization."

First, we need to confirm certain basic facts. Most mine workers came from rural villages. Some had completely severed their links with their villages; others were migrant workers who returned to their villages when they were needed on the farms. The extent to which they had cut ties to their native places differed according to their occupation and the location of those places, but the miners' links with the collective life of their villages had indeed weakened. Further, through working in the mines, they were constantly exposed to the impact of modernization in the form of processes of rationalization, mechanization, and bureaucratization. To this extent, we can agree with Maruyama that the mine workers were indeed undergoing "individuation."

Yet, this does not lead me to accept Maruyama's conclusion that the Japanese miners of the time were a particularly extreme example of "atomization." He seems to consider the repeated riots of miners in 1907 as in themselves proof of their "atomized" condition: "the famous riots in Ashio and Besshi copper mines (both in 1907) were chain reaction explosions giving vent to the pent-up grievances of the workers. . . . these were in fact nothing more than the spasmodic fits of desperately atomized workers and not in any sense part of an organized labor movement."[5] By this key assertion, Maruyama shows that he considers the act of "riot" itself evidence of what he calls "centripetal, dissociative, and other-directed" behavior. The picture that results is one shared by most other researchers to date: workers are devoid of any subjective motivation or sense of independence. In fact, Maruyama does more than assert the mere lack of such subjective qualities. In his view, the workers were not human beings acting on their own volition; as the term *atomized* implies, they were mere bodies, acted upon from without.

Can the riot in fact be characterized in this way? I am extremely doubtful. Are not strikes and even riots both group activities that cannot be considered the behavior of "desperately atomized workers"? If the riots offer evidence of the "associative" tendencies of workers, they can hardly be used as proof of "dissociative" behavior. Thus, to answer these questions, we must investigate the workers' concrete behavior prior to and during the riot.

UNIONS UNDER THE PUBLIC ORDER AND POLICE LAW

The Greater Japan Workers' Association

Nagaoka Tsuruzō, Union Organizer

The most important characteristic of the Ashio miners in the period leading up to the riot is their determination to organize. In the face of numerous obstacles, they attempted to organize a union not once, but three times. Their efforts were finally successful, and the very fact that they achieved this at a time when the Public Order and Police Law made it extremely difficult to organize unions calls into question the assumption that mine workers

Figure 1.1. From left: Minami Sukematsu (1873–1964), Katayama Sen (1859–1933), and Nagaoka Tsuruzō (1864–1914), on their release from prison, 10 February 1908.

were "dissociative." But let us avoid premature conclusions on this matter, and proceed instead to examine the consequences of unionization at Ashio.

On 28 December 1903, a new miner appeared at Ashio. Having presented himself with the customary greetings, he was given a night's board and lodging at each miners' lodge (*hanba*). Accustomed though they were to meeting some strange characters, the men of the lodge were nonetheless amazed by this middle-aged man who was not looking for a job. Rather, he called on them as workers to unite in solidarity with each other. His name was Nagaoka Tsuruzō, and with the intention of forming a national miners' union, he had left his wife and children in Hokkaido to go on the campaign trail (see Figure 1.1).[6] He had chosen Ashio as his first target.

Nagaoka was born in 1864 in present-day Nara prefecture. His father was a doctor of Chinese medicine, who was drawn into the struggles in the closing days of the Tokugawa regime and lost all of his possessions in a fire. He died shortly thereafter. This forced his seven-year-old son Tsuruzō to work, first caring for other children and then as an apprentice in a merchant house. But Tsuruzō was not suited to commerce. In 1880 at age seventeen he began his life as a miner when he took a job as an errand boy for miners at the Munehi mine in Nara prefecture.

Nagaoka joined a mining brotherhood in 1882 and began building his skills, traveling and working at mines throughout Japan. While working at the Arakawa coal mine in Akita prefecture in 1888, Nagaoka's life changed when he heard a sermon about Jesus Christ from a foreign missionary. He was deeply impressed by the story of the crucifixion and the notion that Christ bore the burden of the sins of all humanity. Nagaoka's pleasures until that time had been "drinking, gambling, whoring and fighting," but on hearing this preaching he rethought his deeply sinful life and was baptized as a Christian. Nagaoka resolved to devote the rest of his life to teaching his fellow workers about Christ. To do this, he had to learn to read the Bible. He learned to read from the missionary and continued to study Christianity on his own after he went to Tokyo.[7]

Nagaoka returned to Akita in 1891 and began to work as a Christian missionary himself, organizing a study group of fellow workers. He was particularly impressed that the new Mining Regulations that took effect in 1890 required mine owners to improve safety protections in the mines. Encouraged by this, Nagaoka and his comrades organized a three-day strike at the Innai silver mine in 1893, demanding that the owner strictly follow the Mine Regulations. They won their demands. Later, when the Akita prefectural government imposed a tax on miners, Nagaoka organized workers at several mines in the area in a successful movement for the repeal of the tax. These were Nagaoka's first steps as a labor activist. In the following years he organized strikes against wage reductions, and on moving to Hokkaido in 1897 he made numerous attempts to organize the workers at the Yūbari coal mine. He was a pioneer in Japan's labor movement in the mines.

What led Nagaoka Tsuruzō to Ashio was his meeting with Katayama Sen, who had been a central figure in the Japanese labor movement since 1897, when he had organized the Society for the Formation of Labor Unions. In November 1903 Katayama went on a speaking tour in Hokkaido, giving lectures promoting socialism. At the Yūbari mine he met Nagaoka and Nagaoka's close friend Minami Sukematsu. The three men spent an entire night discussing the future of Japan's labor movement. Katayama was greatly impressed by Nagaoka's obvious talent and rich experience as a union organizer, and he encouraged him to organize miners throughout Japan. Nagaoka took this advice and left Yūbari for Ashio later that year.

For nearly a month Nagaoka went round the four lodge sites urging the miners to unionize. However, he recruited no committed supporters, and after the mining brotherhood's (*tomoko dōmei*) period of customary assistance ran out, the lack of money forced him to continue his campaign while working as a miner. He had been a mine worker since becoming a hauler at the age of sixteen and a miner's apprentice at eighteen, so his fellow miners at Ashio soon got to know of his skill, the product of more than twenty years' experience of the craft. Working together in the darkness of the pits, the men listened more easily to what he had to say than they had done in the lodges, where they were surrounded by others and where the gang bosses and their followers were present. Little by little his fellow workers revealed to him the discontents they vaguely felt in their daily lives.

Of the miners' many grievances, the strongest feelings were directed against company officials (*yakuin*). The relationship between the miners and the officials is extremely important for an understanding of the Ashio riot, and it will be treated in detail below. Stated briefly, the miners' chief grievance related to the bribes they felt forced to offer to influence the low-ranked officials (*genba-in*) who set their wages. Gradually, word of Nagaoka's activities spread among the men, and every evening small groups of seven or eight of them would come to listen to him. Once he had acquired a following, on 11 February 1904 (a national holiday commemorating the mythical founding of Japan by the Sun-Goddess), Nagaoka held his first so-called magic lantern show, a presentation using a slide projector.

Several years earlier, the pioneering socialist organizers Katayama Sen and Nishikawa Mitsujirō had first started using projectors as an attraction to their meetings to discuss labor problems and to their lectures on socialism. In a mining town like Ashio, where entertainment was scarce, Nagaoka's magic lantern shows proved very attractive. He had run similar shows himself in the coal-mining town of Yūbari. Beginning with the show of 11 February, he expanded his activities with a counseling session at Kodaki on 22 February, a second magic lantern show at a Honzan area miners' lodge on the 26th, a meeting at the Hyūganoya restaurant in Akakuramachi in Honzan on 5 March (where he addressed over 150 people), and a third lantern show on 9 March. Then, from the end of March into April, Nagaoka set up the Ashio branch of the Greater Japan Workers' Association (Dai Nippon Rōdō Dōshikai) and gave a series of speeches to launch the organization: at the Iroha-za theater in Akakuramachi on 16 and 17 March, at the Kaneda theater in Tsūdō on 19, 20, and 21 March, and in a shed in Kodaki on 8 and 9 May.[8] His activities had a great appeal; each meeting was attended by some four hundred to five hundred people, and many of these joined the association. To manage the association's activities, Nagaoka quit the mine and set up an office in a room rented from Yamada Kikuzō, manager of the Ashio Printing Works at Akakuramachi. In addition, he opened another temporary office at Kodaki and a workers' clubhouse at Tsūdō. Membership rose rapidly, and by the end of October had passed 1400.

The Goals of the Workers' Association

Nagaoka's hopes for this group can be gleaned from its founding bylaws.[9]

Article 1 The objectives of the Association are to eliminate corrupt practices, promote good relations among workers, serve the people by encouraging faithfulness and good conduct at work, and press to extend workers' rights.

Article 2 The association shall be known as the Workers' Association (Rōdō Dōshikai).

Article 3 The head office of the Association shall be Tokyo Kanda Misakichō 3 chome 1 banchi, and branches will be organized in the provinces.

Article 4 The Association shall elect officers to serve in the following posts: chairman (one), secretary (several), accountant (several), clerk (several), council members (several). A section leader will be elected for every ten members.

Article 5 Association officers shall serve for a period of one year, after which they may be reelected.

Article 6 The names of founding members of the Association and of others who have rendered special assistance to it shall be recorded for posterity so they may be accorded proper honor and thanks.

Article 7 Association members shall conduct themselves at all times in a modest and proper manner and shall fight for justice without resorting to violence.

Article 8 If any Association member impairs the honor and reputation of the Association, a general meeting shall be called at which the offending member shall be expelled.

Article 9 If injury, ill-health, or old age prevents an Association member from working, the Association shall, following consultations, support that member with the sum of 50 yen. This provision will become effective when Association membership has exceeded 1000.

Article 10 The Association shall provide for bylaws for each of its branches.

Article 11 Amendments to the bylaws of the Association shall be made by decision of the Association's general meeting.

These bylaws show clearly that the Greater Japan Workers' Association sought not merely to unionize mine workers, but to organize all Japanese workers. The influence of Katayama Sen accounts for this aspiration. Katayama's lecture tour of Hokkaido in November 1903, when he had visited Yūbari, stayed at Nagaoka's house, and talked well into the night, had led Nagaoka to become a union organizer in the first place. Only a month later, Nagaoka had left Yūbari for Tokyo, where he again met Katayama just before the latter left for the United States. Nagaoka then proceeded directly to Ashio. The Tokyo address that became the location of the head office of the All-Japan Workers' Association was none other than Katayama's private residence and the center of his activities, which included Kingsley Hall, the journal *Socialism,* and the Socialist Society.

When Katayama and Nagaoka met again in Tokyo they doubtless discussed the establishment of the Greater Japan Workers' Association and agreed on its basic objectives, but Katayama probably was not involved in the actual drawing up of the bylaws. If he or his colleague, Nishikawa Mitsujirō, had been involved, the bylaws would not have shown deficiencies such as the lack of reference to eligibility for membership, and they would have been free of a number of spelling mistakes. In drawing up the bylaws, Nagaoka probably referred to the book jointly authored by Katayama and Nishikawa, *Nippon no rōdō undō* (The labor movement in Japan). Articles 1 to 3 of his own bylaws very much resemble the first three bylaws of the Association for the Formation of Trade Unions (Rōdō Kumiai Kiseikai) which are contained in this book.[10]

The two groups nonetheless differed in one significant way. Whereas Nagaoka's Dōshikai was a trade union, Katayama's association was a body formed to "work for the establishment of trade unions." Its bylaws did not therefore include articles relating to financing mutual aid, such as were included in the Dōshikai bylaws. Because there are no surviving records of the bylaws of the Ashio branch of the Dōshikai, which must have been drawn up in accordance with Article 10 of the national bylaws, we do not know Nagaoka's more detailed intentions regarding union organization. However, judging from the objectives stated in Article 1 and the provision for mutual aid laid down in Article 9, we may conclude that the Dōshikai shared the same fundamental character as many other labor organizations of the period, such as the Kiseikai and the Japan Railway Society to Correct Abuses (Nippon Tetsudō Kyōseikai), or the unions that emerged after the Sino-Japanese War such as the Printworkers' Union (Kappankō Kumiai) and the first Friendly Society (Yūaikai). That is, these were all bodies whose main objectives were "to extend workers' rights" and "raise workers' social status," and to this end their bylaws typically spoke of the workers themselves resolving to "remove [their own] long-standing abuses," to be "faithful at work," and to "promote good conduct." All such statements were aimed at gaining the understanding and support of society at large. Furthermore, great emphasis was placed on mutual aid as the means to strengthen workers' solidarity.

Association Personnel

The Greater Japan Workers' Association may have aimed to become a comprehensive, nationwide organization of Japanese workers. In the end, however, it succeeded in recruiting only a portion of the total workforce at Ashio. At the Yūbari coal mine in Hokkaido, Nagaoka had earlier helped to found a workers' organization, and key members of the group held meetings and spoke not only at Yūbari but also at nearby coal mines. They were not entirely isolated in their activity. By contrast, the Ashio branch was the only branch of the Dōshikai organization.

Although documents concerning the Dōshikai are scarce, and they are not very reliable, two points are fairly certain. By October 1904 the branch almost certainly had 1000 members, and most of these were skilled ore diggers. In an interview with branch secretary Nagaoka, the journal *Shakai-shugi* (Socialism) reported that "there are now more than 1400 members," while a report on Nishikawa Mitsujirō's "speeches to the miners of Ashio" in *Shūkan heimin shimbun* (Commoners' weekly) mentioned that "member-

ship has risen to more than 1000."[11] At the preliminary trial hearings following the riot, Nagaoka stated that, "at its peak, membership numbered more
than 1400."[12] Although contemporary official figures are often exaggerated,
it is widely accepted that Nagaoka's testimony was accurate.

What are the reasons for supposing that most of the members were skilled
miners? First, *Socialism*'s interview with Nagaoka gives the full names of
thirteen "Dōshikai officials" and the family names of another four. We can
discover the occupations of the first thirteen from other sources. Five were
skilled ore extractors and one was a shorer's apprentice. Second, Matsuzaki
Genkichi's "Speeches to the Ashio Copper Miners" refers to "the no. 10
miners' lodge at Kodaki from where came most of the members at Ashio."[13]
The representative of Kodaki lodge No. 10 at the miners' council was Kishi
Kiyoshi, later an activist and frequent speaker at meetings organized by the
successor organization to Dōshikai (the Shiseikai). Third, there is the fact
that "more than 60 miners were hired at Ōno Otojirō's lodge precisely because they were Dōshikai members."[14] Ōno was the boss of the No. 14
miners' lodge at Tsūdō. The fact that most of the Dōshikai members whose
occupations are clearly known to us were miners certainly reflects the membership structure of the organization. Moreover, although this evidence is
circumstantial, we also have more substantial and definite information from
Minami Sukematsu's testimony at the preliminary court hearing on the
Ashio riot:

Question: Was it your intention to allow only miners to join?
Answer: No, it was not. We intended it to be open to all workers, but in fact, only
skilled miners did; there were very few members who weren't skilled miners.[15]

Although the vast majority of Dōshikai members were thus surely Ashio
miners, the membership also included a few ordinary citizens. One of these
was Yamada Kikuzō, owner of the premises that housed the organization's
head office. By his own account, he had the role of advisor (*sōdanyaku*).[16]
Another such member was the barber Izumi Yasuji, who not only discounted
his prices to Dōshikai members but also took part in association activities.[17]

Mutual Aid

The Dōshikai used mutual aid to bond its organizing activities together, but
the actual details of the provision of aid were not always clear. Article 9 of the

bylaws stated that if an Association member was prevented from working by "injury, ill-health, or old age," the Association would, "following consultations, support that member with the sum of 50 yen." The question is whether this provision was carried out by the Ashio branch on behalf of the association, or whether the Ashio branch had its own rules relating to mutual aid. Nagaoka's own statements at his trial after the riot support the latter interpretation: "Dōshikai paid out a six-sen-a-day benefit to miners who could not work because of illness. The Association's total income came from the five-sen-a-month subscription paid by each miner. My daily meal expenses amounted to two sen, so because I had to pay the sickness benefit, my wages did not at all cover my expenses."[18]

This statement shows that the association's monthly subscription was five sen. While the provisions for mutual aid are unclear, the most natural interpretation is that those deprived of income owing to illness should have received six sen. If so, then the Ashio branch's mutual aid provisions must have faced a number of difficulties. First, six sen a day as a sickness benefit by no means would have covered a family's expenses; rice alone cost four times more.[19] Nagaoka must have spent twenty rather than two sen a day on food; his statement must have been reported erroneously. Whatever the case, six sen a day as a mutual aid benefit was clearly insufficient to provide a bond for organizing the association. There also existed at Ashio at that time something called the "mutual aid council" (*kyōkyū gikai*). Membership cost ten sen a month, and members who were unable to work for more than five days in cases of injury and ten days in cases of illness received a sickness allowance of ten to fifteen sen a day depending on their work attendance record. The Dōshikai benefit only makes sense when viewed as an increment above this "aid council" allowance.

The second difficulty facing the association was that its subscription was too low to meet its aid obligations. The rate of five sen a month to service a benefit of six sen a day was probably instituted with the "aid council" subscription and allowance in mind, but the latter was financed not only by members' subscriptions but also by additional funds from the Furukawa family and the mine office, plus .3 percent withholding from the company officials' salaries and semicompulsory "contributions" made by traveling salesmen and visitors to the Ashio mines.[20] Further, miners were obliged to join the aid council, and their subscription was deducted from their wages, whereas Dōshikai membership was voluntary and subscriptions could only be collected on an individual basis. The financial failure of the organization was thus inevitable.

Publicity and Educational Activities

Since most miners of the time were barely literate, the Ashio branch of the Greater Japan Workers' Association naturally put most of its energies into publicity by word of mouth. In the three months from February to May 1904 eight meetings and two magic lantern shows were held. In November 1904, Nishikawa Mitsujirō and Matsuzaki Genkichi of the Heiminsha (Commoners Society, a socialist organization) came up from Tokyo and held six meetings, staying until January 1905. No records survive for the interim from mid-May 1904 through October, but an average of some three meetings a month likely took place. Entry to these meetings was not free; for example, an admission charge of five sen per person was taken in November for Nishikawa and Matsuzaki's visit on behalf of the Heiminsha.[21] This was no doubt because of the cost of inviting speakers from Tokyo. A more typical admission charge in Ashio at the time was three sen. The increased admission fee was also necessary to permit the hire of rooms large enough to accommodate a bigger audience, and the later Dai Nippon Rōdō Shiseikai also raised the admission charges to its meetings from three sen to four, and then later to five sen.[22] Despite the high charge for Nishikawa's meetings, the theater was packed, with "hardly room to stand for the more than 1000 people" who came to listen to the speeches. The event, after all, was considered by the miners a form of "entertainment."

What sort of message did these speeches broadcast? A sample account of the content of the speeches of Nishikawa and Matsuzaki survives in the *Commoners' Weekly:*

They spoke in simple terms about several things: the need for miners' solidarity so as to persuade Furukawa to implement strictly the provisions of the new Mining Industry Law; the need for consumers' cooperatives so as to strengthen mutual aid among miners; ways to secure miners' representation on the Ashio town council, since Ashio is a mining town; and the need to petition for ordinary elections to get workers' representatives into the national Diet and to gradually revise laws in order to improve the status of all Japanese workers.[23]

With the exception of enforcement of the Mining Industry Law, these issues—consumer cooperatives, elections for representatives to the town council and national Diet—were not causes likely to mobilize an effective movement of the Ashio miners. Nevertheless, the fact that speakers had come all the way from Tokyo to call for better status for workers must have satisfied many in the audience. Nishikawa noted that the miners "seemed to understand most of what was said and there were many smiling, approving faces."

How did Nagaoka Tsuruzō, the founder of Dōshikai, develop his own message? No records of his speeches survive, but the remarks of Yamane Goichi are of some help. Yamane was editor of the journal *Shakaishugi* (Socialism) in Katayama Sen's absence, and Nagaoka met him when he went to Tokyo to invite leading "socialists" to come to Ashio and address Dōshikai meetings. Yamane summarized Nagaoka's position as follows:

We will always take the side of those who are weak. Whatever the hardship, we will share the plight of the suffering miners. Sympathizing with the miners does not mean opposing the mine owners. We do not understand the actual conditions of the mine as a business operation or the owners' business objectives. Those who are directly responsible for the sufferings of the miners are the company officials and the foremen. Contrary to company policy, they are the ones who act in an authoritarian and arrogant manner, and any penitence on their part would be of direct benefit to the miners.[24]

Does this summary, however, represent Nagaoka's real feelings? Did he really believe that the sufferings of the miners were caused by mine officials and lodge bosses who twisted and distorted company policies? This seems unlikely, judging from his later statements. More likely, he intended to say that the miners certainly suffered terribly as a result of violence and injustice at the hands of the lodge bosses and company officials, with whom they were in daily contact, but that the owners should nevertheless recognize and acknowledge that violence and injustice. Whatever may be the case, this statement was made to a journalist writing for *Shakaishugi* and not to workers at a public meeting. In fact, it is not clear how Nagaoka developed his ideas while he was the leader of Dōshikai. However, at a meeting of its successor group, the Shiseikai, two years later, Nagaoka made a speech that does survive to indicate the direction of his thinking.

At the founding meeting of Shiseikai at a theater in Tsūdō on 5 December 1906, Nagaoka gave a speech titled "Armed Killers and Capitalists: Which Are More Sinful?" Two reports of this speech survive, and we may gain a clear picture of Nagaoka's thinking by comparing them. They reveal both his long-held convictions and also something of the motives that led him to become a union organizer. Despite their length, the reports are worth quoting in full.[25] (The numbers at the beginning of each paragraph were used by the author of a book that cited these reports to indicate their common points.)

Observations at Kodaki of Constable Yamamoto Hisashi

1) First he [Nagaoka] said that when he was a child he knew that he would only live until the age of 44, but then in 1904 he had a dream which showed him to be 44, and he became very pessimistic although he still had three years to go before turning 44. Now he was 44 and still alive. He gave the impression that because he knew he would soon be dead, he had determined to devote himself fully to solving these (miners') problems.

2) He went on to speak about such problems, listing all the cases of injury and death at the various pits and pithead track circuits as he had done many times before. He discussed the reasons for this and even accused the owners of behaving worse than robbers and murderers.

3) He went on to describe the owners' robbery as the theft of miners' money. The 3000 Ashio miners, he said, produced 700 ingots of copper. In other words, each miner produced seven yen and thirty-five sen worth of copper a day, but how much of that did the miner get? It was too much to bear even to mention it. The workers could barely even afford imported rice [viewed as inferior to more expensive domestic rice] and had no mochi rice at New Year. Few capitalists were as mean and heartless as the Furukawas.

4) He commented on the report given by Kojima Jintarō on the working conditions of miners in the United States.

5) Turning to attack the bosses, he said the company had ordered the bosses to recruit miners, but who would want to come and work in a living hell such as this? If any were forced to come, Ashio miners ought to send them away again by singing popular melodies to which they had put their own words about Ashio

6) He went on to raise the case of Jō Seikichi, a loyal worker. Seikichi had been a model worker who worked faithfully for the company, as was widely recognized (he read out a certificate announcing a bonus awarded to Seikichi). But when Seikichi died the other year, surprisingly he left only debts, of 50 yen. He'd worked faithfully for the company for 20 years and yet he'd died with debts of 50 yen. Wasn't it pitiable? So what did the company do for him? They paid a bonus of 35 yen. That

might seem all right by itself, but just think how much money Seikichi had made for the company in twenty years of employment. It must have been about 27,720 yen. What a pittance then was that special bonus of 35 yen! He strongly criticized the owners, saying that greed blinded their eyes to the suffering of the workers.

7) He went on to arouse his listeners' enthusiasm by his explanations of monthly wages, something he had spoken about many times before.

Takeda Tsunagorō's Report

2a) He began by saying that all kinds of evils result from the unequal distribution of society's wealth.

2b) He said that everyone recognizes the evil done by robbers and murderers, but that capitalists' crimes are worse than those. Murderers commit their crimes in various ways, stabbing with a knife or using poison, but the capitalists are different. As everyone knows, they use the trucks that run at Honzan, Kodaki, and Tsūdō. The workers are poorly paid, so they keep the trucks running all the time to make some money. People get hurt by these trucks, because the company makes the workers do impossible jobs. Eight or nine out of ten injuries sustained by old people or children at Ashio are caused by these trucks. Two workers died on the bridge between Hanae-daira and Buzo. The reason why the laborer, Kame, died last year at the Dainichi bridge was that the company had removed the handrails to allow the transport of electricity pylons. A female night soil collector had died in the spring at Honzan Takanosu because the company had not installed the equipment that it was obliged to. The list of such cases was endless, he said. He spoke of the flood six years previously in which dozens of people had died. He said that a total figure of 37 had been reported to the Interior Ministry, but that in fact 30 or 35 people had died at Sunokobashi alone. All these deaths resulted from the company's efforts to cut operating costs. He hoped that no one would be killed at Takanosu and Sunokobashi next year, but he feared they probably would be. Next he spoke about the killing of miners in the pits. The death underground of Yamashita Goromatsu of No. 4 miners' lodge at Tsūdō on the 1st February 1906 had been caused by the fact that there wasn't a single shoring post where he was working. On the same day, Koyama Tsuruzō of Kodaki No. 22 was killed in Kodaki section 4 for exactly the same reason. Two shoring posts were only finally used in digging out the dead bodies.

2c) Wasn't it also appalling, he said, that some men died of their injuries after being taken to the company hospital? Not long ago Tanimoto Kojirō of No. 2 miners' lodge died after receiving an electric shock in a pit at Tsūdō. Dr. Satō at the hospital had written a medical report on the cause of death. The report claimed that Tanimoto had died of cerebral concussion at the lodge. According to the Mining Ordinances, safe pathways are supposed to be laid out underground, but the company still hasn't provided such pathways. Because there are no pathways miners follow the electric truck rails, and because this is dangerous, they ride on the trucks. Officials ride in empty trucks while miners have to ride in full ones, which is also dangerous.

2d) These were all cases of the company's direct responsibility for the deaths of workers, but there were also cases of indirect responsibility, he said, and he went on to describe the company's starvation tactics, saying that workers who became ill as a result of working too long in particularly foul areas underground were denied proper rice or given only imported rice, and that consequently, a miner's life expectancy of 60 years was reduced to 40 in most cases.

6a) He strongly condemned the capitalists for their immorality in not sharing their profits with the miners and for spending them only on their own pleasures and luxurious lifestyles.

7) He gave examples of miners' income and expenditure, bitterly criticizing the debts of more than 18 yen a year which they were forced to run up.

5) He warned his listeners not to lead any new companions into the living hell of Ashio in the next recruitment drive, and he scornfully compared the Ashio gang "heads" to the useless head of a fish from which the capitalists had devoured the succulent meaty flesh.

6b) Next he strongly attacked the company over the amount of money paid to a former Honzan miner, Jō Seikichi.

8) Finally, he concluded by criticizing the ineffective way in which workers at the Akazawa copper mine had staged a strike, saying that if the time came when the company at Ashio tried to force 500 or 1000 miners to quit, workers could avoid the fate of the Akazawa miners by careful preparation beforehand.

I have quoted these two reports of the same speech at such length to get as close as possible to Nagaoka himself and also to show how different two such accounts can be in their emphases. For example, Constable Yamamoto discusses in just one line the fact that Nagaoka listed "all the cases of injury and death at the various pits and pithead track circuits." Yet Nagaoka himself laid the most emphasis on just this point; Takeda Tsunagorō's report reveals it to have been the main point of his speech. The discrepancy stems from the fact that Constable Yamamoto had already attended many of Nagaoka's meetings and was familiar with his basic message. We see from Yamamoto's statement that "this individual had before now made many speeches in various places." By contrast, Takeda was coming to Nagaoka's speech fresh, and he reported it with great interest.

Nagaoka's speech amounted to a strong criticism of the Furukawa Company in that he mentioned the names of victims of industrial accidents and indicated quite clearly the reasons for their deaths. The owners' disregard for the lives of the workers had long been one of Nagaoka's themes; indeed, it was the prime reason he had become a labor activist. His anger at this disregard for human life is expressed clearly in the many accounts of accidents, illness, and death included in the short autobiographical sketch of his life serialized in the journal *Shakai shimbun* (Socialist newspaper).[26] This sketch described the death of Nagaoka's own mentor, and discussed the deaths of many of his comrades from beriberi, the deaths in industrial accidents of a number of Christian miners, and the violent deaths of twenty-six miners in a gas explosion at the Yūbari coal mine. In fact, rather than wage issues, it was the death and sickness caused by industrial accidents that led many miners, Nagaoka included, to think seriously about their situation and, ultimately, to join the labor movement. In passing, it may be noted that another leading Shiseikai activist, Yamamoto Riichirō, was moved to join the labor movement by the loss of his left hand in an industrial accident.[27]

Another noteworthy feature of Nagaoka's speeches was that he legitimized his argument by referring to Japanese law. When people spoke of "rights" in the Japanese labor movement before World War II, they almost never placed labor demands in terms of natural law such as universal human rights. In many cases "rights" were demanded on the basis of the laws enacted in accordance with Article 29 of the Meiji Constitution, which guaranteed freedom of association. Nagaoka's demands were no exception. Repeatedly in his meetings, "he read out a catalogue of the deaths of miners caused by the Furukawa Company and listed the instances in which the company was not implementing the provisions of the Mining Industry Law, claiming that such instances were clear proof of the Furukawas' criminal violations of the laws of Japan." He placed special emphasis on the Mining Industry Ordinances, the Mining Industry Law itself, and the Mining Industry Supervisory Regulations. Passed in 1889 and in force from 1892, the Mining Industry Ordinances included articles relating to workers' protection—what would be referred to today as occupational safety. Section 5 dealt with the supervision of the industry, and it made the minister of agriculture and commerce responsible for supervising the "protection of miners' lives and welfare," laying down by ministerial decree a number of Mining Industry Supervisory Regulations that were to be policed not by the judicial police force, but by the Mining Industry Superintendent's Office. These Mining Industry Supervisory Regulations became law in March 1892 and, together with the Mining Industry Ordinances, were effective from June the same year. The regulations made it compulsory for companies to take safety measures such as the installation within their pits of safety barriers and marked pathways.[28] In blaming the owners' violations of the law for the killing or maiming of their comrades, Nagaoka must have struck a resonant chord with miners who faced danger at work day after day.[29]

At the same time, Nagaoka's call for the company to abide by the Mining Industry Ordinances and the Supervisory Regulations drew attention to the weak points in the Ashio mine operation. Still fresh in the memories of many was the Mine Pollution Prevention Order, which was based on Article 59 of the Mining Industry Ordinances (the order had been issued to deal with the devastating impact of polluted runoff water from the mine on surrounding farmland).[30] Significantly, the Tokyo area superintendent of mines, whose office had issued the order, was none other than Minami Teizō, who had since become the mine director at Ashio. Minami, who had spent his working life as a civil servant, could not totally ignore demands that the company respect the law, and his professional background no doubt played a part in his drawing up, soon after Nagaoka arrived at Ashio, some "splendid letters" that promised "improvements" in respect to the demands Nagaoka was making.[31]

The Impact of the Dōshikai

What did Nagaoka's activities achieve? First, they nurtured a small but very energetic body of labor activists. When the organization later reformed itself as the Ashio branch of the Dai Nippon Rōdō Shiseikai, its leading members were eleven men who had been close colleagues of Nagaoka since the days of Dōshikai. The details of their individual careers are unclear, but all except four were skilled ore extractors, and five served as lodge representatives (*sanchū-iin* or *sanchū sōdai*) to the miners' brotherhood (*tomoko dōmei*) assembly, two of whom were chosen from each lodge. Many were in their thirties and so must have had some fifteen years' experience behind them.

Of the four who were not skilled diggers, one was a shorer and one an ore dresser; the occupations of two men are unknown.

Second, the Dōshikai succeeded in ending unfair dismissals of miners and also effected the dismissal of certain lodge bosses and company officials. Nagaoka is recorded as saying that "until then miners at Ashio had always lost out to the bosses; there was nothing they could do against unfair dismissal, but when Chōkichi was unfairly dismissed, the Dōshikai negotiated with the director, and in the end, Chōkichi won and some of the bosses were sacked instead."[32] Elsewhere, he commented that "six officials were dismissed and two foremen were also forced to leave the mountain.[33] Such claims cannot be verified readily, but we do know that soon after Nagaoka arrived at Ashio, the Dōshikai was in contact with the mine director, Minami Teizō. This is clear from a letter Nagaoka read out at one of his meetings in a speech criticizing Minami: "he drew up some splendid letters, but three years later, he has made no improvements." At that time, Furukawa company policy was changing; the number of officials was being assessed and surplus workers were to be dismissed.[34] Possibly, the company used the Dōshikai's demands to help it carry out this policy. Just over a year later, Nagaoka claimed that "56 minor officials and security staff at Ashio who had shown their loyalty to the company by obstructing our movement were suddenly dismissed as part of a staff reorganization."[35] Taking these things into consideration, it seems probable that in fact Nagaoka and his fellow activists did succeed in obtaining the dismissals of the lodge bosses and the officials through the Dōshikai's activities.

The Breakup of Dōshikai and the Founding of Kyōwakai

The Dōshikai was to last only a short time. The turning point in its fortunes came on 3 November 1904. On that day Yamada Kikuzō withdrew from the organization. He had supported Nagaoka as an adviser to the Ashio branch of the Dōshikai and had lent Nagaoka rooms in his own house to accommodate Nagaoka and his mistress and to serve as the Dōshikai office. As soon as Yamada left the Dōshikai, he launched a series of personal attacks against Nagaoka. According to Yamada, "after setting up the Dōshikai, Nagaoka took a barmaid as wife, his moral standards dropped and there followed many actions which flouted the Dōshikai's idealistic aims." To some extent, Yamada's accusations were true.[36] Nagaoka himself is recorded as saying that he began to live with a woman whom he referred to as "my cook," although it is not known exactly when.[37] The woman was recognized by the preliminary trial judge as "Nagaoka Tsuruzō's common-law wife."[38] The woman in question was Fukuda Fuyo, the widow of a company official at Ashio. She was not merely Nagaoka's "cook"; it is known that she lived with him and supported their household by selling sweets and soap in the streets every day and by working as a factory hand. But this relationship by itself would hardly have justified accusations of a drop in "moral standards . . . and many actions which flouted Dōshikai's idealistic aims." The problem was that Nagaoka already had a wife and family of seven, and that his activities at Ashio were made possible only by their sacrifice.[39] Moreover, in the Association's "Rules for Members," Nagaoka called on Dōshikai members to "improve the dignity of workers," to "walk in the path of justice, help the weak and combat evil in the world." Thus, Yamada Kikuzō's criticisms were indeed justified in part.[40]

But Yamada had an ulterior motive as well. Until 1903, the Yamada Printing Works, "as the only such business in Ashio had been the sole supplier to the copper mine. A multiple workshop operation, the works were able to produce both Japanese and Western-style books. Mr. Yamada Kikuzō . . . studied the printing business in Tokyo for many years and with great skill had brought his company to the point where it was constantly deluged with orders."[41] In 1904, however, another printing company started operating in Ashio, and Yamada's position as "sole supplier to the copper mine" was threatened. Yamada could see clearly that his business would be endangered if he continued to support the Dōshikai. The day Yamada made his speech from an upper balcony of his house attacking Nagaoka and refusing him continued accommodation on account of alleged misconduct in his private life (3 November 1904) was also the day scheduled for a general council of the fifty Dōshikai representatives. At that meeting, twenty-nine supported Nagaoka, and while it is unclear whether the remaining twenty-one took Yamada's side, it is likely that most of them quit Dōshikai and joined the Kyōwakai (Cooperative Harmony Society) formed by Yamada and a number of lodge bosses.

The organizational and campaigning ability of the Kyōwakai was weak. Bringing up lawyers from Tokyo to make further personal attacks on Nagaoka, "getting newspaper reporters to write scandalous stories"—such was the limit of its activity. Nagaoka quickly replied by going to Tokyo himself and inviting Nishikawa Mitsujirō to come to Ashio. The fact that Nishi-kawa and Matsuzaki were able to draw crowds of one thousand to their meetings shows that the formation of Kyōwakai did not deal any sudden blow to Dōshikai. A month later, audiences at Dōshikai meetings were greatly reduced but still numbered from 150 to 350 participants. Despite the fact that the lodge bosses were now openly declaring themselves opposed to the Dōshikai, the organization's ability to maintain itself surely points to a weakening of the bosses' control over the miners. Nevertheless, the bosses' campaign of opposition to Dōshikai was without question a severe blow. Membership declined from a peak of 1400 members at the beginning of 1904 to 1000 at the beginning of January 1905. Declining membership and attendance at meetings pushed the organization's finances, which were always weak, into a critical position.

The Restraining Order

The final blow to the Dōshikai came when the police intervened in its affairs. On 7 May 1905, the Ashio station of the Nikkō Constabulary issued a restraining order against Nagaoka in the name of the governor of Tochigi prefecture.[42] Restraining orders, which dated back to January 1892, originally had been introduced by an emergency imperial edict prior to the infamous second general election of that year to influence the outcome of the election. The edict listed four activities warranting restraint:

(1) those who have no fixed occupation and seek to disturb the peace by inflammatory speeches and arguments; (2) those who disrupt, or who conspire to disrupt, any lawful assemblies; (3) those who interfere or who conspire to interfere in the lawful occupational activities of others; (4) those who, with the intention of causing the offenses cited in clauses (2) and (3) above, circulate writings likely to lead to the offenses cited in clauses (1), (2) and (3) above.[43]

Which of these four offenses applied to Nagaoka is not clear, but at his preliminary court hearing, he told how he had been detained in police custody for three days in the very same month that the restraint order had been served against him.[44] Three days in custody was the lightest punishment handed down for violations of a restraint order, and it applied only to those found guilty of the first of the four offenses. Nagaoka was no doubt found guilty of being "of no fixed occupation [and of seeking] to disturb the peace by inflammatory speeches and arguments." For those found guilty of this offence, the restraint order prescribed the following: (1) the offender was required to seek employment in a lawful occupation and to be employed in that occupation for a stipulated period; (2) the offender was forbidden to attend lawful gatherings and assemblies organized by others; (3) the subject was not permitted, under any pretext, to engage in attempts to extort money, to make unjustified demands for meetings with others, to send threatening or suggestive letters, or engage, by any means whatsoever, in attempts to force others by violence to alter their opinions, nor to prevent or conspire to prevent citizens going about their lawful business.

Thus, legislation originally designed to restrain ruffians and hooligans was now being used to control labor activists. Nagaoka was no longer able to devote himself to Dōshikai activity, because the law did not recognize the labor activist as being employed in "a fixed occupation." There was also the danger that verbal or written requests for meetings with the mine director to demand the implementation of safety procedures would now be subject to legal sanction. Nagaoka said that "for the time being I decided to lie low to gather strength for the future." He went into the grocery business, "selling various kinds of beans from a hand cart." However, police surveillance prevented his business from having much success. It did the same for the ice selling that he started as a side job in his home.

The tightening police control exemplified by the issuing of the restraining order led to an exodus of members from Dōshikai. Apart from a few leading activists, most workers stayed away from Nagaoka. He described this distressful situation to his old friend Nishikawa Mitsujirō in a letter late in 1905: "The pressure from both the owners and the police has been ferocious; all those among us normally given to boasting and bragging have had their legs knocked from under them and are in a daze. I've really been put through it. It's a very painful period. No one has anything to do with me. The employers have been trying to starve me out and I've often had to fast. Friends have given me 5 gō or 1 shō of Chinese rice, but I've had to live like a beggar these last 150 days here at the mine."[45]

As a result of his experiences, Nagaoka's attitude toward workers in general hardened considerably. When questioned at his trial about the reasons for the Dōshikai's demise, he cited the group's financial deficit, but went on: "Very few joined with any real feeling for the needs of the Association. They just joined because they were welcome and made a lot of noise like at festival time without thinking about the future."[46]

In those days, when Nagaoka's activities turned to peddling, he used to walk about selling sweets and singing songs, the words of which he had composed himself and set to the "Rappa bushi" melody popular at the time. One of these, "The Song of the Ashio Workman," reveals something of his feelings toward his fellow workers.

In their struggle for existence, are my friends swooning, or just stupefied? Are they asleep or have they died?

Pale as ghosts, all skin and bone, clothes stained with filth, brows lined with pain.

Not enough food for their families, working day and night, their strength sapped by other men—such is the fleeting life of my friends, empty in its despair.[47]

The Greater Japan Mine Workers' Association

The Amalgamation of the Dōshikai and Kyōwakai

In November 1905, the situation at Ashio took an unexpected turn. The Dōshikai, now reduced to only a few activists, merged with the Kyōwakai, the group formed to destroy the Dōshikai. How did this come about? The judge at Nagaoka's trial made a point of asking this question. Nagaoka replied that not only was the Dōshikai in a bad way, the "Kyōwakai also was disorganized and in decline, and so after some mutual consultations, the two groups decided to merge."

The man who facilitated these "mutual consultations" was Ishida Kishirō, boss of Tsūdō's No. 1 lodge. The groups agreed to amalgamate following Ishida's "personal suggestion that if Dōshikai was in danger of going under, it should mend its fences with Kyōwakai."[48] That Ishida, who helped lead the movement against the Dōshikai, would suggest "mending fences" with Kyō-wakai is surprising but not incomprehensible.[49] "Crush the strong and help the weak" was a saying that summed up one of the characteristic qualities of chivalry demanded of a gang boss. With over one hundred miners, Tsūdō's No. 1 lodge was the largest at Ashio, and it can easily be imagined that Nagaoka, who described Ishida as "a very strong-willed fellow," judged him to be the type of man with just such qualities. Nagaoka's own words and behavior reveal clearly that he and Ishida shared the same mentality.[50] Ishida, for his part, no doubt felt that Nagaoka, who carried on with his activities even in the most trying and painful circumstances, was "a valiant foe" and that to ignore his distress would be too shameful for the boss of Ashio's largest *hanba*.

On 17 and 24 November and 10 December, "nearly 1000 miners from the Ashio Tsūdō pit area chose two representatives from each lodge" who then "held three assembly meetings which drew up the [amalgamation] agreement."[51] The "amalgamation implied that the organization had somehow collapsed, and that was embarrassing, so it was decided to change the name, and on the 1st January 1906, the Greater Japan Mine Workers' Association (Dai Nippon Kōzan Rōdōkai)" was formally instituted.[52]

The points to note are the "nearly 1000 miners from the Ashio Tsūdō pit area" who "chose two representatives from each lodge" and "held three assembly meetings." First, the expression "nearly 1000 miners" suggests that whereas miners joined the Dōshikai and the later Shiseikai singly, as individuals, the Greater Japan Mine Workers' Association recruited the miners of the Tsūdō area lodges en masse. Second, the activity in which were chosen "two representatives from each lodge" who "held three assembly meetings" duplicated the functions of the miners' brotherhood (*tomoko dōmei*) at Ashio. Since the names of the association's lodge representatives are unknown, we cannot confirm whether or not they were the same men as the lodge representatives to the brotherhood, but the body of members was the same, as was the size of the units choosing representatives and the number of representatives selected. Very likely, the same people were elected in both cases. Third, unlike Dōshikai and Shiseikai, the Mine Workers' Association was an organization of Tsūdō men only, and it was clearly organized from the top down by the lodge bosses. The organizational units of the Ashio brotherhoods were the four pits at Tsūdō, Honzan, Kodaki, and Sunokobashi. Each had its own agreements and its own organizational management. However strong a lodge boss Ishida Kishirō may have been, and whatever influence he may have had over other bosses, he was only able to exert direct control over the men at Tsūdō.

What then was the connection between the Mine Workers Association and the Tsūdō brotherhood? Extant sources offer no concrete evidence for such a connection, but a report on the founding of the association in the journal *Hikari* [The Light] makes clear that while it subsumed some of the functions of the brotherhood, it by no means replaced it. The association fulfilled none of the mutual aid functions of the brotherhood or even of the Dōshikai. The *Hikari* report lists the following goals of the association:

(1) To engage the services of suitable lawyers who can act as legal consultants to press persistently for legal rights in accordance with the provisions for workers' protection laid down in the new Mining Ordinances due to take effect from the 1st July this year. (2) To put aside as much as possible of members' monthly dues as insurance for the future. (3) To introduce workers to new ideas by occasionally inviting academics to lead study and discussion groups. (4) To establish an asylum for the elderly and the infirm. (5) To safeguard the welfare of unemployed miners through workers' solidarity. (6) To take action against illegal operations by employers and against unjust and unfair treatment by company officials by reporting such operations and behavior to newspapers and magazines. The organization aims to recruit all Japanese miners.[53]

It is difficult to form any judgment based on such scanty material, but we may conjecture that the association was an attempt to use the brotherhood organizational structure and transform it into a modern trade union.

However, the Mine Workers' Association flourished for only a very short period and soon disappeared under company pressure. Surprised by the new group, the company threatened to cancel Ishida Kishirō's appointment as gang boss.[54] It would seem that Ishida's chivalrous spirit wilted before the threat of dismissal, and he soon pulled out of the association.

THE FORMATION AND ACHIEVEMENTS OF THE DAI NIPPON RŌDŌ SHISEIKAI (GREATER-JAPAN SOCIETY OF DEVOTION TO JAPANESE LABOR)

The Ashio Branch of Shiseikai

Minami Sukematsu and the Change in the Movement's Aims

On 27 October 1906 an old colleague of Nagaoka from his time at the Yūbari coal mine came to Ashio. His name was Minami Sukematsu. He had been to Ashio once before, in July, to hold meetings, and had since decided to move the base of his activities from Yūbari to Ashio. He arrived at the mine with his wife, Misao, rented rooms on Matsubarachō, Tsūdō's main street, and immediately put up a sign in the name of the Greater-Japan Society of Devotion to Japanese Labor (Dai Nippon Rōdō Shiseikai; hereafter, Shiseikai). Minami spent his first month at Ashio in preparation, holding only a small meeting on 29 October, gathering information, meeting with the remaining activists from the Dōshikai period, most notably Nagaoka, and visiting company officials and lodge bosses to try to obtain their cooperation. Finally, on the evening of 5 December, the Ashio branch of Shiseikai was formally declared open at a big meeting in Tsūdō's Kaneda theater.

Invited to the meeting were all Ashio lodge bosses, mining brotherhood stewards, and company officials, as well as leading townspeople. Teams with flags and drums were sent around to advertise the event and hand out leaflets. Even those who were accustomed to such advertising tactics from three years of Nagaoka's activities were keen to know what this new man, who had come all the way from Hokkaido, was going to say. Company guards estimated that five hundred were in attendance, including some four hundred who paid the four sen admission charge.[55]

The meeting began at 6:15 P.M., more than one hour behind schedule. First, workmen's songs were sung, and then Minami Sukematsu opened the meeting with a few words, followed by congratulatory addresses and five telegraph messages from Shiseikai members in Hokkaido, read by Hayashi Kotarō and Imori Shingo. The formal opening over, the meeting proper began with speeches from Imori and Hayashi, Kishi Kiyoshi, Nagaoka, and finally Minami Sukematsu, who delivered a fiery oration entitled "An Appeal to the Miners of Ashio." Minami proposed a platform for the Shiseikai, focusing on three issues: conditions at Ashio, the goals of the movement, and the means to achieve them.

Minami's view of the situation at Ashio was the opposite of that of Nagaoka during the days of the Dōshikai. Nagaoka used to say, "It's the officials and the foremen who are most directly responsible for the miners' suffering. They go against company policy, throwing their weight around in an arrogant manner." Now Minami argued that "the lodge bosses can't be blamed for being the way they are, and the reason why company officials demand bribes is because they are paid a pittance. Even the mine director and the white-collar staff are badly off. The management are given an initial budget of 100,000 yen and they are expected to save 10,000 yen of that. The more they save, the better their prospects, so that's what they do out of loyalty to the company, and as a result, the miners' wages stay low. It's the company that's to blame for everything."[56] This analysis seems more accurate than that of Nagaoka. As a result of the Mining Pollution Prevention Ordinance of 1897, Furukawa company policy changed from one of expansion to one of retrenchment and stabilization; the company sought to cut expenses in all aspects of its operations. Thus, despite inflation and a sudden rise in the price of copper, the company held down miners' nominal wages and their real wages fell.[57]

Minami presented two goals of the movement: wage increases for workers and officials, and improvements in workers' food rations. The call for improved quality of the workers' food needs some explanation. At that time Ashio employees obtained their daily necessities mainly from the four company stores (see Figure P.10), which supplied such things as rice, miso paste, soy sauce, salt, firewood, and straw sandals. Cash was not accepted at the stores; each worker was given a booklet in which the value of each purchase of goods was entered. At the end of the month, the total was deducted from his wages. Although the system meant that workers could buy goods at relatively stable prices, which were actually lower than the ones in town, and although it offered a form of credit to obtain such goods with no cash in hand, it created several problems. When the goods were handed out "the clerk would calculate the worker's daily wage and assess whether or not the wage was enough to pay for the goods. The worker was only allowed to buy the amount he was capable of paying for, and no more, thus strictly regulating expenditures as well as 'encouraging' workers to report for work." That is, those who missed work, even if due to injury or illness, would have their rations restricted.[58] Workers were also chronically discontent with the unfair administration of this system and the poor quality of goods.[59] Further, officials and ordinary workers did not receive the same rations. Officials were supplied with domestic rice, rated as "top quality," while the workers were allowed to purchase only "standard quality" foreign-grown rice (so-called Nanking rice), no matter how high their wages. Not only was the foreign rice nonglutinous and therefore not to the liking of the Japanese, it also had a particular odor owing to shoddy packaging during transport. Eating it was said to be like "chewing plaster."[60]

In a life of unremitting hard labor, appalling living conditions and quite limited entertainment, meals had always been one of the miners' few pleasures. Many observers commented on "the extravagance of their eating and drinking habits" and "the bad habits of their excessive eating and drinking." Exactly when Japanese rice was replaced by foreign rice is not clear, but several sources indicate that the change came with the new Furukawa company policy in 1897 that made all sections in each of the company's mines responsible for their own budgets.[61]

Skilled, highly-paid miners who disliked the "standard quality" imported rice sold at the company store could, if they lived with their families, buy more expensive domestic rice from rice merchants in town. Single men could enjoy themselves in local restaurants and eat better rice there. If these men had been brought up on foreign rice, and if all those around them were also eating it, then they would have been less frustrated. But miners knew that the only way they could eat domestic rice was by increasing their output and wages, and frustration built up over the company's policy of selling them only foreign rice. Further, even before this issue surfaced, the relationship between miners and officials had been tense. The miners harbored particularly strong resentments against the lower-ranked officials with whom they came into daily contact. Most of these grades were filled by men who were chosen from among the miners, and their wages were often lower than those of the most productive miners. As Minami Sukematsu pointed out, the low wages of these officials led them to solicit bribes from their men. But when ordinary miners had any dealings with these men, they had to act dumb, bow low, and "keep repeating yes boss, yes boss, with heads bowed."[62] If a miner upset an official in any way, this could immediately affect his work assignment, his output, and thus, his income.

So when Minami Sukematsu drew attention to the fact that "in Hokkaido workers get Japanese rice. They can get rice easily and sake too, but here it's foreign rice and if you're off for three days, you get nothing, so workers are forced to go down the mine even when they're ill," and called for the withdrawal of foreign rice, he was rubbing salt in a raw wound.[63] The workers were angry about foreign rice not just because it tasted to them like "bits of plaster." They were angry over the way the company hedged in their lives with its rules and unfairly discriminated against them. Their response reflected anger at the contemptuous way in which low-ranking officials treated them.

What was the substance of Minami's third point, the methods to be used to realize of the group's objectives? He proposed the tactic of mass resignation, which amounted to a strike. When the membership of Shiseikai exceeded one thousand, he said, "we shall in the proper manner put forward our demands and press for gradual improvements," and "even if the company chooses to regard us as rioters, we shall not resort to violence. We shall also not go on strike, although we shall not deny ourselves the option to do so if the situation were to become extreme. What we shall do in most cases is quit and move on to other mines. In that way the company cannot bring in the police to suppress us, but if they did, as workers exercising our right to withdraw our labor, we would be justified in defending ourselves against those who attempted to stop us and would certainly be prepared to fight."[64]

The Public Order and Police Law of 1900 prohibited "attempts to incite or to agitate others" to go on strike, and it laid down penalties for infringement of "between one and six months' imprisonment with hard labor." In response to this, Minami, Nagaoka, and other Shiseikai activists often commented at their meetings on cases of strikes both in Japan and abroad, and called for "complete solidarity in pressing demands to the limit." They insisted that the simultaneous withdrawal of labor was lawful, because it was "self-directed, not other-directed" through incitement and agitation. Hayashi Kotarō, an activist since the Dōshikai days and a lodge representative at Tsūdō, straightforwardly declared, "If they still won't listen to our demands, then we'll have to xxxx [strike]."[65]

That the Shiseikai shared a number of characteristics with the Dōshikai and other labor organizations of the period can be seen from the four articles of its "constitution" drawn up at the time of the founding of the organization in Hokkaido in 1902. These called for (1) raising the status of workers, (2) fostering a spirit of independence and self-control, (3) encouraging habits of thrift and savings, and (4) mutual respect and mutual aid among members.[66] However, there was one clear difference between the Ashio branch of Shiseikai, founded after Minami's arrival at the mine, and all previous workers' organizations. This was its emphasis on becoming a union determined to realize its demands for higher wages through the withdrawal of labor, rather than a group that made raising the social status of workers through mutual aid and education its priority. Nevertheless, there is absolutely no evidence that Shiseikai at this stage made any concrete plans for strikes. It simply called on workers to constantly maintain the resolve to see their "demands" through.

Clearly, however, this Shiseikai objective was decisive in renewing a union organization at Ashio that had already suffered two major setbacks. Not only did Minami clarify the central demand of workers who had only expressed themselves in a vague manner until then. He also made them aware that this demand was both justifiable and achievable. In particular, Minami gave the workers strength when he guaranteed them reemployment in other mines if they were fired for their union activity.

The change in union objectives was not, of course, the only reason for the growth of Shiseikai. The considerable sum of union capital that Minami had been building up was surely of no little significance. When he left Yūbari, he had "borrowed" 250 yen and 150 yen, respectively, from two executives of the Hokkaido Coal and Steamship Company, and after moving to Ashio he "borrowed" two further sums of 50 yen each from one of these men.[67] This money enabled him to rent rooms on Tsūdō's main street and treat lodge bosses and brotherhood representatives to meals in noodle shops where he explained the Shiseikai to them. How Minami was able to secure the "loans" from the Hokkaido Coal executives is still unknown. Possibly, they were a form of "severance pay" to get him to give up his union activities at Yūbari, but if so, it was hardly necessary to pay him a further 100 yen after he arrived at Ashio. More likely, Minami convinced the coal executives to send the money in return for a promise to persuade Ashio workers to quit Ashio and move up to Hokkaido. In his speeches, Minami made frequent references to the high wages paid in Hokkaido, and he assured the audience that "even if 1000 or 2000 miners left Ashio, it wouldn't make the least difference." Minami also made no secret of having received this money, and his colleagues often mentioned it. At a meeting of the Tsūdō brotherhood assembly, for instance, Imori Shingo "boasted that there was no need to worry because if Shiseikai's demands were rejected at Tsūdō or by the main office at Honzan, Minami Sukematsu would be able to get 200 yen from Hokkaido, and these remarks strengthened their resolve and gave them the impetus to make their demands."[68] At Shiseikai's inaugural meeting, Nagaoka also declared that "even if 500 or 1000 men go down the road, it'll make no difference as long as we're prepared."

Shiseikai's Influence on the Bosses and Brotherhoods

The Shiseikai believed that to win a pay increase it especially needed the cooperation of the lodge bosses and the brotherhood assembly representatives. As described in the prologue, at Ashio there were about one hundred lodges for all those workers belonging to the Pits Department: all underground workers such as miners, shorers, carters, and haulers, and also the male ore dressers. There were a further seven lodges for the ore-refinery workers, and several more for Engineering Department workers and workers such as carpenters and the laborers who belonged to the Supply Department.

These lodge bosses (who will be discussed further in Chapter 2) still held the power to hire and fire the workers. They loaned money and equipment to the men and generally "looked after" them, and their influence over the men was considerable. Their attitude had to be taken into account by anyone attempting to reach the workers as a whole. It was clear to Shiseikai leaders that the understanding and cooperation of the lodge bosses would greatly help them realize their demands, since the bosses acted as the official channel through which the frustrations and desires of the workers were conveyed to the company. While the miners' brotherhood was an organization of miners only, the assembly representatives did not have managerial authority over the workers, as did the lodge bosses. The miners, however, constituted the most essential nucleus of the entire workforce and far outweighed other workers both in numbers and importance. The company could therefore not ignore the brotherhoods. The assembly representatives, precisely because they were elected from among the men themselves, had influence among the men greater than that of the lodge bosses. The Shiseikai leaders therefore looked to secure the support of these two groups.

Of course, the lodge bosses had opposed the Dōshikai and cooperated with the Mine Workers' Association to this end. Certainly it would be a delicate matter for Minami's group to deal with them. To obtain their cooperation, Minami paid courtesy calls on the most authoritative bosses and showed understanding for their "hardships." He invited them to meals and paid them all due respect. To some extent, his efforts paid off. He and his colleagues did not expect the bosses wholeheartedly to support the Shiseikai, but for a time the bosses held back from opposing the group publicly.[69]

Compared to the lodge bosses, the miners' brotherhoods cooperated readily with the Shiseikai. These brotherhoods at Ashio had never formed a united body. The groups centered around the four pits at Honzan, Kodaki, Tsūdō, and Sunokobashi each responded to Shiseikai in different ways. Tsūdō cooperated most energetically, followed, in descending degrees of cooperation, by Honzan, Sunokobashi, and Kodaki, but even the last two were by no means hostile. Many of Tsūdō's brotherhood assembly representatives had attended Shiseikai's founding ceremony, and after the speeches, all took part in the social gathering. Minami is recorded as commenting:

"Having decided to hold a party at an admission fee of 20 sen per person, we all went to Komatsuya. On that occasion there were about 25 assembly representatives (names unknown), myself, Nagaoka, Imori, Hayashi, Yamamoto, Izumi Yasuji, Katō Hidematsu, and Yamazaki Inuhei."[70] Imori, Hayashi, and Katō were all brotherhood assembly representatives from the Tsūdō lodge, as well as members of Shiseikai. Of Tsūdō's thirty-six representatives, twenty-eight attended the Shiseikai party. The fact that the Shiseikai office was located in Tsūdō, near the theater where the founding ceremony was held, is certainly part of the reason for such a high rate of attendance. But a more important reason for the friendly relations between the Tsūdō brotherhood and the Shiseikai is that, although the Mine Workers' Association had collapsed, its organization had been virtually identical in membership to the Tsūdō brotherhood. Although the association had been organized "from the top down," it was nonetheless an organization of Tsūdō miners that was separate from the brotherhood and was "officially" recognized by both the lodge bosses and the brotherhood. It is surely no coincidence that most Dōshikai and Shiseikai activists were Tsūdō miners.[71]

In mid-December, Shiseikai made a final effort to gain the support of the lodge bosses. All the Tsūdō bosses were invited to a meal at a restaurant where "they were asked to support a petition of 1000 to 1500 workers for better rice and higher wages." The bosses replied that "as individuals they would be sympathetic, but as lodge bosses, it was difficult for them to show support."[72] These were not individual replies of Tsūdō lodge bosses; it was their common view, one they had agreed on in their own meeting prior to the dinner. Minami then went to a meeting of all the Honzan lodge bosses on 18 December, where he made the same appeal for support. The bosses replied that they "would discuss the proposal well and give him a reply, and after he left, they opened a discussion and decided that, given their relations with the company, they could not openly lend their support, but neither would they put any obstacles in the way."[73] Minami later said of this meeting, "I was not expecting the bosses to support Shiseikai. I just went to see if they were going to oppose us or not."[74]

In fact, even with Minami observing all the proper courtesies, it is still surprising that for some time the bosses refrained from attacking Shiseikai. After all, Minami's promise to lead one or two thousand men off to Hokkaido if necessary amounted to a public declaration that he would remove the source of the bosses' income. Probably the bosses felt that talk of one or two thousand resignations was excessive and unrealistic, while at the same time, they could not deny Minami's argument that calls for improvements in wage levels and in the quality of rice were justified.

In any case, by late December, Shiseikai had abandoned hopes of gaining the support of the lodge bosses and turned instead to the brotherhoods. On 22 December, after a public meeting at the Iroha theater,

the Honzan assembly representatives were invited to the Azumaya restaurant. Those attending were Kawase Shohei, Maruyama Sukematsu, Tsuruta Uchinosuke, Kaneko Hisakichi, Tabata Kamenosuke, and some thirty other miners. Minami Sukematsu put to them the following proposals: (1) to secure wage increases and better working conditions all round which would be to the advantage of the workers, it was necessary to build up the Shiseikai membership and workers' solidarity, and if the assembly representatives joined, all the other workers would too. He therefore hoped that the representatives present would cooperate on behalf of those who were not.

Minami went on to suggest that "all membership dues would go to the union and would not be used for any individual's personal expenses, as had happened when Nagaoka formed the Dōshikai." Certainly, one of the accusations made against Nagaoka as leader of Dōshikai was that he had "appropriated union funds and lived off the workers." After listening to what Minami had to say, the Honzan assemblymen "were all in agreement with it, and Tsuruoka Ushinosuke formally gave that agreement to Minami Sukematsu on behalf of all of them."[75] The next day, 23 December, Minami met with the Kodaki assemblymen, but without success. They gave him a letter "which said that Kodaki could not join Shiseikai."[76] On 26 December he sent a letter to the Sunokobashi treasurer, asking for a meeting. He received another letter of refusal, which asked him "to understand that if the Sunokobashi brotherhood treasurer were to cooperate with Shiseikai, the lodge bosses would make trouble." But on 2 January 1907, accompanied by a group of Sunokobashi miners who were all "Shiseikai enthusiasts," Minami visited Sunokobashi, gathered about ten miners when the treasurer was away, and called for their participation in the demand for higher wages. "All of those present demonstrated their agreement."[77]

The Company's Response

The company had been monitoring Shiseikai's activities from the start. A constable was always present at Shiseikai meetings, taking notes of the content of the speeches, recording the listeners' reactions, and checking the names of the most prominent members of the audience. But despite these information-gathering efforts, the company seemed to lack any clear plan of action against Shiseikai's ongoing activities. Surviving sources that reveal anything of how management saw the situation are poor, and we have nothing like a clear picture.[78] Nevertheless, the decisions implemented by managers at this time strongly suggest that Furukawa executives as well as the local managers at Ashio did not understand the seriousness of the situation. On 6 December 1906, when frustrations over low pay were spreading rapidly among the Ashio workers, the Furukawa family "decided at a family council to donate 1,060,000 yen to building funds at Fukuoka College of Engineering, Sendai College of Science, and Sapporo College of Agriculture."[79] This sum exceeded the annual profit for the year 1905 from the entire Ashio operation, and was equivalent to the total Ashio wage bill for 1906. Such an enormous donation infuriated the Shiseikai leaders, and they were soon condemning it in their speeches.

The Furukawa Company pays out 7,000,000 [sic] yen to build schools for the children of the rich, but it gives nothing to the place where we miners work. Our organization is still young, we must unite to fight against the company. (Kishi Kiyoshi)

Furukawa has donated the colossal sum of 8,000,000 [sic] yen to three universities in Fukuoka, Sapporo, and Sendai, but to we who are suffering here, they give nothing but lies. Why did they only spend 2,050,000 yen to build the places we, the exploited, have to live in? (Hayashi Kotarō)[80]

These donations to help establish three imperial colleges in Kyushu, Tohoku, and Hokkaido had been made at the suggestion of the home minister, Hara Kei.[81] At this time, Furukawa Ichibei's adopted son, Junkichi, had died, and his natural son, Toranosuke, had been appointed president of the company. But Toranosuke was still young and, furthermore, was still abroad studying. Real power in the Furukawa family was in the hands of Junkichi's natural brother, Mutsu Kokichi, at whose request Hara Kei became pro tempore vice president and "advisor to the Furukawa family." Hara Kei, who had no knowledge of or interest in the problems of Furukawa management, could hardly have appreciated how inappropriate his timing was. One who did was Kimura Chōshichi, chief auditor of the company, Toranosuke's guardian and a participant in family council meetings. But Kimura would not have presumed to oppose the "suggestion" of the home minister. At the same time the donations were made, fresh cases of the company's discriminatory treatment of its workforce poured yet more oil on the fires of the miners' frustrations as, at the end of 1906, the company paid a special year-end bonus to "officials" only. This naturally fed the anger of Shiseikai members.

From all its profit at Ashio and elsewhere, the company paid out a special bonus of between 10 and 30 yen on 26 December, but who do you think produced that money? The workers who had sweated for it were told nothing. What are they playing at, giving it to errand boys who spend all their time dozing and to thieves who steal oil? (Imori Shingo)

Because the price of copper was good, the company was able to pay out a special bonus of 300,000 yen, and where did they get that money? From the skill of you miners working in the darkness of the pits, that's where. From the sweat of workers in ore-dressing and refining. They weren't able to produce that money from officials who spend all their time dozing. They got it because of us workers. Yet they look down on us as if we were oxen. (Yamamoto Riichirō)

Thanks to an unprecedented rise in the price of copper, on the 26th December last, the company awarded each grade of staff a special bonus. That was wrong. They should have paid it to ordinary workers like the underground miners who have to hammer away with their chisels in the darkness or the refinery workers who have to work in the raging heat of the furnaces. This is an example of the company's abuse of its workers. (Yamamoto Riichirō)[82]

Clearly the company's top managers did not recognize how serious the situation had become. Ashio's director, Minami Teizō, traveled to Tokyo on 17 January for a meeting with top company executives to discuss the problem of wage increases, but reached no early decision. He remained in Tokyo, idling away his time. According to newspaper reports after the riot, he "went to Tokyo on the 18th of last month on company business and for treatment of his diabetes, and was planning to go on to the resort town of Atami for rest and recuperation."[83] He finally arrived back in Ashio on 5 February, after the outbreak of the riot.

The Response of Ashio Mine Managers

Of course, the company was not entirely without a labor policy. Around 25 December 1906, the pit managers at Tsūdō and Kodaki informed the lodge bosses under them that "if Shiseikai submits a formal set of demands, rather than accepting demands from people unconnected to the company, they should adopt the line that demands will only be accepted through the lodge bosses who are the direct intermediaries between the company and the workforce."[84] About the same time, the Honzan lodge bosses announced as a group that they "would explain to the Honzan pit manager the need for improvements in the quality of rice and for wage increases, and would formally submit demands [to him]."[85] From the records it seems as if these demands resulted from a spontaneous initiative by the lodge bosses, but the timing and contents of the demands would suggest that they were prompted by management.

By pushing the lodge bosses to submit demands ahead of the Shiseikai, the company in effect forced the bosses to drop their erstwhile "neutrality" and take a position that clearly opposed the Shiseikai. The problem with such a policy was that the final decision over any wage increases lay with the company board, not with local Ashio managers. Because the board had not agreed to any improvements in wages at the time the lodge bosses were encouraged to put forward their demands, no prompt reply was possible. Therefore, from the time the bosses submitted their demands, on 7 January 1907, nearly a month went by with no response from the company, and the riot took place in this interim. Why did it take so long to decide on a wage increase? Probably because compared to the pit managers in direct contact with the workers, Director Minami Teizō was lukewarm about offering a wage increase. He did not have the enthusiasm or the power to persuade board members who feared the impact of an increase at Ashio on the company's other mines. Even after the riot, Minami was saying that "the decision to increase wages was far from easy and due consideration had to be given to the need to preserve the balance with wage levels in other mines. On this occasion it was therefore necessary, whatever the risk of a riot, to proceed with the utmost caution in order to avoid creating worse problems for the future."[86]

The Supply of Japanese Rice to the Workers

The company's second tactic to deal with the Shiseikai was to supply Japanese rice to the workforce. This step was announced at the beginning of January and put into effect on 1 February. Authority to make this decision probably did lie with local management, and here again the intent was to preempt a formal demand from Shiseikai. Here as well, however, the managers who handled the issue failed to perceive accurately the depth of the anger that fueled the demand for "improvements in the quality of the rice provision," for the company merely offered the workers access to poor-quality Japanese rice, and it limited to company officials access to rice designated "top quality." Shiseikai activists all took up this issue in speeches criticizing the company on 1 February.

The other day, passing the company store, I saw the announcement of the rice supply [written on a blackboard]. It said that best quality rice was limited to officials only, at a cost of 18 sen per sho, while ordinary Japanese white rice would cost 16 sen 5 rin. What an example of the cold and heartless way the company treats its workers! This is nothing but a way of emphasizing the gap between the officials and the rest of the workforce. What a way they've chosen to do it! By this unfair distribution of rice, which can only be described as a contemptuous and hard-hearted act, they've built a wall around every individual miner who can't afford to concern himself about the dangers to his health and who has to breathe filthy air, working long hours in the dark with only his lantern as a companion. The quality of the white rice is poor, and husks are left in the mere 3 sho 5 gō that we are allowed [he showed them a handful, about 2 gō of husks]! Such base methods are despicable and hateful. Their outrageousness is intolerable. We must all band together and demand a system of cash payments. (Yamamoto Riichirō)

As the previous speakers have already said, the Ashio managers have finally begun to sell Japanese rice to working miners, who are, after all, Japanese citizens. Many of you will have no way of judging the quality of this rice, but from what I've seen of the rice some colleagues of mine got, I can tell you I was really shocked at the poor quality of it. So many husks are left mixed in with the rice and although I can't claim to judge the quality of all of it, what I have seen is proof enough for me that there was never any careful selection of the rice. Whether it was careless selection, or rough handling by the suppliers, or whether it was the familiar habits of the officials, I'll leave to you to judge. So much for Japanese white rice. It is hard to see what is the real motive for saying that what was "quality rice" is now to be called "best quality rice" and sold to officials only. Dividing Japanese rice into two classes and discriminating by supplying officials with class 1 rice and workers with class 2 is clearly contemptuous of workers and amounts to the tyrannical enforcement of a system which sees the workers as slaves! What is the reason for not supplying workers with best quality rice? We must have a system of cash payments. Then the worker can buy the rice that he wants with his own money. (Nagaoka Tsuruzō)

There are now two classes of quality Japanese white rice, and best quality is for officials only. Why have ordinary workers been denied this privilege? This is a clear sign of the increasingly vicious system of slavery which is being imposed. (Minami Sukematsu)[87]

In response to Shiseikai's claims that "foreign rice" was a symbol of discrimination between officials and workers, the company (i.e., the officials), while appearing to recognize Shiseikai's demands, actually held fast to its policy of discrimination. I noted above that managers failed to understand the depth of the workers' frustration, but it is probably more accurate to say that managers may indeed have understood the workers' grievance, but that they could not redress this grievance due to their sense of their own authority as managers. Ultimately managers were forced by the riot to learn the hard and (literally) painful lesson that the miners were human beings. Without question, the Furukawa Company board, the local Ashio managers, and especially the presumption and slowness of the mine director, Minami Teizō, pushed the situation inexorably toward riot.

THE EVE OF THE RIOT

The Lodge Bosses' Petition

On 7 January 1907, bosses of all the lodges attached to pits at Tsūdō, Honzan, and Kodaki petitioned for an increase in the wages of their men, plus an increase in the bosses' own "pit entry commission." Nearly two weeks had passed since 25 December, when the Tsūdō pit manager had suggested that they should preempt any demands from Shiseikai by putting forward a petition themselves. Why this delay, given that the bosses favored both an increase for their men and, of course, an increased "pit entry commission"?

The festive season of year's end and the New Year explains part of the delay. Further, since there were over one hundred lodge bosses spread out among the three pits, it took time to coordinate joint action. But a more important reason was the weakness of the lodge bosses in relation to the company. Over the previous decade or longer, the bosses' position had markedly deteriorated, to the point where the bosses surely feared losing their jobs if they upset Ashio's management. We see this fear clearly in the behavior of the Tsūdō bosses. When they selected five members of their Committee to Petition for a Wage Increase, the Tsūdō bosses decided to collect 2500 yen in contributions, to be invested in government military bonds and distributed to committee members if they were fired.[88] Lodge bosses who felt the need for such a precaution despite the fact that Ashio management had directed them to make this petition were hardly in a secure enough position to convey their subordinates' discontent to the mine management. This weak status was one reason the miners distrusted the bosses and were drawn to Shiseikai.

The Tsūdō bosses were the first group to submit a petition, and they encouraged the other bosses to follow suit. Tsūdō, of course, was the site of the greatest Shiseikai influence, so the Tsūdō bosses likely felt the greatest threat. Their petition was the boldest and also the most detailed of all those submitted by the lodge bosses. Although it is rather long, it is worth quoting in full to convey the bosses' view of the situation at Ashio on the eve of the riot.

At this time, when our nation makes progress with each day and month that passes, we are astonished by the great strides being made in industry on land and at sea. Abroad, our armed forces are expanding; at home, the foundations of a rich nation are being securely laid. All patriots profoundly wish to encourage all forms of industry and to further strengthen and protect public order and tranquillity. This is especially so in the mining industry, the foundation of the nation's wealth and the sole domestic source of wealth for post-[Russo-Japanese]-war management of the nation. The Ashio mine has become one of the greatest mines in the world and has been fully equipped in all specialized areas of operation after due consideration and study of the most modern Western machinery. It is expanding its operations and is making ever greater progress, so that it appears to be an exemplary mine, giving no cause for shame. Yet, the working and living conditions of the mine operatives are unbearable to observe. For this we feel sincere regret. Consequently, for some time we have desired to petition in respect of these conditions. As we have procrastinated until today, the situation has already become turbulent owing to the mischievous agitation of the workforce by elements unconnected with the mine, who, by their rash behavior, have seized on the opportunity provided to draw attention to workers' fatalities and have raised calls for the maintenance of equilibrium between wages and prices. We labor contractors cannot remain indifferent to this situation. On this occasion, therefore, we request through the proper procedure that this petition may be granted so that we may be given proper wages and allowed to take our own initiatives to ensure that workers' fatalities and accidents be reduced in order that the mine may become genuinely exemplary in all respects. Since management and we in the workforce are in relationship like the two wings of a bird, it is a matter of sincere regret to us that work cannot make progress when one wing is extended while the other is restrained. Since the recent hostilities between Japan and Russia, the cost of living has risen, prices have increased sharply and the burden of taxation has almost doubled. There has, however, been no corresponding increase in workers' wages, which have remained at previous levels, and it has become manifest that owing to the exceeding destitution of their circumstances, an ever greater number of workers are finding themselves beset with difficulties. Under the present circumstances, the workers' bewilderment forces them to resort all the more to desperate and reckless measures which make it difficult to prevent dishonor falling upon the company. Consequently, since it is not possible for them to sustain their livelihoods at the current level of wages, they fall into debt with the company and have no means of discharging their liabilities. In short, we are of the opinion that the situation derives from the low level of workers' wages. We therefore fervently hope for the company's approval of a wage increase, so that with both wings outspread and a policy of cooperation adopted between superiors and subordinates, our chief ambition may be realized, namely, the successful development of the company's business. Accordingly, we humbly request that, after due consideration of the following articles, the company grant the increases listed therein.

Articles

1. An increase in the miners' piece-work rate of an average 1 yen 20 sen

2. A 60 percent average increase in miners' basic pay

3. A 60 percent average increase in wages for haulers, ore dressers, and other grades

4. An increase in the miners' pit entry commission of 1 sen 5 rin retroactive from July 1905

5. A similar increase of 1 sen in the basic haulers' pit entry commission retroactive from January 1907

We would respectfully request that in regard to these articles the company make comparisons with other mines and we humbly ask for the company's sympathetic understanding in the present difficult circumstances. To facilitate this we have taken the liberty of appending a table of model daily expenses on a separate sheet.

7 January 1907
The Greater Tsūdō Lodge Bosses Petition Committee[89]

The Brotherhoods' Movement for Wage Increases

The brotherhood assemblymen soon learned of this attempt by the bosses, prompted by a pit manager, to petition for a wage increase without consulting the brotherhoods' assemblymen. On 3 January, actually before the bosses had formally submitted their petition, Imori Shingo, Yamamura, and others argued, "The fact that demands are being put forward by the lodge bosses is no reason for us to postpone our own action," and they pressed the assemblymen of the lodge responsible for brotherhood funds to summon a general assembly of the brotherhood. Consequently, it was decided "to hold a meeting tomorrow the 4th [January] with an admission charge of 30 sen at the Komatsuya restaurant in Akazawa, rather than at the lodge in the presence of the bosses."[90] Normally, such brotherhood assemblies were held in the presence of the lodge boss responsible for the "treasury box" of the brotherhood (the *hakomoto*, or steward). But the miners held this assembly without consulting the bosses. Imori Shingo led the meeting, reading out a proposed petition of sixteen articles that he had prepared. The petition was amended slightly, ending up with seventeen articles. The assembly decided the petition should not be from Tsūdō alone, but should call for participation from the brotherhoods at Honzan, Kodaki, and Sunokobashi, so as to represent all Ashio miners. The meeting also addressed the question of the actual presentation of the petition: Should it be put forward in cooperation with Shiseikai, or via the lodge bosses after obtaining their approval, or should the brotherhoods themselves submit it to the company directly?

Imori "pressed [for the petition] to be presented in cooperation with Shiseikai," but he failed to gain much support. The group finally decided to go via the bosses.[91] The next day, 5 January, assembly representatives from Tsūdō approached the fund stewards at Honzan, Kodaki, and Sunokobashi to inform them of the Tsūdō decisions and ask for their cooperation in the petition for wage increases. According to the police record the replies were as follows:

Honzan

On the 5th January this year two stewards from Tsūdō called on Hattori Sōshirō, steward of the [Honzan] mine, bringing with them a 17 article petition, and requested that this petition be considered since it was desired that it might be presented on behalf of all miners, it being unlikely to achieve its object if submitted by Tsūdō alone. Hattori conveyed the substance of this communication to all the assembly representatives and a meeting was held on the 7th of the month. This adjourned when the participants resolved to take a final decision after returning to their lodges to consult with lodge members. On the 9th of the month the representatives met together again and announced that, all their members in each lodge having declared their agreement, they would take part in the joint petition, and accordingly, the stewards informed the Tsūdō stewards of this fact.[92]

Kodaki

On the 5th January two keenly pro-Shiseikai assembly representatives from Tsūdō, Asahi Fujitarō and Kawakami Tsurushige, showed the 17 article petition to [Kodaki] representative, Yamada Shinjirō, and requested that it should be a joint petition. Yamada, while himself agreeing, said that no decision could be reached without consulting everybody. When, on 28 January the matter had still not been resolved by normal means after careful consideration, Asahi and Azuma went to consult with the stewards of the [Kodaki] mine (two whose names are unknown and Yamada Shinjirō), and it was arranged that a joint meeting would be held at Tsuruya in Matsubarachō, Ashio town on the 2nd February.[93]

Sunokobashi

At the first meeting of the year on 5 January, attended by assembly representatives Kawasaki Seiji and Yamaguchi Kamenosuke of lodge 11, Kiyama Chōemon and Ozawa Kazuzō of lodge 12, and Hamatake Jirō and Kanazawa Eiji of lodge 13, brotherhood representatives from Tsūdō turned up bringing their 17 article petition and asked that it be submitted jointly on behalf of all the mines. They were told that those present could not resolve the matter upon their own initiative, but would have to refer it for consultation with all the men before replying. The representatives who received the request then explained its purport to the men in each lodge, who all signified their agreement. On 7 January, this sentiment was conveyed to the steward of Tsūdō lodge 8 by the steward of Sunokobashi lodge 12.[94]

It is important to recognize that in every case, the stewards and the assembly representatives did not decide the matter by themselves. They returned to their constituencies, the lodges that had elected them, and reached a decision only after winning the agreement of the ordinary miners. Conventional historical judgment has seen the brotherhoods as constituted by a premodern patron-client system of hierarchical relationships, but this perspective exaggerates a single aspect of the brotherhoods. The evidence here suggest that a more characteristic feature of their decision making was precisely the system of consulting all their members.

Sunokobashi, on 7 January, was the first of the mines to signal its agreement to the Tsūdō petition. Honzan decided to join in with Tsūdō two days later. There were only three lodges at Sunokobashi, and the Tsūdō petition was put to them at a general meeting when all their representatives were present. This allowed them to respond two days earlier than Honzan, but the attitude of the two groups toward the Tsūdō initiative was virtually the same. The problem was Kodaki. More than three weeks after receiving the request from Tsūdō, the Kodaki miners had not produced a clear response. The fate of the effort to present a joint petition of all brotherhoods was up in the air.

The Shiseikai and the Brotherhoods Join Hands

On 7 January the lodge bosses of the three Tsūdō pits together submitted their joint petition for wage increases, and the Tsūdō assemblymen held a meeting at Donryūji Buddhist temple in Kakemizu. Also present at the meeting, ostensibly a party to celebrate the New Year, was Yoneya Ichihei, boss of Tsūdō lodge No. 8 and the current senior boss of the Tsūdō lodges.[95] Naturally enough, the subject of discussion was the joint petition from the brotherhoods. Yoneya argued, "If the brotherhoods presented a petition as well as the bosses, it would only aggravate the situation and would conflict with the aims of the bosses. The brotherhood assemblymen should wait for a while."[96]

His words angered many of the assemblymen, who asked why he opposed their petition. The Shiseikai activists present, who had been the first to call for wage increases and had worked through channels by requesting the bosses to join the petition campaign, fiercely criticized this unilateral action of the lodge bosses. They clashed head-on with Yoneya, insisting that the bosses should return control of the brotherhood finances (the treasury box) to the assembly, a matter that had long been in dispute.[97] At that point Imori proposed that Minami Sukematsu of the Shiseikai be invited to come and state his views. The proposal was immediately taken up and a messenger dispatched.

The police report by Inspector Tamura offers the following description of this situation:

On the 7th day of the month at a meeting at Donryūji, Minami and Nagaoka tearfully said that they had organized the Shiseikai to fight for wage increases and other benefits for the workers. To this end they had risked their lives and concentrated all their efforts. They had steadily pursued their goal and had continually pressed the company for wage increases to the point where a pit manager had been forced to inveigle the lodge bosses into submitting a petition. When they themselves were already in the process of wage increase talks with the bosses, for all their efforts to come to nothing when success was at hand was a bitter disappointment.[98]

While this report conveys to us the substance of the two men's remarks, it does not capture their tone. We get closer to this tone via the following record of speeches at a Shiseikai rally the next day, in which Minami and Nagaoka spoke directly to ordinary miners.

Apparently the bosses have taken out 2500 yen worth of government army bonds which they'll pay out to the five committee members as severance pay if the petition fails. They've put in for wage increases, and while they were about it, for a 3 sen increase in their own commission rate. The bosses have no idea of right and just behavior. Old Sakura Sogoro [seventeenth-century martyr in a peasant rebellion] never tried to cover himself like they are doing. He didn't ask for any increases in his commission rate. However, we may hate their behavior, but we do not hate the bosses themselves. From now on we too intend to make substantial demands. We'll lay down our lives if need be for the cause of what is right and just. (Nagaoka)

The bosses have put in a petition for a 1 yen 20 sen wage hike, and if the company pays up, all well and good, but it's still a pittance. Or else it's a plot against Shiseikai by the company and the bosses. (Minami)

The devious way in which the bosses have presented their petition without consulting us even once is truly the mark of men who know nothing of morality. It also truly obstructs our Shiseikai movement. Some of you may think that the company will listen to petitions presented by the bosses and by the brotherhood assemblies, so there's no need to join the Shiseikai, but the bosses have acted this way to break our movement. Of course, we don't know whether the company will accept the bosses' petition, but we can be sure that the agreement won't last forever. (Minami)[99]

The meeting of the Tsūdō assembly on 7 January greatly strengthened the relationship between the Shiseikai and the brotherhoods. Toward the end of the meeting, there was "a request from one of the assemblymen that they should all state their opinions one by one."[100] In response, "Katō Hidematsu and Ōhashi Chūzō of Tsūdō lodge No. 10, Maeda Tokutarō and Teraguchi Yukichi of No. 4, Imori Shingo and Matsumura Yukichi of No. 2, and all the representatives of the other lodges as well as the other assemblymen [present] all signified their personal approval."[101] The bosses' submission of their petition without consulting the assembly and their treatment of the brotherhoods' petition movement rebounded against them. In the end, the Tsūdō brotherhood assembly firmly lined up with the Shiseikai. That evening, together with many other assemblymen, Ōnishi Saichi, one of the representatives of the No. 1 lodge, Tsūdō's largest, and a man with great influence among the miners, joined the Shiseikai. Of the 36 Tsūdō assemblymen, 32 or 33 were now Shiseikai members.[102]

This day's events were a great boost to the movement, and at a public meeting the following day at the Kaneda theater "there were more than 1160 people in the audience, and the miners who came to hear Minami and Nagaoka speak were very excited and applauded loudly."[103] Their excitement no doubt derived from the sharp criticisms leveled by the Shiseikai leaders at the bosses and their pro-company stance. The district attorney in charge of the investigation into the riot also recognized that this 7 January meeting of the Tsūdō brotherhood assembly marked a significant turning point: "After the meeting at Donryūji on the 7th January, the brotherhood assemblymen became increasingly involved with Shiseikai. Many miners joined the movement and their sense of confrontation toward the lodge bosses increased." Men such as Katō Hidematsu, an assemblyman from Tsūdō's lodge No. 10 and a former Dōshikai activist, were key figures in this surge of opposition who, "after the 21st January were absent from work feigning illness and went about recruiting new Shiseikai members, campaigning for higher wages and even forcing people to buy the *Commoners' Weekly,* the organ of the Japan Socialist Party."[104]

The Return of the Treasury Box

Disturbed by the unexpected turn of events, on 10 January the Tsūdō lodge bosses held a secret meeting in the storehouse of the Izumiya Inn. They discussed how to destroy the Shiseikai. Ishida Kishirō, boss of lodge No. 1, and Yoneya Ichihei, boss of No. 8, insisted that "force must be used; Minami and Nagaoka must be killed." But others disagreed, and a fierce debate followed. The result of this supposedly secret meeting was that "the [Shiseikai activist] Katō Hidematsu went to see what was going on, having heard that the bosses were arguing."[105] The bosses met again on the 13th and "agreed that all Shiseikai members should be fired." Most bosses did not, however, go along with this decision, and only at three lodges (Nos. 4, 14, and 15) were notices posted announcing that "Shiseikai members will be dismissed. By company order." On hearing the news, Minami, Nagaoka, and Hayashi went to see Kawachi, the general manager at the company office. They asked if the notices were indeed sanctioned "by company order." Kawachi "said that no such order had been issued and immediately countermanded the notices."[106] Nagaoka complained that by seeking to prevent people from joining Shiseikai, the bosses were violating Article 17 of the Public Order and Police Law.[107] Thus the Tsūdō bosses' plan to dismiss Shiseikai members ended in failure, not only because the bosses were unable to gain the public support of the company office, but because the bosses at Honzan and the other pits had not cooperated.

Another secret meeting in mid-January between bosses from Tsūdō and Honzan, called by the Tsūdō bosses, decided that "at this time when Shiseikai is displaying an aggressive energy, to avoid provocation our policy should be one of nonintervention rather than active prevention." At this meeting, two proposals were made: (1) the company should be pressed to consent to the bosses' own petition already drawn up, before Shiseikai was able to present its petition for wage increases, and (2) if it were true that general manager Kawachi had told Minami Sukematsu of the company's intention to raise wages, discussions should take place between Kawachi and the bosses, because they had not been consulted. However, the Honzan bosses disagreed with these proposals, saying that they were "improper" and that they did "not at all meet with approval."[108] Thus in the confrontation between the *hanba* bosses and the brotherhood assemblymen, the intrusive behavior of the Tsūdō bosses only aggravated both sides.

For ordinary miners, even those influential men who served as assembly representatives, to oppose the lodge bosses who had direct authority over them was no easy matter. But once a large number of men had made a collective decision, their pent-up frustrations boiled over. The bosses had exploited them and had drawn unfair profits from room and board charges. But what angered the miners more was the excessively weak behavior of the bosses toward the company, which prevented them from adequately representing to the company the miners' desires and demands. Indeed, far from representing those demands, the lodge bosses had slyly sought to suppress the movement for higher wages. In particular, many assemblymen could no longer bear the fact that the bosses joined the brotherhoods, supposedly the miners' own independent organization, and meddled in their affairs. This was especially the case with the brotherhood funds, which were entrusted to the supervision of the bosses. If control over the "treasury box" were wrested from the bosses, they could be excluded from the brotherhood. Imori Shingo and others proposed this idea at a regular meeting of the Tsūdō assembly on 7 January. Earlier on, a steward (*ōtōban*) chosen from among the assemblymen had managed brotherhood funds, but in 1902 one of these stewards had run off with the money, and the lodge bosses who made up the loss insisted that from 1903, the boss of the lodge to which the steward belonged would control the treasury box.[109]

Owing to the stubborn opposition of the current chief steward (and lodge boss), Yoneya Ichihei, at the 7 January meeting the proposal to transfer control of the box was not resolved, but when Yoneya refused a request to hold an assembly meeting on 25 January in lodge No. 8, the issue flared up again.[110] Yoneya probably felt that since many Tsūdō assemblymen had joined Shiseikai after the 7 January meeting, to lend space to another brotherhood assembly would be equivalent to aiding and abetting the Shiseikai.

From the assembly's viewpoint, however, this was another case of unreasonable meddling in their affairs and obstruction of their rights. Imori Shingo brought up the matter at a Shiseikai public meeting the next day, 26 January. He made the following criticism: "One of the bosses has been to see the assembly representatives, and while he said 'I am not seeking to restrict your freedoms or ignore your rights,' he created problems by also saying that unless the assembly's emergency meeting were calm, he wouldn't let them use the lodge."[111]

This meeting was held in the first place because Minami Sukematsu, chairman of the Ashio branch of the Shiseikai, had issued an open letter to Minami Teizō, director of the Furukawa Company Ashio Mines and former chief superintendent of mines in the Tokyo area, and in it, he had challenged the director to speak at the meeting. A rumor then spread that "the workers would see an interesting sumo [wrestling] match 'between a rich man and a poor man,'" and "already by the start of the meeting at 6 o'clock, more than 1100 people were crammed into the hall with hardly room to stand." The director, of course, did not turn up. Yet for some reason, in his speech that evening Minami Sukematsu criticized Minami Teizō far less than usual and certainly less than expected. Instead, he launched a sharp public attack on the lodge bosses, whom he had generally refrained from criticizing in the past:

Among the bosses, two or three are talking about some particularly underhanded methods. They are spreading all kinds of rumors that Minami Sukematsu will be put under a restraint order by the police because of his recent activities. In this way, the Shiseikai is being obstructed. One Tsūdō boss has refused to allow a meeting of assembly representatives to go ahead, but what right do the bosses have to meddle in such meetings? These are free activities of the representatives of us working men. This is nothing but arrogant insolence. The time has come for you to act. You must get back the letter of proxy and reclaim control over the receipt of your own wages.[112]

Stirred by Minami's speech, the Tsūdō assemblymen met later that evening backstage at the Kaneda theater and asked Minami and Nagaoka how they could reclaim the treasury box. The next day they met again at the Komatsuya restaurant. They discussed the reluctance of the Kodaki brotherhood to support the wage hike petition, and they also decided to reclaim control over the box from the bosses. They set out to do this immediately, as their opponent, Yoneya Ichihei, later testified:

After a meeting at Komatsuya on the 27th January, to which I was invited but did not attend, the Tsūdō assemblymen all came to my lodge at three o'clock that afternoon and attacked me, demanding to know why I hadn't come and why I had refused permission for their meeting at the lodge. The real reason why they came was that since the bosses were entrusted with control of the treasury box and the payment of brotherhood expenses, and since it was the custom not to pay out if we felt that payment was not justified, the assemblymen wanted to take this right away from the bosses. This is what they demanded, so on the 28th, the next day, all the bosses got together and agreed that on 5 February, when [stewardship of] the box was due to be rotated again, they would relinquish their right to control. The ones who were most insistent on the return of the box were Ōnishi Saichi, Imori Shingo, and four others.[113]

For the bosses, the issue of "control of the treasury box" was not just a question of whether or not to guarantee the brotherhood the right to speak on the matter. A considerable financial loss was involved as well, because the finances of the Tsūdō brotherhood were bound up with the lodge bosses' system of subcontracted labor. Miners were obliged to pay to the bosses a 1 yen 50 sen monthly surcharge known as the "*hanba* charge."[114] Out of this lodge charge the bosses paid the men's bathing charges and their other brotherhood expenses, called "social expenses." The amount of social expenses each month was not fixed. Each lodge boss paid a total amount every month that reflected the number of men in his lodge. This was called a "subcontracting system" because if the outlay exceeded the total collected, the lodge boss was responsible for making up the difference, but if expenses fell short of total income, the money saved went not to the brotherhood but into the lodge boss's own pocket. Not surprisingly, under this system the lodge bosses tended to keep 25 to 35 percent of the income from the lodge charge, that is, 40 to 50 sen per man per month. This was more than the legitimate amount of 1 sen 5 rin per worker per day paid to the boss as a "pit entry commission."

To profit from this lodge charge, the bosses had to retain the "right to control the treasury box." Precisely because "the bosses were entrusted with control of the treasury box and the payment of brotherhood expenses, and it was the custom not to pay out if [they] felt that payment was not justified," the bosses profited from handling the brotherhood funds. If such control were transferred to the assemblymen, and especially to those who were members of Shiseikai and thus hostile to the bosses, the bosses would be asked to cover any fellowship charges that exceeded income from the lodge charge, and might have ended up paying out of their own pockets. And if the social expenses fell short of the lodge charge, assemblymen who came to understand this through their new control of the box would naturally demand a reduction of the lodge charge.

When, then, did the bosses relinquish this vitally important right of control of the treasury box? Above all, they did so because they could not deny that originally the lodge charge had been intended to cover brotherhood expenses, and that assemblymen had held the right to control the charge. Also, the bosses engaged in the discussions, Yoneya Ichihei of lodge No. 8 and Ishida Kishirō of No. 1, were bosses of very large lodges with over one hundred men under them. The considerable output from these lodges meant that their bosses could get by despite the loss of income from the lodge charge. But it is also possible that many bosses simply did not immediately grasp the significance of surrendering control of the box.

However, on the following day, 29 January, a shocking report spread among the Tsūdō bosses. The men of lodge No. 1, led by Ōnishi Saichi, had presented a demand for a reduction in the lodge charge to their boss, Ishida Kishirō. He had responded by abolishing the lodge charge system in his lodge altogether.[115] Giving up control over the brotherhood funds by handing over the treasury box did not in itself immediately mean a financial loss for the bosses, although it threatened such an outcome. But the outright abolition of the lodge charge was another matter. This meant the loss of a stable source of income, and bosses of the smaller lodges of forty to fifty men felt this as a particular threat. They feared going bankrupt. Driven by such apprehension, the bosses sought to force lodge No. 1 to reinstate the lodge charge and desperately tried to convince Ōnishi to go along with this. That evening, Kamata Nobutarō, boss of Tsūdō's lodge No. 19, met Ōnishi and another assemblyman from the No. 1 lodge at the Izumiya Inn.[116] He asked them "to return to the existing system of contracting with the lodge boss." Kamata appealed to Ōnishi to remember "his obligations and the favors he had received" from Ishida Kishirō, "boss of lodge No. 1 who had cared for him for many years." Kamata "tried forcefully to persuade [Ōnishi] to accept a return to the lodge charge system." "After careful consideration, [Ōnishi] replied that if he were to agree to such a request, he would be selling out the other miners. It would be like forcing infants to drink hot water. It was impossible. If they sought to force him to agree they would have to kill him first. He was determined not to change his mind." The meeting that evening broke up without agreement, but Kamata did not give up, and on 30 and 31 January he tried again to persuade Ōnishi: "On the 30th January Saito Kanezō, the boss of lodge No. 13, called [several men] from lodge No. 1 to his own lodge for further discussions about the 'lodge charge.' As they reached no agreement on the essentials, they arranged to hold a mass meeting at lodge No. 1 for yet further negotiations. This meeting duly took place the next day, 31 January, when all the men of lodge No. 1 met. But again the negotiations ended without reaching a decision."[117]

This brief "court testimony of witness Kamata Nobutarō," contained in the prosecution's statement of appeal, makes clear how significant the abolition of the lodge charge was. The bosses were going to desperate lengths to prevent its abolition.

The Four Brotherhoods Agree on a Joint Petition

The first objective of the Tsūdō assemblymen at their emergency meeting on 27 January was to find a practical way to press ahead with the petition for a wage increase being held up by the procrastination of the Kodaki miners. The main topic of discussion in fact turned out to be the return of the treasury box, but they decided as well to propose a meeting of assembly representatives from all four mines for 1 February to agree on a joint petition. Accordingly, representatives from Tsūdō visited the other mines the following day and asked for their cooperation. Honzan and Sunokobashi agreed immediately, but the reply from Kodaki was "we should wait to see the result of the bosses' petition." At this, the Tsūdō representatives asked representatives from Honzan to accompany them on another visit to the Kodaki stewards. Together, they persuaded the Kodaki men that they should all "hold a joint meeting anyhow whether or not we go ahead with a petition." The result was that Kodaki promised to reconsider its position, and a "joint solidarity meeting" could finally take place.

A total of fourteen representatives (four men from each of the mines at Tsūdō, Honzan, and Kodaki, and two from Sunokobashi) took part in the meeting, held at the Tsuruya Inn in Tsūdō from 9 A.M. on 1 February. The first problem was whether to ask Shiseikai for help with the petition, or to put it forward via the bosses. Asahi Fujitarō, steward of Tsūdō's lodge No. 8, argued that they should "get Shiseikai's cooperation for the petition," but Yamada Shinjirō from Kodaki opposed this, saying that "if Shiseikai was going to be involved, Kodaki could not take part." The Honzan representatives, who had foreseen this problem, suggested that "since no documents presented to the company will be accepted unless they come from the bosses, the petition should be presented by the bosses, but should bear the names of assemblymen," and "if the petition is rejected, it will not be too late to ask for Shiseikai's cooperation." Kodaki and Sunokobashi went along with this. When the Tsūdō men asked what would be done if, as seemed likely, the Tsūdō bosses refused to present such a petition, the reply was that "all the mines would rally round and seek to persuade the bosses."

At this point a Tsūdō steward, Azuma Kichijirō, proposed that if the question of the petition was to be more than a formality, we should first draw up articles of federation and engage in a frank and open-hearted discussion. Thus saying, he took up his pen and drafted the following article of federation: "The course of action to be taken by us will be decided by all of us." The Kodaki stewards then proposed adding the words "following joint deliberation and decision." This was then finally agreed on as representing the final version and signed by all: "The course of action to be taken by us will be decided by all of us following joint deliberation and decision." After this, the articles of the petition were discussed and drawn up. The resulting twenty-two articles included three proposed by Honzan, two by Kodaki, and one by Tsūdō, in addition to the seventeen drafted by Tsūdō at the meeting at the Komatsuya restaurant on 4 January.[118]

The group further decided to present the petition at 9 A.M. on 6 February and make a verbal request for a reply by 10 February.

Thus, the brotherhoods from the four mines had finally resolved to go ahead with a joint petition for a pay hike. The petition document itself had now to be drawn up in quadruplicate; this presented another slight problem when the group meeting at the Tsuruya Inn realized that not one of the men present was actually able to write such a petition. This difficulty was overcome when Imori Shingo stopped by the inn to check up on the meeting's progress. Taking advantage of this "happy coincidence," the group invited him to write the petition. Thus, the detective's report notes that "Imori Shingo wrote down the articles of the said petition to which all had agreed, and he himself added the preamble and concluding paragraph." After a marathon session of thirteen hours, the meeting broke up at 10 P.M.

The next day, 2 February, each mine sent a representative to another meeting at the Komatsuya restaurant, where they all put their formal seals to the "article of union."[119] The Tsūdō and Honzan brotherhood assemblies heard reports of the discussions and decisions of the "joint meeting" on 3 February, and the Kodaki brotherhood met for a report the following day. After a long and laborious struggle, the brotherhoods' petition was finally ready to present to the company.

The Miners' Demands

The brotherhoods' petition catalogued the grievances felt by the miners at the time of the riot. It clearly reveals to us the points at dispute between the miners and the company. Surviving copies of the petition can today be found in the file headed "Classified Documents Relating to the Ashio Riot Incident" in the archive of the Utsunomiya district attorney's office and in an Ashio mine office document entitled "Outline of the Ashio Riot," published in volume 2 of *Historical Documents of the Japanese Labor Movement*. The first is a copy of the petition handed in at Honzan, and the second is a copy of the one handed in at the Kodaki pit by the Kodaki brotherhood's assembly stewards at the height of the riot on 6 February. The first has twenty-three articles and the second twenty-four, and the texts differ in a number of details as well. The following is the complete text of the more detailed copy found in the "Outline of the Ashio Riot." I show in square brackets [ ] those sections that appear only in the company document and not in the version held in the district attorney's archive, while portions in the DA version but not in the company's copy are bracketed thus { }. Although demands in the original petition are not numbered, for the sake of clarity, I have done so here.

As the result of a meeting of representatives of the three mines, which noted the difficulties and inconveniences of workers at those pits, we hereby petition the company for consideration as follows:

Articles

1. A base rate wage increase of 60 percent for fixed-rate workers.

2. A raise in the piecework rate of 1 yen 20 sen for the lowest grade workers.

3. In cases where, despite considerable exertions, a worker's daily wage falls below 80 sen, it will be adjusted to at least 80 sen.

4. All piecework rates for ore diggers will be reviewed periodically.

5. Workers absent owing to sickness or injury for more than two weeks will receive financial support commensurate with costs of medical treatment.

[6. Adequate financial compensation will be offered those workers who, through illness or injury in the course of their duties, have no prospect of a full recovery.]

7. In accord with mutual aid rules, [within limits] {in this case} of mutual aid resources, daily necessities will be provided to sick and injured workers.

8. Owing to the frequent miscalculation of workers' wages, certificates will be issued to workers that record the result of work [length of excavation].

9. Daily necessities from the company stores will be sold on a scale reflecting the miners' basic wage. Cases of unfair practice in this connection will be forbidden, such as the provision at the same price of inferior goods to workers and of superior goods to staff.

10. In all cases of unfairness in the payment of piecework wages and in the allocation of piecework or of inappropriate rates for ore, assemblymen will have the right to mediate and investigate the circumstances.

11. Adequate safety precautions will be taken to prevent illness due to foul air and poor sanitation.

12. Workers absent without notice for five days a month will be subject to no penalties.

13. Drinking water installations will be sited in every pit tunnel.

14. All main galleries in the three pits will be illuminated by electric light.

15. Washplaces in the miners' accommodation areas to be fitted with roofs and washbasins.

16. Workers at the three mines will receive accommodation [as a matter of course] {to a considerable degree}, and financial assistance will be provided to those workers forced to live elsewhere when company accommodation is lacking.

17. Safe walkways will be provided underground in all three mines.

18. Careful maintenance of equipment and safety provisions will be strictly enforced [during working hours] {at the work site} so that miners are able to work free of undue concern for their safety.

19. A lean-to shack will be erected at pit entrances where explosives are disbursed and attendance is checked.

20. Miners working at depths of more than 300 shaku (100 meters) will work a six-hour shift [however, changes of shift will take place at the pithead].

21. Wages will be paid out twice a month every fifteen days.

22. Bonuses will be paid to fixed-rate miners as well as to ore extractors.

23. Mutual aid councils will elect their members, conduct their affairs, and render accounts at the end of each month.

24. Henceforth, workers will be notified in advance of the announcement of new company regulations affecting them and the execution of such regulations will be contingent upon our agreement or disagreement.

The above articles having been affirmed by joint decision, the representatives of all the mine workers hereby respectfully petition for their consideration, and contingent upon the company's receipt of this petition, the mine workers of the three pits reserve the right to hold a mass meeting.

Your humble and obedient servants,
the miners of Kodaki
the miners of Honzan
the miners of Tsūdō
the miners of Sunokobashi

For the attention of the Kodaki pithead manager's office

[Additional articles
—Chisel sharpening will be without charge
—Bathing will be without charge

6th February 1907
Kodaki assembly stewards

Petition Addendum
The assembly stewards humbly request your consideration and acceptance of the articles enclosed herein, 6 February 1907.

From the Kodaki gang bosses
For the attention of the Kodaki pithead manager's office]

The issues addressed by the petition can be divided into six categories: (1) wages, (2) safety and sanitation, (3) aid for the sick and the injured, (4) the supply of daily provisions, (5) the rights of the representatives of the workers' brotherhoods, and (6) miscellaneous issues.

Demands concerning wages focus on a pay increase and the method of determining wages. These matters are raised in article 1 calling for a 60 percent pay raise for regular workers (those working on a fixed daily rate rather than a piecework system), article 2 demanding that piecework rates for the lowest grade workers be fixed at 1 yen 20 sen, and article 3 calling for the minimum piecework rate to be set at 80 sen. The problem here is that articles 2 and 3 contradict each other. This probably stems from the weak writing ability of the framers of the articles. By "1 yen 20 sen for the lowest grade workers," they meant that the amount of the standard wage, which served as the criterion for determining the piece rate, should be raised from the then current level of 65 sen to at least 1 yen 20 sen. A clearer phrasing of the article would have called for a wage increase "of not less than an average 1 yen 20 sen."

Articles 8, 10, and 4 impinge on the wage issue. Most miners' wages were paid on a piecework basis. Mine officials set wage rates for the different faces being worked, and miners keenly felt these assessments were unfair in several respects. Thus in article 10 they demanded that brotherhood representatives be given the right to intervene and investigate when miners felt the official rates were unfair or the quality of extracted ore was graded inappropriately. The demand for such a right was similar to that of European and American coal miners' unions, which had called for "check weighmen" to ensure fair weighing of extracted coal. Also important in this connection was article 24, calling for the brotherhoods to be consulted before any new company regulations that affected miners were instituted, and article 23, which called for the mutual aid funds, supported by regular worker contributions, to be administered by workers' representatives elected from among the workforce. Article 23 also called for public accounting of the use of the funds.

The phrase *collective bargaining* was not used in this petition, but the substance of the demands comes very close to it. If articles 10 and 24 had been accepted, then the Ashio brotherhood would have been functioning just like a trade union. Because of these three articles (10, 23, and 24), I consider "the rights of the brotherhood representatives" to have been one of the main areas addressed by the petition. Article 21 was also concerned with wages, calling for wage payments twice a month rather than the existing practice of once a month.

A number of articles (11, 13, 14, 15, 17, 18, and 19) concerned health and safety. These no doubt owed something to the influence of Nagaoka Tsuruzō, who had always considered safety to be a major issue and never ceased to call workers' attention to it in his speeches. The same can be said of articles 5, 6, and 7, concerning the welfare of the sick and the injured.

Also of great importance to the Ashio workers were articles 7 and 9. These reflected the miners' frustration that without cash they were forced to buy food and other daily necessities at the company stores or at their lodge. As noted earlier, the workers' strongest grievance lay in the fact that prolonged absence from work led to restrictions in the amount of goods they were allowed, including basic food supplies such as rice and miso. Just like the system of fines imposed for unreported absenteeism, this control of supplies was another means of increasing workers' attendance, and article 12 addressed the question of these fines.

Other articles concerned shorter working hours at the faces that took a long time to reach and financial assistance with housing costs. After 1 February, when representatives from all four mines decided on the content of the petition, the Kodaki brotherhood added demands of their own for the dropping of charges for "chisel sharpening" and for "bathing."

THE RIOT

The Course and Character of the Riot

4 February: Tsūdō

On the morning of 4 February just after 8 A.M., nearly three thousand meters underground from the Tsūdō pithead, a group of shouting miners attacked the foreman's cabin for the no. 3 and no. 4 sections.[120] The miners threw stones and smashed windowpanes and electric lights. The officials made a desperate escape, but the miners did not chase them. They chose to remain in the cabin, cutting telephone cables, thoroughly destroying the rest of the window glass and the door, and scattering and tearing up all documents and papers. They finally threw dynamite into the empty cabin. This was the beginning of the Ashio riot. It raged for three days.

Hearing the noise, other miners joined in, gradually swelling the number of rioters. One after another, miners attacked and destroyed the transport station in no. 1 shaft, the section 2 cabin, the tunnel intersection-point cabins, the truck inspection station, and all the underground stations, cabins, and horse barns in the Tsūdō pits. About 11 A.M. the rioters formed groups of ten or twenty men and left the pit. Three hundred men gathered near the pithead cabin, loudly decrying the abuses of the officials. After the once proud officials had been forced to run for their lives, the men roared with delight as they recalled to each other that unsightly spectacle. Some threw stones at the pithead cabin, and the violent mood continued.

Minami Sukematsu and Nagaoka Tsuruzō soon heard of the trouble and hurried over. They reportedly addressed the rioters "in loud voices," saying, "The crimes you have committed cannot be helped; what you need after all is a pay raise! We'll be responsible for seeing that you get it, but we need you to calm down." Hearing this, "the miners became quiet."[121]

At 10 A.M. the same day, the Ashio mine office issued an order forbidding Tsūdō miners from entering the pit. The men who were still underground continued to run wild, releasing their long-pent-up anger and frustrations in further attacks on the underground offices, cabins, and stations. Around 3:30 P.M. they began to leave the mine in small groups, and by 5 that evening more than two hundred men had again gathered in the pithead area. They threw stones at the main Tsūdō pithead office and at the pithead cabin, breaking a number of windows. Meanwhile, the local Ashio constabulary had informed the Prefectural Police Department of the outbreak of the riot and had appealed for assistance. It had also called in all the Tsūdō lodge bosses, censured "the disorderly improper conduct" (of the miners), and ordered the bosses to calm their men. However, the center of the disturbances was the dark and now chaotic mine. Frightened by the fact that the miners had access to dynamite, the policemen merely tried to negotiate with them at a distance. The stone throwing at the pithead office went on throughout the evening, but by 10 the rioting had ended. Returning to their lodge, the men were still in a buoyant and aggressive mood. "They ate and drank voraciously in a most unusual mood. The bosses were unable to control them for fear of being attacked themselves and were forced to look on passively."[122]

5 February: Sunokobashi, Honzan

The following morning just after 8, a group of miners again attacked officials' cabins. The targets this time were the pithead cabins at Sunokobashi. Miners threatened the staff, and after they had run off, cut telephone lines and threw stones. At about 7:30 A.M. several hundred miners gathered in the Honzan Ariki pit area, and the electric trucks stopped running. Just before noon another group of about seventy to eighty miners beat up some officials in the underground section 1 cabin, three of whom sustained light injuries.

The staff, already frightened by the news of the previous day's attacks at Tsūdō, all ran to escape. Once again, miners set upon the empty cabins, threw stones, and smashed windows.

These events of 4 and 5 February are usually included in descriptions of the riot, but in fact only cabins and barns, actually little more than shacks, were destroyed or had windows smashed. Dynamite was used only against empty shacks, and after explosions, the miners were careful to douse any fires with water. Eight trucks were overturned, some mechanized drills were removed, and some equipment was strewn about, but otherwise machinery was left untouched. The miners evidenced no intent to put the mine out of operation or to damage company buildings. The "rioters'" targets were the overseers and foremen, the low-ranking officials on whom they wanted revenge. Apart from two or three officials at Honzan who were beaten up and lightly injured, there were no injuries at all. The total number of people involved must have been about one thousand, but usually no more than two or three hundred were active at any one time. A special correspondent from the *Commoners' Weekly*, Nishikawa Mitsujirō, began his first report, sent on the evening of 5 February, with the words "The disturbances are on a surprisingly moderate scale."

6 February, Honzan: From Underground to the Surface

The situation at Honzan changed dramatically after 9 A.M. on 6 February. "Rioters" who had wrecked underground foremen's cabins before 8 that morning split into two groups and came to the surface, one group emerging from the Ariki pithead, the other from Hongochi. Their targets were no longer mere foremen's cabins but the Honzan pithead office and stores located near the Ariki pit entrance, or else the buildings of the Supply Department and the Pits Department, the two departments at the center of the administrative structure of the Ashio mine office. At first they gathered around the buildings and broke window glass with stones or sticks and damaged doors, without actually entering the buildings.

Their behavior altered soon after 10 A.M., however, when rioters seized Mine Director Minami Teizō in front of his residence and hit him over the head with an iron bar. Not only was the director, in addition to the officials, now a victim of the miners' fury, but an angry group of miners also set upon a policeman who attempted to arrest the "criminal" who had attacked the director. They rescued the "criminal" and badly beat the policeman. This was an open attack on authority itself. During the melee involving the police-man, Director Minami barely managed to escape into his residence, where he hid himself under the floorboards for more than three hours. During those three hours, the rumors went round that the director had been mur-dered. "Rioters" searching for the director wrecked his residence, destroying furniture and scattering his clothes. Minami's own account of this incident throws an interesting light on the character of the riot.

As far as I could make out their movements from under the floorboards, they were smashing everything. I heard a calmer voice among the rioters, who must have been one of the ringleaders, saying: "Eat and drink your fill, but there must be no looting, because that would shame us. But let's make sure we smash everything thoroughly." After that the destruction went on more violently, and I even saw them looking for me under the floor.

Eventually, Minami saw his chance and tried to get away, but he was caught and again beaten up. He later testified:

A crowd of the rioters saw me and shouted "Get him!" "Do him in!" But one man, who looked like a rail car driver, said, "There's no point in killing him; take him to the hospital." While one good man calmed the others down, the one who looked like a driver took hold of me and another worker lent a hand. "Right, let's get him to the hospital," they said, and they helped me up the hill to the hospital, a bunch of them actually carrying me on their shoulders . . . they got me to the Honzan medical station. Then Kaneko Gakusaburō [the doctor] came out and said to the miners, "Don't you know that injured people are protected under this Red Cross flag?" The rioters obeyed him and pulled back a little.[123]

Minami's testimony makes clear that at this point, the "riot" was no disorganized rampage. Among the men were those who exercised leadership at certain times. Particularly noteworthy is that one of these leaders told the men that wrecking, eating and drinking are all right, but there must be no stealing. This was a behavioral norm common to peasant riots of the eigh-teenth and early nineteenth centuries.[124] It is also certain that the men who beat Minami must themselves have exercised some self-control when they did so, for Minami was hit over the head with an iron bar, yet made "a complete recovery, with no sign of any organic injury five weeks after the event."[125] In fact, a mere two weeks later, on 18 February, he was told that his "wounds [were] healing well," at which point he left Ashio for Tokyo.

The Riot Spreads

Around 11 that same morning, the character of the event certainly changed. A group of men broke into the company store at Honzan and started looting from the piled-up stocks of rice, miso, soy sauce, and sake. Not only did some proceed to get blind drunk and start acting wildly, but the riot began to spread when bystanders, who had been watching the "rioters" at a distance until the day before, now suddenly joined in. Some went around the miners' shacks rounding up those inside, yelling: "Come on out! What are you waiting for! Stop skulking in there!" This swelled the numbers of "rioters" at a stroke to more than five or six hundred.

The main victims of the violence until this point had been officials such as overseers and foremen who lived in daily contact with the miners and made a practice of soliciting bribes. The attack on Director Minami was the event that signaled that all "officials" were now targets. The rioters began to challenge all men with beards or wearing Western-style clothes, and they started to attack all those found to be company "officials." At first, rioters only verbally abused or intimidated their victims, but gradually this turned to physical violence, as men took the opportunity to settle old scores. On 6 February the "rioters" were, at the outset, still taking care to "choose buildings that were not close to people's houses when they set fire to documents and clothes."[126] But as the disturbances spread, more and more bystanders joined in, many moved only by the effects of alcohol. These rioters were more interested in eating, drinking, and looting than in beating up officials. Shortly after 4 P.M. the company fuel warehouse was set on fire. With no one to put it out, the fire rapidly spread to the surrounding buildings and the flames lit up the sky all evening. One group of "rioters" hunted for "officials," pursuing their quarry as far as the inns and shops of Mato district. Officials' living quarters were wrecked and some set on fire. That evening, Nishikawa Mitsujirō, one of the few newspaper reporters on the spot (actually on the other side of the river from Honzan), reported the following: "To get a view of the fire I went off in the direction of Honzan. On the way I saw a lot of drunks in the crowd. They must have looted sake from the company stores. I did not see one policeman. I wondered, where on earth are they? I saw 50 or 60 bags of rice that had been thrown in the river. They must have been taken from the stores too. Looking at the fire burning furiously on the other side of the river and at the many drunken miners coming and going on my side, I was profoundly shaken by the whole spectacle."[127] Noteworthy here is the moblike character of this final stage of the "riot." The first police report noted: "It would appear that many of those committing acts of arson, looting and violence are masons, construction workers and day laborers, and that relatively few miners are involved. It is believed that many acts of arson are currently being committed by drunken laborers, masons and other such workers, and as a result of investigations, a cleaner from Kiyo-o lodge, Kimura Tajirō, has been arrested along with three other individuals."[128]

The Authorities' Response

The Powerlessness of the Police

When the "riot" broke out on the morning of 4 February, the authorities had at their disposal the mine's forty security guards and no more than twenty officers of the Ashio police station of the Nikkō constabulary.[129] Since the disturbances had broken out deep underground and involved the use of dynamite, the police officers did not immediately hurry to the scene, but rather remained in the pithead area and merely issued verbal warnings against stone throwing. The only other action they took was to call all the Tsūdō lodge bosses into the Ashio police station and order them to calm their men down. The disturbances that day were restricted to only one part of the Tsūdō mine and did not last long, so shortly after 2 P.M. two police officers were taken down into the mine by officials to inspect the damage. Hearing of the emergency that afternoon, the Tochigi Prefectural Police Department ordered out a special contingent of about fifty officers and three inspectors, headed by Superintendent Mizuno. The following morning, District Attorney Yoshida of the Utsunomiya District Court and preliminary court judge Kakinuma set out for Ashio accompanied by clerks and four policemen. At 1 P.M. that afternoon Uematsu Kaneaki, chief superintendent of the Tochigi Prefectural Police Department, also left for Ashio.

The Prefectural Police Department was now moving in earnest. There were over 11,000 workers at Ashio, and experienced socialists like Minami Sukematsu and Nagaoka Tsuruzō had been very active—men whose influence could by no means be underestimated and on whom the police had long been keeping a careful watch.[130] In addition, the home minister, Hara Kei, had a special relationship to Ashio. All this meant that the police could not afford to treat the situation lightly. Nevertheless, the prefectural police took nearly nine hours to reach Ashio, leaving Utsunomiya for Nikkō and then traveling to Hoso'o, crossing the mountain valleys. Despite the calls for assistance, for more than half a day they were therefore unable to respond effectively, at a time (5 February) when the local police had only twenty men to cover the three widely separated pit areas of Honzan, Tsūdō, and Kodaki.

Until the morning of 6 February, the activities of Shiseikai activists such as Minami and Nagaoka had been the main objects of police surveillance, so most officers had been assigned to Tsūdō, site of Shiseikai's head office. The police were most suspicious of those leading Shiseikai members who were members of the Japan Socialist Party and in contact with leading socialists in Tokyo. Although Minami and Nagaoka both made repeated visits to the Ashio police station on 4 and 5 February with the message that Shiseikai had nothing to do with the destruction of the underground foremen's cabins, and were at the same time desperately urging the miners to exercise restraint, their protestations did not allay police suspicion. In the prejudiced view of the police, Nagaoka's desperate efforts were simply seen as a case of "pretending to damp down the fire with one hand while stoking it with the other."[131] The following is a report of a telephone message to Utsunomiya District Attorney Mukai at 2 P.M. on 5 February, from fellow attorney Yoshida, then on duty in Ashio: "Although the causes cannot be ascertained in detail, the present disturbances have resulted from the speeches made to the miners by the socialist Minami Sukematsu who arrived here from Yūbari coal mine in Hokkaido."[132]

When he heard foremen's cabins at Honzan were attacked on the morning of 6 February and that trouble was spreading outside the mine, Chief Superintendent Uematsu of the Tochigi Prefectural Police requested the prefectural governor to send reinforcements. He also ordered the arrest of Minami, Nagaoka, and six other leading Shiseikai activists. Nagaoka was taken into custody at 10 A.M. and Minami followed thirty minutes later. Both men went "voluntarily." They were charged with "incitement" to cause damage to the foremen's cabins on 4 and 5 February.[133]

The Request for Military Assistance

At 11:10 A.M. on 6 February, District Attorney Yoshida in Ashio sent an urgent telegram to District Attorney Mukai in Utsunomiya: "Situation deteriorating. Request troops. Police Chief has telegraphed the Governor. Urgent. Assistance required."[134]

By this time the situation at Honzan was completely beyond the authorities' control. At 9 A.M., when the miners had turned from attacking underground cabins to buildings above ground, "although the authority of the police had not yet completely collapsed, [the rioters] were simply ignoring the admonitions of the police and moving on to places where there were no police and continuing their violent acts there."[135] However, when the crowd rescued the "criminal" who had been arrested for attacking Director Minami, the last vestiges of police authority collapsed. When Minami Teizō was recaptured after trying to escape from under the floorboards of his house and was attacked again, "the small groups of policemen nearby were powerless to prevent it and could only look on."[136] Facing crowds of six hundred or one thousand with no weapons other than their sabers, and under orders from the governor "to keep swords sheathed at all times," the fifty police officers were effectively helpless.[137] After the Honzan storehouses had been set on fire at about 4 P.M., "the many police on duty could do nothing but look on, and the Honzan-Matō area was completely unpoliced." With telephone lines to Honzan cut and the violence now widespread, rumors flew everywhere. One of these held that the director had been murdered. This rumor may have started when Minami, after being hit over the head, had pretended to be dead to avoid worse treatment. Other rumors flying around with no substance whatever included reports of a plan of underground miners to blow up the mine, of plans to destroy the power station at Hoso'o, and plans to burn Ashio town to the ground.[138] Most worrying to the police in this confused atmosphere were reports of an impending attack on the Ashio police station to force the release of Minami, Nagaoka, and the others.[139]

When this information reached the police station some time after 3 P.M., the station chiefs disagreed as to how to deal with such an attack. "Some argued for arresting [the rioters] by a forthright attack with drawn swords, killing if necessary, while others urged a tactical retreat to plan a strategy for effective arrests, or wondered what further measures would be possible if they themselves were all killed. The debate was heated, but eventually it was decided to transfer all important documents elsewhere, to defend the station until it was destroyed and then to withdraw."[140]

The panic at the police station was hardly alleviated by the arrival of reinforcements and the crowding of the Ashio police station with some sixty officers. When District Attorney Yoshida and examining judge Fujinuma, who were staying at an inn in Ashio town, heard a rumor that those inns sheltering officials were to be burned to the ground, "they put down the chopsticks with which they had been hurrying through their meal and finished the rest with their hands, then they shaved off their beards and moustaches, changed their clothes, and fled."[141] The police also issued a warning to the journalists who had gathered to cover the "riot": "If it comes to the point where we are no longer able to protect you, it will be every man for himself. Even if you feel you must go out, we advise you that because of the possible danger, it would be better if you stayed at the inn."[142]

Earlier, at 10 A.M. on 6 February, Prefectural Governor Nakayama was arranging to mobilize all prefectural police forces and send them to Ashio. Over 505 officers were serving in the prefectural force in the nine stations and nine substations. From just 193 men in 1896 the force had increased by 260 percent to its strength of 505 at the time of the riot.[143] Fully two-thirds of this force was now to be sent to Ashio. Following an emergency message from Ashio that read "Riot out of control. Mine Director Minami murdered," at 11 A.M. the governor received a telegram from Chief Superintendent Uematsu asking for troops to be sent.[144] The senior police officer on the spot had thus judged that the police would be unable to manage by themselves. Article 8 of the Local Government Regulations stated: "In cases of dire emergency, when the Governor requires the deployment of military force or the use of military equipment by the police, he is to notify the commanding officer of the local garrison and make a formal request for such deployment or supplies." The governor urgently contacted the home minister and around 1 P.M. made formal request of the commanding officer of the first division. The man who had appointed Governor Nakayama Miyozo was none other than Hara Kei, and it was Hara who decided on sending in troops after consultations with Army Minister Terauchi.[145] At 3:30 P.M. the army's divisional chief of staff ordered the regimental garrison commander at Takasaki to send three companies to Ashio.[146]

The Ashio riot was the first time troops were sent to deal with disturbances at a single industrial company. This outline of discussions at the highest levels explains the speed with which this unprecedented decision to send troops was taken and executed. Nevertheless, after Major Yoshino and his battalion of three companies (three hundred men) had left Takasaki railway station for Nikkō via Omiya at 11 P.M. on the 6th, they did not arrive at Ashio until 1:20 to 3 P.M. the following day.

The Troops Suppress the Riot

By 7 February the operations throughout the Ashio mine were at a complete standstill. Even at the Kodaki pits, which had been running normally the previous morning, the men were paid wages in the afternoon and given two days off. By 2 A.M. on the 7th, the fires at Honzan had burned themselves out, but in the ruins of the stores and warehouses piles of rice were still smoldering among the burning cinders. The police, still fearing attacks from "rioters" believed to be hiding in the mines, anxiously awaited the arrival of the army. The one action the police did take early that day was to take into custody the *Heimin shimbun* reporter Nishikawa Mitsujirō, who had been staying at the Tsuruya Inn near the Ashio police station.

The troops who had left Takasaki station the previous night arrived at Nikkō station at 8:30 A.M., and, leaving behind their blankets and knapsacks, hurried on to Ashio with only light equipment. Arriving at Hoso'o at 11 A.M., they proceeded on foot over the mountain pass to Tochigidaira, from where they took horse-drawn carts to Ashio, arriving finally at 1:30 P.M., thirteen hours after leaving Takasaki. The three companies marched to take up posts at Honzan, Akakuramachi, Ashiochō (Ashio town), Kodaki, and the Hoso'o electricity generating station.

On arrival at Honzan, the main center of the disturbances, Company No. 1 fired salvos of blank ammunition to intimidate any "rioters," but in fact by this time there were none. Many miners had worked off their frustrations the day before by getting drunk and running wild all day with their mates, and when they woke up the next day to see the ruins of the burned-out mine offices and stores, they felt only unease at what might lie ahead. News of the soldiers' arrival quickly spread. At the height of the attacks on the hapless officials, some miners had no doubt called for a charge on the police station and would have actually gone on to carry out such an attack. But at 7 A.M. on the morning of the 7th, no such voices could be heard. The fact that the "rioters" took no further direct actions between 7 A.M. and the arrival of the troops clearly suggests that the burnings and destruction had not been premeditated or organized. "The police who, until the arrival of the army, had only been onlookers during the riotous disturbances, quickly recovered their confidence and in groups of 30 or 50 went to the Honzan miners' shacks where they began to conduct searches."[147] The authorities declared Article 18 of the Public Order and Police Law to be in force, giving them de facto powers of martial law.[148] Some three hundred people were arrested and interrogated that day, and the arrests and interrogations continued on 8 and 9 February. Altogether, 628 were arrested and 182 were prosecuted.[149]

The Cost of the "Riot"

Company investigations revealed that a total of sixty-five buildings had been destroyed, including the offices of the Supply Department and the Pits Department, the Honzan pithead office, stores and warehouses, officials' living quarters, the ore-dressing station, and the refinery buildings. Of these, forty-eight buildings had been burned down. The fires had mostly spread from the stores; only the officials' quarters were recognized as having been "subject to separate acts of arson."[150] Three townspeople's houses in Matō and Akakuramachi were also damaged. In addition to Minami Teizō, whose head wound took five weeks to heal completely, a Honzan official, Takashima Toragoro, had sustained severe injuries, and the general manager, Kawachi, and the pits manager, Kibe, had both been wounded by blows to the head. Six other officials, both underground and office staff, were also injured. Of the twenty mine workers with head injuries, most were underground miners, but there were also electricity workers, laborers, and haulers. Three policemen were wounded, all of them at the time of the attack on Director Minami. There was only one fatality: a laborer from Tsūdō named Takeuchi Takejirō apparently burned to death while drunk.[151]

The immediate financial damages totaled 283,058 yen: buildings, 52,500 yen; machinery, 118,756 yen; warehouse goods, 45,000 yen; and employees' personal belongings, 66,802 yen.[152]

The Aftermath

Mass Dismissals and Selective Rehiring

The miners had set 10 February as the limit for a reply to the brotherhood petition. They had presented the petition on behalf of all miners, and although only the Kodaki pits had been uninvolved in the "riot," all waited with some trepidation to see how the company would now respond. Shortly after 1:30 P.M. on the 10th, Tajima Yukichi, the pit manager at Honzan, and

Kojima Jintarō, the manager at Tsūdō, called together all the lodge bosses and two miners' representatives from each lodge and read out to them a written statement of the company's decision. In essence, the company fired all Honzan and Tsūdō miners and apprentices, whether or not they had actually taken part in the disturbances. Those wishing to be rehired were to submit "requests for employment" the following morning, the 11th.[153]

The company's statement noted the wage proposal of the lodge bosses but neither mentioned nor replied to the brotherhood's petition for a wage increase:

The matter of wage increases submitted by the lodge masters was considered in various respects and forwarded to the company's head office where, after further extensive investigations, it was decided that although wage levels at this mine are higher than those of other company-owned or private mines, the current favorable operation of the [Ashio] mine makes it possible for the company to share the happy results with the workforce and accordingly, the company resolved to grant a wage increase in the very near future. It was on the point of announcing this fact when the miners unhappily chose to oppose the company by resorting to the recent acts of violence. In consequence, the company regrets the division that has opened up between itself and the miners and apprentices.[154]

The severity of this response—firing all workers, requiring them to ask for their jobs back, while utterly ignoring the wage increase issue—shocked both the miners and the lodge bosses. Most of them duly submitted "requests" for reemployment, and some even wrote words of apology: "Henceforth I shall obey officials' instructions and shall not heed those calling for solidarity to achieve whatever benefits for workers." But the workers had no idea whether submitting a "request for employment" would actually lead to rehiring. Some in the lodge argued that unless all were rehired, they all should reject Ashio's pressure and quit on the spot, going instead to the Kosaka or Akazawa (Hitachi) copper mines. Debates raged within the lodge, and no consensus could be reached.

Eventually, however, the majority came to favor accepting the demand to submit "requests" for reemployment. At Sunokobashi, all miners signed such "requests," and at Honzan, nearly all the 1200-plus miners submitted their "requests," including those who had been arrested or retained in custody. The company, for its part, would not agree that all the miners were "good men." The mine indicated to the bosses that the petitions of "all those

Table 1.1. Reemployment of Fired Ashio Miners

	Honzan		Tsūdō	
	Estimates by the		Estimates by the	
	Company	Police	Company	Police
Total no. of workers, as of 31 January 1907	1217	1217	1151	1151
Number requesting reemployment	1158	1158	1062	1046
Number reemployed	1157	1158	971	1046
Number not reemployed	1	0	91	0
Workforce reduction	60	59	180	87
Number detained by police		57		39

Sources: For company data: "Ashio dōzan bōdō gaiki" (Outline of the Ashio Copper Mine riot), in NRUS, vol. 2, p. 221. For police data: Utsunomiya District Attorney's Office Archive, "Ashio sōjō jiken ni kan suru himitsu shorui" (Confidential documents relating to the Ashio riot incident).

detained by the police [and] those likely to be difficult employees in the future" should be rejected. The Honzan bosses were concerned that "if workers submit signed petitions with the understanding that they will be reemployed, and are then told that petitions will be accepted after investigation, the workers will be upset, the lodge bosses will lose face and forfeit their trust." The bosses asked for an agreement to extend the deadline for submissions until 10 A.M. on the 12th. Their request was denied and the company had its way.[155] At 3:30 P.M. on the 12th, the company again summoned all the bosses to the Honzan and Tsūdō pits and announced the names of those workers who were to be reemployed. Table 1.1 shows considerable discrepancies between the company and the police records in the number of workers reemployed.

The company's figures show that eighty-nine men at Tsūdō did not submit petitions for reemployment and that the company rejected ninety-one men, while at Honzan only one man was not reemployed. Yet the police records show that all petitioners were accepted at both Honzan and Tsūdō. There is no evidence that allows us to decide which count is correct. The police record comes from an official "notice" published the day of the company announcement of rehirings, and newspaper reports gave a figure of 1064 for the number of workers reemployed at Tsūdō.[156] In contrast, the company's figures were compiled by Supply Department staff and released two months later. Probably the police figures are therefore be more reliable.

Whichever numbers are correct, the significant fact remains that Ashio dismissed more men at Tsūdō than at Honzan, where the worst "rioting" took place. The great majority of the men dismissed at Honzan were those who had been arrested, but at Tsūdō many who had not joined the "riot" were among those dismissed. This difference no doubt reflected the influence of the Shiseikai among the Tsūdō miners. That is, in the initial aftermath of the "riot" the company targeted the Shiseikai as much as the rioters. Protected by the police enforcement of the Administrative Provisions Law, Ashio's hard-line policy was to get rid of activists and postpone any talk of wage increases.

However, on 12 February, the day the lists of reemployed workers were announced, a problem emerged through an action of one of the Honzan lodge bosses that would greatly affect the Ashio brotherhood and later, the bosses themselves. A police report records the following: "A certain lodge boss from Honzan named Yamamoto is to call a meeting today in the lodge at 10 A.M. At the meeting he will call for the abolition of the brotherhood assemblies, because assembly men acted as leading intermediaries between the miners and Minami and Nagaoka, whose agitations have corrupted the miners' morals."[157]

That same evening groups of Honzan miners met in their own lodge and decided to present the following written covenant to the lodge bosses:

To: Esteemed Lodge Masters

12 February

As a result of our agreement in the lodge meeting today, we establish the following articles and shall henceforth strictly abide by them:

1. We shall not commit injurious acts in any form of union.

2. We shall not disobey the company's orders.

3. If a boss judges that an injurious act has been committed and issues a suspension, we shall abide by that suspension.

4. We shall apply to the bosses for permission to hold lodge meetings and bosses shall be present at such meetings.

If any of the above articles are infringed we shall ask for the perpetrator to be dismissed.

The Lodge Members[158]

The locus of authority implicit in the phrases "If a boss judges that an injurious act has been committed and issues a suspension" and "we shall ask for the perpetrator to be dismissed" indicates that the articles of this "covenant" were written by a lodge boss.

On 13 February, company officials, lodge bosses, and miners made their way to the guardian shrines at each of the mines at Honzan, Tsūdō, and Sunokobashi, offered up libations of rice wine, and, "after purifying the mountain that had been polluted by the riot," recommenced work at the mine. However, at Honzan, "30 men who were due to report for work today were all absent, pleading illness." The reason given—"they were probably anxious for their safety after the recent violence"—was in all probability correct. That morning, the troops left Ashio for Nikkō.

The Implementation of Wage Increases

Thus, the mine returned to normal operations after roughly ten days of disruption, but Ashio's problems had not been solved. With each passing day, the atmosphere at Kodaki, where miners had not taken part in the riot, became more uneasy, as company records noted:

By the middle of February the situation at Kodaki had not calmed down. Few were coming to work, and the number of men going down the pits and the amount of ore coming out had not only declined significantly, there were signs, even if only moderate ones, of disobedience to police officers and company officials. The men would not pay attention to the strenuous efforts of the police and the pit manager's officials to pacify them.

The author of this "Outline of the Ashio Copper Mine Riot" attributed this behavior to the fact that the Kodaki miners

despite the obligation to act in unison with all the [Ashio] miners, had been pacified by the pit manager and his staff, had therefore lost their opportunity to participate in the explosion, and had in effect betrayed the agreement made with their fellow miners. If they were to remain passive, they would be forced to acknowledge their lack of spirit to the miners of the other pits. This fear of losing face in front of their fellow miners led the men at Kodaki to remove the stain of their breaking of the miners' agreement by securing the implementation of the terms of the original petition in their own power.[159]

This view of the riot as having been fomented by an agreement among the four Ashio brotherhoods is contradicted by the facts. The reason representatives from the four brotherhoods had signed the "joint agreement" with its stipulation that "the course of action to be taken by us will be decided by all of us following joint deliberation and decision" was because the miners had agreed their petition would be "presented by the brotherhood assembly stewards, accompanied by the lodge bosses, in accordance with custom, at 9 A.M. on 6 February and they had made a verbal statement to the effect that a reply [would be] expected by the 10th February." The Kodaki miners resented the fact that the company had used the riot as an excuse to squash the petition. Why should they, who had submitted their petition peacefully and had not taken part in the riot, be involved in its consequences? Such was their reasoning. If the wage increase had already been decided on before the riot, why not go ahead and implement it? Had not Pit Manager Esashi said, "If you present your demands fairly and squarely without recourse to violence, you will not be treated badly"? Why then did the company in effect cut wages by paying only the "base rate" when the mine was at a standstill? The mine could not address such frustrations simply by suppressing them.

On 25 February, Kondo Rikusaburō was reappointed mine director in place of Minami Teizō. The following day, he went to Kodaki and invited all the Kodaki lodge bosses to a meeting. Greetings were exchanged on the occasion of his appointment and "he declared that the fact that Kodaki alone had been unaffected by the recent incident was due to your (i.e. the bosses') strength. He said that they therefore had earned a bonus." The thirty lodge bosses were each paid a total of 45 yen: a bonus of 5 yen for food and drink, ten days' daily allowance (30 yen) and an extra allowance of 10 yen. Similar but smaller bonuses were paid to the Kodaki assembly representatives in amounts of 5, 20, and 5 yen. Miners were paid bonuses of 5 yen, their apprentices 3 yen, base rate workers 3 yen, part-timers 1 yen 50 sen, male ore-dressing workers 1 yen 50 sen, and female workers 30 sen. The total, 9475 yen 20 sen, was paid along with regular wages on 28 February.

Director Kondo visited Honzan on the 27th and Tsūdō on the 28th. After being greeted on the occasion of his appointment, he declared that "the recent riot incident was extremely regrettable. Wage increases for the workers of this mine should be implemented in the near future." Bonuses of between 5 yen and 50 sen were paid to those workers who had not disobeyed the company. A total of 1086 yen 85 sen was paid to 465 workers at Honzan and Tsūdō.[160]

Some among the Honzan and Tsūdō miners "were agitating miners in drinking sessions, saying that the award of the bonus only to the Kodaki pits was favoritism and discrimination and that the wage increases should be paid immediately." The police soon "dealt with these unruly elements by proceeding against them with the force of the law." The details of the wage increases were confirmed by the company on 27 February and officially announced on 1 March:

1. The miner's daily standard rate is hereby fixed at 80 sen, effective from the 16th of this month. The "base rate" wage category is abolished, effective the 16th of this month.

2. The wages of other workers will be increased significantly beyond their present levels, effective from the 16th of this month.

3. Financial provision for medical expenses and sickness allowances will be improved for those workers absent from work on account of injuries and illness sustained in the performance of their duties.[161]

The pay raise averaged 19.4 percent over the previous level of 67 sen. Company records that detail the increases for other workers have not survived, but a police report noted that the maximum wage level for other workers had been raised from 1 yen 5 sen to 1 yen 20 sen and was paid according to job classification.[162]

PROBLEMS POSED BY THE "RIOT"

Theories on the Cause of the Riot

What were the direct causes of the riot? More specifically, how and why did the attacks on the underground overseers' cabins in the Tsūdō mine take place on 4 February? Were they entirely unplanned and spontaneous, or did someone plan the attacks and carry them out deliberately? If the latter, who made the plans? These questions must be addressed in any examination of the direct causes of the riot. We cannot expect the conclusions to be crystal clear; after all, the events took place over ninety years ago, and it is almost impossible to get to the truth of the matter. Rather, we should be able to examine the analyses that have been put forward by scholars so far, and assess their validity.

The Spontaneity Theory

The first such explanation can be called the spontaneity theory. This was the view taken by the preliminary trial court after extremely detailed examination of the course and the causes of the riot. Judge Miyamoto Rikinosuke of the Utsunomiya District Court described the harsh treatment of the miners by Director Minami Teizō. The miners, he said, had endured this for many years, but "despite their resentments and frustrations, they had no means of giving vent to their feelings" until the Shiseikai activists, and especially Minami Sukematsu, "told the miners that if they were dismissed, then thousands of them could go with them [Minami et al.] to Hokkaido." This "great agitation of the miners," Miyamoto said, lay behind the riot. He drew the following conclusion: "The feelings of these violent, ignorant, intemperate but vigorous miners, consumed with the frustrations of many years and without hope of better treatment, suddenly flared up in an explosion of violent self-indulgence."[163]

The Tokyo Court of Appeals and the Supreme Court upheld this verdict, and the spontaneity theory also appeared in many newspapers, such as the *Kokumin shimbun*. All versions of the theory stressed how intensely the miners resented company officials, especially the low-ranking ones such as foremen and overseers. These feelings, it was claimed, suddenly took the form of the attacks on the underground cabins at Tsūdō. Interestingly, spontaneity theorists varied widely in their descriptions of specific details of the incident that actually sparked the attack on the cabins. One version blamed "an argument over wages between officials and miners,"[164] another pointed to "contemptuous language used by an official,"[165] and a third singled out "officials allowing water only to those miners who had given them bribes."[166] Certainly any one such incident could have been the spark that lit the fuse. The overseers' use of bribery in the determination of wages was one of the miners' main grievances, and the workers had to put up with the officials' arrogance and contempt day in, day out.[167]

But the spontaneity theory has several weaknesses. First, a few days before the riot began, "a rumor [spread] of plans to wreck an underground cabin." This rumor was actually mentioned in the findings of the preliminary inquiry:

Inquiry Protocol of Chiaki Genzō [a miner]: at the end of January, he occasionally heard some of the men down the pit at Tsūdō saying that if any of the officials treated men unfairly, they should be roughed up a bit. He heard men down the mine saying that if the deals with the officials were no good, the cabins or something else should be smashed up. On 3 February a rumor went round that a foreman's cabin was to be wrecked; he went with four other men to Ōnaname, below the cabin at the intersection of sections 3 and 4. Three or four other men were there. He said he had come because he had heard that a cabin was to be wrecked and he asked what was happening, but the conversation did not come to a conclusion, because it was time for everyone to start at the faces. He was told to wait until someone came to get him, but he left.[168]

The "deals" mentioned here refer to a particular method by which officials determined wages. The men were saying that if the officials tried any tricks in setting wages, "the cabins or something else should be smashed up." If this testimony is accurate, it confirms the possibility that the riot was planned in advance.

Chiaki Genzō's testimony was borne out by the three men who accompanied him on this visit to Ōnaname. Their testimonies too were cited in the findings of the inquiry:

Inquiry Protocol of Onoda Tomesaburō [a miner]: About 9 A.M. on 28 or 29 January this year, there were seven or eight miners at the foot of the pit entry shaft. Chiaki Genzō said that he had heard that a plan to smash up some foremen's cabins was going to be discussed at the walkway intersection in section 3 and that he'd gone there, but found nothing going on. He (Onoda) went down the pit at 8 A.M. on the 3rd February, and at the assembly point, Chiaki Genzō said that there would be a meeting that day at the intersection crossing between sections 3 and 4 to talk about wrecking some foremen's cabins and suggested that they go along together, which they did. More than ten miners were there. Chiaki said there was supposed to be discussion of a plan to wreck some cabins today—what had they done about it? The others replied that the men down the pit that day had met to talk about it but could not reach any conclusion because they had had to go to their positions at the faces. Hasegawa

Kenkichi and Kurihara Umekichi, in their testimonies to the inquiry, gave similar accounts of the events of 3 February to this account by Onoda Tomesaburō.[169]

For some reason, despite having heard such testimonies, the inquiry judge failed to investigate further this claim that the attack on the underground cabins at Tsūdō, which after all had sparked the entire riot, had been premeditated. Instead, the judgment merely stated that "there were those who talked about wrecking underground foremen's cabins and of threatening officials, in consequence of which, as has been explained, acts of violence were committed against underground foremen's cabins at Tsūdō on 4 February 1907." The "plan to wreck some cabins" was considered merely an example of the "great agitation of the miners."

The second weakness of the spontaneity theory lies in the fact that there was indeed a ringleader in the attack on the underground cabins on 4 February. He was none other than Ōnishi Saichi, brotherhood assembly representative of Tsūdō's No. 1 lodge and an enthusiastic member of "the Shiseikai hard-line activists, the Group of 14." The inquiry verdict noted that:

The defendant, Ōnishi Saichi, was an influential representative of Tsūdō's No. 1 lodge who had been a leader in the efforts to restore the "treasury box" and to reform the lodge organization. There had already been much talk among the Tsūdō miners of wrecking the underground foremen's cabins which had not yet been translated into action. But at approximately 8 A.M. on 4 February, a large group of miners happened to gather at the diagonal level crossing below the foreman's cabin at the intersection of sections 3 and 4. There was talk of an attack on the cabin. The defendant concurred with this and cried out that because they were going to wreck the cabins today, the first shift man shouldn't go up (to the surface) and the second shift man shouldn't go down (from here). There were many restless and angry miners present and when the uproar became extreme, the defendant lent his influence to the agitation for violence by shouting above the tumult that the cabins were useless and should be destroyed, whereupon, beginning with the cabins at the intersection of sections 3 and 4, the rioters wrecked all the underground foremen's cabins, and the violence developed into a full-scale riot.[170]

Ōnishi was prosecuted under article 137 of the Penal Code, accused of fomenting and agitating a "riotous assembly," and sentenced to five years' imprisonment with hard labor. Considering that there were plans to wreck the cabins beforehand and that Ōnishi Saichi just happened to be at the scene and played a leading role in the attack, it would seem implausible to maintain that the riot began as a spontaneous event.

The Shiseikai Agitation Theory

The prosecution consistently presented this view, and the company shared it. The "Shiseikai theory" held that Minami Sukematsu, Nagaoka Tsuruzō, and others had laid the plans, and that Ōnishi Saichi at Tsūdō and Tsuruoka Ushinosuke at Honzan had executed them by leading the miners in their attacks on the foremen's cabins. The Shiseikai, it was claimed, had planned and instigated the riot, having deemed that a "show of strength" was necessary to soften the company up prior to submitting the brotherhood assembly petition, which was, in effect, written by the Shiseikai.[171]

This claim has weaknesses as well. First, the behavior of Minami and Nagaoka during the riot contradict the theory. As noted above, on 4 and 5 February, Minami, Nagaoka, and the other Shiseikai leaders were desperately trying to calm down the "rioters," a fact recognized by both the police and the prosecutor.[172] These authorities, however, labeled this a ruse masking the Shiseikai men's ongoing agitation of the miners. If we bear in mind Nagaoka's constant admonitions to audiences at his speeches that their movement should be based on "the principle of making the law work for them," then this is not a persuasive claim. Nagaoka always maintained that his activities and arguments were justified by the Mining Industry Ordinances and even by Article 17 of the Public Order and Police Law. He stated that he had not changed his views despite suffering personally under the weight of the state's authority (he had been made the subject of a restraint order and forbidden to speak at public meetings). Nagaoka feared any outbursts of violence by the miners, because he foresaw how these could be used by the police to break up organized labor movements.

Thus, when the campaign for a raise was rapidly gathering steam on 11 January, and again on 1 February, Nagaoka had spoken as follows at public meetings:

The whole workers' movement is getting stronger and stronger! But we should avoid bloodshed and rash behavior as in the Tokyo streetcar riots . We must press on with our assault and bring it to a successful conclusion without spilling blood. . . . Let us maintain a serious attitude and avoid all ignoble methods.

Shiseikai now has over a thousand members. With more than six hundred partly paid-up members and over two hundred members who have not yet paid their membership fee, but who have completed the formalities for membership, Shiseikai has become a large and powerful body, great beyond our expectations! . . . We have always believed that if we follow the path of justice, we shall ultimately triumph. We must therefore never resort to violence and must refrain from all rash and foolhardy behavior.[173]

We should not, however, view Nagaoka simply as a legalist. Both Shiseikai's policy concerning strikes and Nagaoka's speech of 8 January, which the prosecutor attempted to use against him, contradict such a view: "If the company doesn't accept the petition, then I have made my decision. We have the right to buy matches and the right to buy oil. Furukawa's 20,000,000-yen property here will suddenly be reduced to ashes." The prosecutor took this as proof of Nagaoka's incitement to riot, but Nagaoka replied, "I said that we have the right to buy matches and oil simply to bolster the men's self-confidence. It was no more than that." Nagaoka's "decision" in this statement could be read as implying that if he failed to achieve his objectives through Shiseikai, then he would sacrifice himself as peasant rebel and martyr, Sakura Sogoro, had done.[174]

Another difficulty with the theory pinning responsibility for the riot on the Shiseikai is the lack of a credible motive. Shiseikai had absolutely nothing to gain and much to lose in resorting to a riot. In fact, the riot destroyed Shiseikai, and the organization's leaders recognized this danger clearly. In his speeches, Nagaoka warned against repeating the mistakes of the workers at the Osaka arsenal, who had allowed their dispute with the management to turn violent and whose struggle had failed as a result.

The prosecution argued in court that Shiseikai had planned the riot to intimidate the company into accepting the twenty-four-article petition drawn up by the brotherhood assemblymen. This argument lacks credibility. First, the petition did not come from Shiseikai, but was presented in the name of the brotherhoods, supported by the lodge bosses. With over one thousand members, Shiseikai was planning to hold a mass meeting and present its own demands. If Shiseikai had planned the riot as a way of pressing its demands, it made no sense to do so before its own mass meeting, planned for approximately 11 February. Second, even granting the prosecution's contention that the brotherhoods' petition was a Shiseikai creation and that Shiseikai had planned the riot to get the petition accepted, we can see clearly that the timing of the riot made no sense from Shiseikai's point of view. The group intended to present the petition on 6 February and demand a reply by the 10th. Even if one were determined to foment a riot, it made more sense to do so after the petition had been rejected, or else (in an attempt to force the company's hand) just after it had been presented. To riot even before presenting the petition could only have a negative result. On 6 February, when all the pits were supposed to present their petitions, the only one that did so was Kodaki, and this was the only pit not involved in the riot.

The Theory of Lodge Boss Responsibility

The final scenario places the responsibility for the riot with the lodge bosses, on the theory that they sought to discredit Shiseikai by getting some of their own men to act as agents provocateurs. At the preliminary trial hearings, Ōnishi Saichi testified in support of this position:

Ōnishi Saichi belatedly agreed to speak about the cause of the riot. He said that Kamata Nobushirō [actually, Nobutarō] had been sent by the Tsūdō boss Ishida Kishirō to see him and that they had gone together to the Izumiya inn. A boy from Izumiya had been sent to summon Sakai Kazukichi to join them. Kamata said that he had come as a representative of the lodge masters, and asked Ōnishi to be a man and listen to his request. He would receive 300 yen if he would agree to stir up the younger men, because the bosses were presenting their own petition.

What Kamata said to me was . . . "Everyone knows that you are a member of Shiseikai, and the boys in the lodge will listen to what you say. If you'll go along, they will too. Stop them from getting worked up about Shiseikai. We'll give you about 30 men. I'm asking you, man to man, to lead these young ones and smash a few cabins."[175]

My own view is that, of the various scenarios, this "lodge boss provocation" theory is the most persuasive. First, we have a motive. As noted, on 28 January the Tsūdō bosses agreed to the assembly demand that control of the treasury box of brotherhood funds be returned to them. On the following day the lodge charge was abolished at Tsūdō's No. 1 pit, and it is easy to imagine the disastrous economic consequences for the lodge bosses of a general abolition of these charges. The bosses were also keenly aware of related danger: Minami Sukematsu's insistence that the miners "must reclaim the letters of proxy" that gave the bosses authority to receive the workers' wages from the company. At that time, the Ashio's pit miners were formally termed "category 1 workers" and had contracts of employment with the company that specified that wage payments go directly from the company to the miner. But many of the men were in debt to the lodge bosses, and as security on the debt they handed over to the bosses letters authorizing the latter to act as proxies who would receive the wages on their behalf. The bosses used these letters to claim from the company a man's total wage and then deduct from it the amount owed. Not only did many miners in this way receive their wages from the bosses, they also depended on them for the provision of their food and daily necessities. The cost of living at the lodge was comparatively high, and the men had trouble paying off debts. The letters of proxy kept the workers in a semipermanent state of debt slavery.

In this context, the bosses (particularly those at Tsūdō) perceived Shiseikai to be the cause of many of their problems. They were convinced that Minami and Nagaoka meant to influence the Tsūdō assemblymen to reclaim the treasury box and abolish the system of lodge charges. The bosses feared that if they did not contain or destroy Shiseikai, they might be forced to surrender the letters of proxy. They must have seen Shiseikai as a threat to their very existence.

Second, in addition to offering a plausible motive, the lodge boss theory provides a reasonable explanation for the timing of the riot. Whereas 4 February was the worst possible choice for a Shiseikai-led riot, for the bosses this day represented their "last chance." On the following day, the treasury boxes were due to be handed back to the brotherhood assemblies.

Third, the lodge bosses in fact turned out to be the only people who actually profited from the riot. The Shiseikai leaders were fired, the brotherhood assemblies were abolished, and the bosses gained firm control of the brotherhoods.[176]

Fourth, by adopting the lodge boss theory we are able for the first time to make sense of the confusing behavior and statements of one key individual. This is Chiaki Genzō, introduced above in discussing problems with the spontaneity theory. He testified that there was talk among the miners at the end of January of an attack on the cabins. On 3 February he heard of "rumors that some cabins were to be wrecked," and he deliberately invited some of his mates to go with him to the meeting below the cabins between sections 3 and 4 where the plan was to be discussed. Whatever his reason for going, he clearly had a keen interest in smashing the cabins. Chiaki said that "he had come because he had heard that a cabin was to be wrecked and he asked what was happening, but the conversation did not come to a conclusion, because it was time for everyone to start at the faces. He was told to wait until someone came to get him"; however, he did not wait. Rather, for some reason, "he left." This same Chiaki Genzō testified to a policeman after the riot that one day in mid-January, Shiseikai activist Imori Shingo "had said that the pithead cabins are necessary, but those underground are not, so they should all be destroyed." All of Chiaki's statements appear calculated to give the impression that Shiseikai had planned the attacks before the event.

Finally, there is the behavior of Ōnishi Saichi, who was identified in court as having stirred up the miners to attack the cabins. According to a police report in the immediate aftermath of the riot:

At approximately 8:30 A.M. on the 4th of this month, at the time of the outbreak of the violence in the Tsūdō mine, at the cabin at the intersection of sections 3 and 4, Ōnishi Saichi called out to ask if there were any men from no. 19 (among the men gathered there). He said repeatedly that the men of no. 19 were insincere and two-faced, and he led the men to commit repeated acts of violence, of which Motochika Toratarō, a miner from lodge no. 19, was a witness. Ōnishi ordered Nishimura Fujinosuke and 13 or 14 others from lodge no. 8 to wreck the cabins at the bottom of no. 2 shaft in section 3, saying that all the underground cabins were unnecessary and should be destroyed. Although he had stirred the men up to engage in these acts of violence, Saichi left the mine ahead of them, which angered the miners.[177]

This testimony clarifies two points. First, Ōnishi had worked the men up to attack the cabins and then had immediately left the mine himself. Second, the men who wrecked the cabins after his prompting were not men of No. 1 lodge, which he served as assemblyman. They belonged to lodges No. 19 and No. 8. On the matter of Ōnishi's leaving the mine ahead of the other miners, another police report contains the following:

Ōnishi Saichi, a miner from no. 1 lodge, put on a jacket near the pithead cabin and pretended to look on as an observer who had not been down the mine. After midday, although the day and night shifts at that particular pit were divided in four periods of six hours, and the second shift was supposed to work from 6 A.M. to 12 A.M. (on a normal working day the men coming off shift usually reported to the pithead cabin at 12:30), (Ōnishi) collected his card at 10:40 and left the mine.[178]

In addition, if the attack on the cabins had been unplanned, why had the assemblyman from another lodge, that is, Ōnishi, who was supposed to be working at the face and who then directed the attacks, come to the cabins? Stranger still is the fact that the bosses of these lodges (Nos. 8 and 19) were Yoneya Ichihei and Kamata Nobutarō, both leading advocates of the destruction of Shiseikai and the same two who prevailed upon Ōnishi Saichi to stop the abolition of the lodge charge at No. 1 lodge. Further, Kamata not only persuaded Ōnishi to restore the lodge charge, he also prevailed on Ōnishi to wreck the foremen's cabins in order to discredit Shiseikai. The question of whether Ōnishi was persuaded by Kamata and the Tsūdō bosses to stir up the men to attack the cabins actually surfaced in the final stages of the first court proceedings, but for some reason the verdict of the court did not mention it, instead referring only to the spontaneity theory. Interestingly enough, an appeal statement by the prosecution expended some six thousand words on denying the possibility that the lodge bosses provoked the riot.[179]

The prosecution's argument consisted of two main points. The first of these was extremely convoluted and not very convincing. Without presenting the details here, we may note that the prosecution focused first on a series of conversations between Kamata and Ōnishi which purportedly exonerated the lodge bosses.[180] We have no way of knowing, of course, whether or not the idea of the attack on the cabins came up in the conversations between the two men, but Ōnishi clearly did provoke those attacks. In view of the fact that he would hardly have done so with the blessing of Shiseikai, we must conclude that the plan was more than likely hatched by the lodge bosses.

The prosecution's second point in denying the bosses' responsibility for the riot is that Ōnishi was a Shiseikai activist and that if he "had been asked to bring down Shiseikai" by the bosses, he would naturally have informed Minami and Nagaoka of any such request. The prosecutor said of Kamata's request to Ōnishi: "It was like letting your enemy know your strategy; it didn't seem like common sense." As a member of Shiseikai, Ōnishi had certainly played a leading role in the campaign for the return of the treasury box and the abolition of the lodge charge. But he had joined Shiseikai on 7 January 1907 and had been an active member for only three weeks when Kamata persuaded him to change his mind over the issue of the lodge charge.[181] He had also been a "favored protégé for over ten years" of Ishida Kishirō, the boss of No. 1 lodge, and "had been helped out by him many times."[182] Like Ōnishi, Kamata Nobutarō was a miner who belonged to Ishida's No. 1 lodge. He and Ōnishi "used to eat out of the same bowl." The fact that the meetings between the two men took place over three days shows that Ōnishi was not easily persuaded, but in the end it would seem that he was unable to say no when faced with the debt of obligation to his boss that had built up over more than ten years.

The details of all the favors Ōnishi received from Ishida are not known, but according to a *Shimotsuke shimbun* newspaper report of 5 August 1907, he "was arrested and imprisoned last year [1906] for failing to appear in court to answer charges of assault and battery committed in February 1900." He had been on the run for six years, a fact that no doubt had something to do with his relationship with Ishida.

The Reasons for Kodaki's Nonparticipation

In contrast to the participation (to varied degrees, to be sure) of miners from the other three mines, why did the Kodaki men not take part in the riot at all? A number of factors are important. First, compared to Tsūdō and Honzan, the Kodaki brotherhood had been less than enthusiastic in their support for Shiseikai. In short, it could be said that Kodaki's critical attitude toward Tsūdō and Honzan was reflected in its nonparticipation in the riot. But this answer begs another question: Why was Kodaki critical of Shiseikai? One reason lies in the fact that Kodaki had no theaters or public spaces available for large meetings. Certainly this helps explain why, since the days of the Dōshikai and the Mine Workers' Association, Tsūdō rather than Kodaki had always been the base area of Nagaoka's activities. For the same reason, Shiseikai's influence in the district was also weak. However, a lack of facilities cannot fully account for Kodaki's nonparticipation.

A second and more persuasive explanation is that the pit manager at Kodaki, Esashi Shigeki, was more skillful in handling the miners at Kodaki than his colleagues at Tsūdō and Honzan. A number of documents attest to this, among them a report by Inspector Tamura Kan'noshin dated 19 February: "The pit manager at Kodaki was himself a worker promoted from Honzan; he therefore knew the feelings of the men under him, and the workers at Kodaki therefore had less of a sense of unfair and ill treatment compared to those at Honzan, Tsūdō, and Sunokobashi. Workers were less

dissatisfied and more likely to expect good treatment by the manager."[183]
A newspaper reporter who interviewed an arrested miner made a similar
observation:

All the trouble at Tsūdō and Honzan happened because the managers with all their
educated ideas couldn't understand the actual situation in the pits, but the Kodaki
manager Esashi Shigetoshi [sic: Shigeki] took the line of the previous manager but
one, Kimura, who had been down the mines himself and knew the men well. Thus
either his officials didn't take bribes, or else he knew about it beforehand. He was a
responsible man and raised the piecework rate to an average of 1 yen per man. That's
why there was no rioting at Kodaki.[184]

The Shiseikai leaders also recognized that Esashi, unlike the other pit
managers, had been sufficiently concerned by Shiseikai's campaign for a
wage hike to accept those portions of the demands that lay within the bounds
of his own authority. At a meeting at Kodaki on 11 January, Imori Shingo
recognized that, "Since his arrival at Kodaki, manager Esashi has set about
making up for the lack of facilities here. He has redressed abuses, and
won the miners' sympathies by installing pithead lighting and electric lights
underground wherever the wind is strongest and by making it easier to get in
and out of the mines."[185] Nagaoka Tsuruzō and Hayashi Kotarō also recognized that "there had been some improvements at Kodaki since [Esashi]
had become manager" and warned the workers "not to be deceived by
honeyed words."[186]

Yet it was not only Esashi's everyday treatment of his workers that influenced them not to join the riot. More important were his actions immediately after the riot broke out. On the evening of 5 February, the day after the
first troubles at Tsūdō, a meeting was held at Kodaki attended by the lodge
bosses and more than ninety assemblymen. The pit manager requested the
meeting, and Esashi, who also attended, said that he wanted the men to
decide if they "were going to resort to uncivilized violence or whether they
would take a more modern and enlightened view and opt for action that was
open and above aboard." "After debating until one o'clock in the morning of
the 6th which of these two paths to choose, the 90 delegates decided that the
disturbances at Honzan and Tsūdō amounted to pointless violence. [They]
chose to pursue their demands in a manner that was fair and above board
and declared themselves resolutely against any resort to uncivilized behavior."[187] The key point here is that Esashi did not depend only on the bosses,

but sought to involve the assemblymen directly in the decision. He thus managed to get the Kodaki miners to decide themselves not to join in the "riot." He probably reasoned that the power of the bosses alone would not suffice against the brotherhood, which had pledged joint action in league with the other three mines. His judgment was vindicated by the fact that not one Kodaki miner joined the "riot" and by an episode early the following morning. The men went down the mine at 6 A.M. as usual but were angered to find that the bosses, who normally did not go underground, had turned up at the ore faces too. The men refused to start work and instead held a meeting:

Our representatives having taken a decision last night that we would pursue our demands in a manner that is fair and above board and having pledged that we would not indulge in the kind of foolish violence that has taken place at Honzan and Tsūdō, we have come down the mine this morning to find that, contrary to normal practice, the bosses have also come down in order, we suspect, to spy on us and keep us in order. The bosses have always been accustomed to us obeying their orders without question. Their presence here to keep an eye on us must have been on the instructions of pit manager Esashi. If this is indeed the case, it is a gross insult to us, and whatever the cost, we should make our views known to all the bosses.[188]

Wrongly assuming that the men had called this meeting to discuss joining the "riot" at Honzan, the officials immediately went off to report to the pit manager. The surprised Esashi contacted the brotherhood stewards, three of whom hurried to the scene and apparently succeeded in calming the men down without further incident. The whole episode indicates the weakness of the bosses at that point, and also clearly shows the independent spirit of the brotherhood. Esashi Shigeki, himself a former miner, not only recognized these realities, but sought, through the brotherhood, to establish direct and effective contact with the miners. This is the most important reason the Kodaki miners did not take part in the riot.

Background to the Hostility between Miners and Officials

Attacks on company officials were among the chief features of the riot. Targets ranged from senior staff such as the mine director and the heads of the Pits and the Supply Departments to low-ranking officials such as foremen and overseers. Officials' living quarters and residences were also singled out in the destruction of buildings. Why did these attacks take place?

In the case of lower-ranking staff, testimony of the attackers is unanimous on one point: Officials took frequent unfair advantage of their huge authority in wage setting to demand bribes.

The taking of bribes in connection with pay raises and promotions is known to have been widespread among foremen and even sometimes engineers in prewar Japanese mining and manufacturing industries, especially before World War I, so the disease of bribery was not confined to Ashio. Nevertheless, the fact that bribery was one of the main factors involved in the riot indicates that at Ashio, the problem was particularly acute. What accounted for this?

The first reason lies in the complexity of the piecework system based on predictions of a miner's forward movement in extraction and of the amount of ore extracted. A system based on predictions left great scope to the supervisors' discretionary assessments. Management used this complex system because of the tremendous difference in the width of Ashio lodes and in the hardness of the surrounding rock and the veins containing the ore, all of which determined the pace of extraction and the effectiveness of blasting. Consequently, the amount of ore extracted by each miner varied widely. For example, in the first half of 1907, miners at Sunokobashi extracted a minimum of just 3.75 kilograms of ore, as against a maximum of 168.75 kilograms.[189] And even in the case of a fairly even lode, the quality would change from place to place. In such circumstances, the use of a simple piecework system that did not attempt to account for these differences would inevitably produce unjustifiably large pay differentials.

The physical characteristics of the Ashio mine were very different from those of other mines such as the Besshi copper mine with its stratified deposits and the Ani copper mine with its highly uniform lodes; at Ani there were no sudden changes in the width of veins and the amount of ore extracted remained virtually the same wherever one dug.[190] Ashio's managers had tried various systems over the years, seeking to develop a wage system that would meet the mine's unusual conditions. The history of these efforts is itself an interesting story, but at this point I will offer just a brief explanation of the wage system applied to the stoping method of extraction in general use at the time of the riot.[191]

Twice a month supervisors would assess the criteria for setting wages at each ore face. They took three factors into account: the projected length of the face dug, the projected amount of ore, and the projected cost.

The *projected length* was a prediction of how far a single miner would advance along a certain face in a given period. This depended on the efficacy of explosive charges in the surrounding rock, the relative hardness of any veins, the frequency of cracks and crevices, and also the actual width of the face itself. In the stoping, or tier method of extraction, the normal height of a face was 1.82 meters, whereas the breadth varied with the width of the ore-bearing vein from 45 centimeters to 3.63 meters.[192] These factors also accounted for the number of men employed at each face.

The *projected amount* referred to the quantity of top-quality unprocessed ore expected to be dug by a single miner along a projected length of face. "No. 1 quality ore" was the highest grade ore-bearing rock; the miner at the face selected it, put it into sacks that bore his name, and carried it out. The "projected amount" of this ore was not the simple weight of the top-grade unprocessed ore dug at a particular face. Rather, it designated the weight of "approved 25 percent content ore" that resulted from it. For example, 75 kilograms of top-grade unprocessed ore of 12.5 percent content would be assessed as 37.5 kilograms of "approved 25 percent ore."

Projected costs designated the expected costs incurred by an individual miner in the course of his work along a projected length of face. The cost of explosives and chisels and of transporting the extracted rock from the face to the main underground trackways was deducted from the miner's wage. Chisels were used up at varying rates depending on the quality of the rock, and the consumption of explosives also varied. Wherever there were a lot of water bursts, more expensive dynamite had to be used in place of ordinary black blasting powder.

Once these three projections of length of face, amount of ore, and individual costs had been decided, each man's piece rate, designed to produce an average income for average work (65 sen in 1906), could be determined for every face. The piece rate refers to the value of 3.03 meters (10 *shaku*) of face dug. The value assigned to "approved 25 percent grade ore" was uniform throughout the Ashio mines (in 1906 it stood at 5 sen per 3.75 kilograms).[193] Thus, if the projected amount of ore to be extracted was also fixed, then its value would be automatically determined, although the price obtained for the length of face dug did differ according to the quality of the face. The piece rate was calculated as:

Table 1.2. Piece-Rate Calculations

Face	Projected Length	Projected Amount	Cost
A	6.06 cm.	18.75 kg.	15 sen
B	9.24 cm.	37.50 kg.	20 sen
C	12.12 cm.	112.50 kg.	25 sen

{standard wage (65 sen) + costs − (amount of ore per unit cost)}/projected length dug

A practical example of this is given in Table 1.2. We see that for face A, a miner is projected to extract 18.75 kilograms of "approved ore." At 5 sen per 3.75 kilograms (1 *kamme*), the miner's output is worth just 25 sen. Further, his costs (deducted from this amount) are 15 sen, leaving him just 10 sen. To earn a standard wage of 65 sen, his piece rate must yield an additional 55 sen. Because he is expected to dig 6.06 centimeters (2 *sun*) of face, his piece rate works out to 27.5 sen per *sun* (3.03 centimeters).

The miner at face B gets 50 sen for his output of ore-bearing rock, minus 20 sen costs. To earn his standard 65 sen, he must dig unprocessed ore with a piece-rate value of 35 sen. He is expected to dig 9.24 centimeters (3.5 *sun*), so that his conversion rate works out to 10 sen per *sun*.

Digging goes easily at face C, and the lodes are rich, so the miner is able to extract 112.50 kilograms of "approved ore" in one day. The value of the unprocessed ore is 1 yen 50 sen, so deducting his costs of 25 sen leaves 1 yen 25 sen, exceeding the standard wage of 65 sen. Consequently, in this case, 15 sen are deducted from the value of the ore for every 3.03 centimeters dug, and the result is a negative piece rate. At Ashio this was called a "red piece rate" or an "excess assessment."

The assessments of the "conversion rate" for each face were made twice a month by the foremen and their immediate superiors, the section chiefs. The pit manager confirmed the decisions. However, "in fact, the pit manager's confirmation was no more than a formality; he never checked whether the assessment was correct or not. The assessments were mostly a matter of the arbitrary whims of the officials."[194] The "conversion rates" were no more than best guesses that could easily miss the mark, so so-called small assessments were carried out every five days to check the actual rate of digging. The ore face at which a man worked was, in principle, chosen by lot. This of course had originally been a system devised to prevent unfair practices such as bribery to secure good work assignments. However, we have reports that "formal lotteries were not really held."[195] And in any case, any lottery would have been rendered irrelevant because the foremen and section chiefs were able to change the "conversion rate" for a miner's allotted face every five days. It was easy for foremen to favor those miners who paid large bribes with high "rate" assessments as well as high reports of their actual rate of extraction.

All this is not to say that bribery was inevitable given such a piecework system. If the section chiefs and the pit managers charged with supervising the foremen had constantly been going around the pits, keeping in touch with the day-to-day situation, they could have prevented or halted unfair practices. Indeed, the men at Kodaki respected pit manager Esashi precisely because he did this.[196] Such was not the case at Honzan and Tsūdō. The prosecutor's statement of appeal contains the following:

As for the unequal treatment of the miners by the officials, that depended on the amount of the bribe a man was able to pay. Many defendants have made similar claims about unequal treatment by officials at the preliminary investigations and also in court. Over half the defendants have testified that the said officials demanded bribes which, if paid, would lead to a man being allotted a productive face to work. If they were not paid, he would be allotted an inferior face. Of these defendants, many have testified that they paid bribes on demand to the officials. Discontent over this treatment is certainly widespread.

In addition to the foremen who had primary responsibility for assessing miners' wages, the overseers, charged merely to supervise the miners' entry to and exit from the pits, also demanded bribes. It seems that the less his actual authority, the more grasping the overseer's demands. For example, if a man was late to work, he would be fined one-tenth of his pay for that day, so the overseer was able to use the threat of the cancellation of the miner's good attendance bonus to get a bribe.[197] "If a bribe was paid, the penalty would be overlooked, but if no bribe was paid, then the penalty would stand even if the man had only been one minute late. Miners also had their pay docked if they were late leaving the pit."[198] The refusal of drinking water was another irritant: "If we asked for drinking water, we were told, 'there is none,' but those who paid bribes were given as much as they wanted."[199]

The surprisingly low level of officials' wages was another reason for the widespread bribery. A lack of data rules out an accurate assessment of officials' wage levels, but one newspaper reporter discussing the causes of the riot wrote of "company officials such as (underground) section chiefs who earned 14 to 15 yen a month."[200] This translates into a daily rate of no more than 50 sen, less than a miner's average wage. Even taking into account the facts that deductions were taken from miners' wages for expenses such as explosives and tools and that officials received bonuses, one could still consider the officials' wages to be low. With the changes in company policy introduced in 1897, officials' salaries had been severely restrained, and Shiseikai leaders drew attention to this fact in their speeches: "Officials take bribes because their own wages are poor" (Minami Sukematsu).

Many low-ranking officials, however, were themselves former miners or shorers who had won promotion. Originally, the company had intended to fill such posts with graduates of technical schools, but as few such candidates came forward and as managers noticed that promotions from within the workforce raised morale, quite a number of workers were promoted. In common with most Japanese workers, the men of Ashio were strongly motivated to improve their status, a fact noted in the first court verdict: "Since (the arrival of) Director Minami, the employment of (low-ranking) officials has been limited to shorers. While Furukawa Ichibei was alive, promotion was open to any worker depending upon his skill." Those who were promoted tended to be the most skilled workers, and because of the piecework system, they would have been earning high wages. If legitimate wages alone are compared, promotion often must have entailed a drop in wages. The many miners who nevertheless choose to become officials made up for this by taking bribes.

Reasons for the Attack on Director Minami Teizō

The Personality of "Former Bureaucrat" Minami

Of all the attacks on company officials, the most significant was that upon the person of the mine director, Minami Teizō. It proved to be the turning point in the whole riot. The violent clash between the miners and the foremen and overseers would have stayed underground had it not been for this attack, which even stimulated open defiance of the police and violence aimed at all company officials, not just those of low rank. To grasp the nature of the Ashio riot and its causes, we must understand how the mine workers felt about Minami Teizō.

Fortunately, the first court verdict gives us a clear view of this matter. At the beginning of that verdict, Judge Miyamoto Rikinosuke of the Utsunomiya District Court stated that the first cause of the riot had been Director Minami's exceedingly harsh treatment of the mine workers. He compared this to the regime at the mine under the late Furukawa Ichibei as follows:

The many thousands of workers employed by the Furukawa Mining Company's Ashio Copper Mine were glad to work there while Furukawa Ichibei was alive, because they had been well-treated. But after [Furukawa] became fatally ill, the miners' wages did not keep pace with the dramatic rise in prices. Without due regard to this fact, the company appointed Minami Teizō director. He treated the miners harshly, with not the slightest consideration for their circumstances. For example, the company guard Ishikawa Ukichi has reported that after the appointment of Minami Teizō, miners were fined for taking away small bits of rotten timber which they had found underground for use as firewood. Such things did not happen when Furukawa Ichibei was alive. Second, Director Minami allowed only shorers to be promoted to the rank of company officials. Furukawa Ichibei had promoted workers of various grades depending on their skills alone. Third, during Furukawa's time, even if a worker was absent from work for two or three days a month, his rice ration was not affected, whereas under Minami, a single day's absence meant that a miner had to forego 1.98 liters of his rice ration (1 shō 5 go). Fourth, under Furukawa, workers worked a six-hour day. Minami introduced the eight-hour working day. Fifth, Ichibei allowed two rest days a month; these were abolished by Minami. Sixth, while Furukawa Ichibei was alive, a man was paid an [attendance] bonus of two days' basic wage of 50 sen even if he were absent for two days in addition to the two monthly days off. But under Minami, those who had incurred penalties of a mere 5 sen were not paid this allowance. What is worse, regulations were enforced whereby those who were five minutes late either entering or leaving the pit were to be fined from 5 to 25 sen. Seventh, Furukawa Ichibei had provided for all workers to be given sake and fish at New Year and on shrine festival days; under Minami this practice was totally abolished. In his first report, Inspector Kawashima Hyōsaburō described the character of Director Minami Teizō as being extremely rash. He would often slap the face of workers whom he had found to have gone against his wishes and spoke to them with great harshness. Inspector Tadokoro Tanemi's report notes that in 1895 the basic wage rate of workers at Ashio had been fixed at 50 sen and that there had been slight increases since then. . . . but while owing to dramatic price rises, there were subsequent calls for wage increases in 1899, and again in 1903, [the company] did not respond to these calls. . . .[201]

While all the "misdeeds" attributed to Director Minami in this verdict—penalties for taking old timber, the penalty system for lateness, the denial of bonuses to workers who had already been penalized, [202] the rules on rice supply to those absent from work, and the abolition of rest days[203]—were indeed measures introduced during his tenure as director, as was the freezing of the basic wage rate at 50 sen, we must question whether all these "misdeeds" should be laid solely and squarely upon the shoulders of Minami Teizō alone.

The Background to the Changes in Company Policy

That Minami Teizō carried "the odor of a feudalistic bureaucrat" is no doubt true.[204] Further, for Minami to tighten the system of penalties was very much in character. Nonetheless, the court's verdict places too much blame for the riot on Minami. For example, the longer working day—from six to eight hours—was introduced before Minami arrived at Ashio in 1901.[205] Likewise, the decision to peg the basic rate at 50 sen is thought to have been taken by the company board and not by Minami himself, a conjecture that is supported by the company's response to the bosses' petition. More significant than Minami's personal role was the change in Furukawa company policy prompted by the 1897 Third Mine Pollution Prevention Order.

From its founding in 1875, the company had been under the personal control of Furukawa Ichibei himself. His principal aim was to maximize market share in the production of copper, to which end he made large-scale investments centered on Ashio and bought up all the metal mines he could, especially copper mines. However, there were those around Ichibei, such as Shibusawa Eiichi and Mutsu Munemitsu, who were concerned about this aggressive policy of expansion. After the Mine Pollution Prevention Order of 1897, Shibusawa's Daiichi Bank made further investment in plant construction conditional on changes in Furukawa company policy, and control passed from Ichibei into the hands of his adopted son, Junkichi, Munemitsu's own second son. Junkichi adopted a policy of "consolidation, now that the company's initial expansionary phase is over," and he introduced a number of measures designed to cut costs and promote savings. Longer working hours, the freezing of wage levels, reductions in holidays, and the tightening up of penalty regulations were all measures reflecting this change in company policy.

In this sense, the court verdict was not wrong to sharply contrast the period of Ichibei's control to Minami's era, although it would have been more correct to say "when Ichibei was in sole control" rather than "when Ichibei was alive." If the new regime was indeed a kind of polar opposite to the old, as far as the workers were concerned, then the nadir came with the arrival not of Minami Teizō, but of Furukawa Junkichi. Minami was merely a manager carrying out part of Junkichi's overall "policy for the consolidation phase." At the same time, the workers were certainly justified to feel that after the death of Ichibei in April 1903 and the appointment of Minami Teizō five months later, their working conditions had worsened considerably. Although the change in company policy had been made before Minami was appointed, it took some time for the effects of the change to reach the workers, so the change appeared to coincide with Minami's arrival.

Shiseikai Criticism of Minami

The public verbal attacks on Minami made by Minami Sukematsu, Nagaoka Tsuruzō, and the other Shiseikai activists reinforced the workers' impression that Minami Teizō was the "source of all evil."[206] Initially, Shiseikai criticized the Ashio management but qualified the charges by noting, "the reason why officials take bribes is because they are poorly paid. The director and his highly educated staff are actually to be pitied, their pay is so low." But beginning in January 1907, Shiseikai criticisms of the Ashio management, in particular of Minami Teizō, began to intensify.

Minami was cited as the "villain" who had signed the Third Mine Pollution Prevention Order, which had threatened to close the entire Ashio mine operation, and Minami's words and behavior were censured. Minami Sukematsu, in a speech on 8 January, claimed: "Director Minami is one of the most unloyal, traitorous men in the country. What better proof could there be than the fact that he is afraid of the Shiseikai—loyal and patriotic subjects of the nation? It is said that Minami has requested that 800 policemen be sent by the head office. It will cost the head office ten thousand yen to send 800 policemen. The miners would be happy if they could each get one yen of that money. Members of the public have said that they would prefer that too."

Minami Sukematsu further criticized Minami Teizō at a public meeting on 12 January: "Minami's record in his previous job is not very convincing. As head of the Office of Superintendent of Mines, he knowingly ignored the inadequacy of the company's anti-pollution measures. He [text missing] the company's illegal profits, and then as the man in the top seat here at Ashio, he has ignored the Mining Industry Ordinances. There's no end to his illegal acts."

An open letter addressed "to the former head of the Tokyo Area Superintendant of Mines Office and Director of the Furukawa Ashio Mine, Minami Teizō, from Minami Sukematsu, head of the Ashio branch of the Greater Japan Workers Shiseikai," had called upon Minami to attend the Shiseikai meeting of 26 January. Of course, Minami did not turn up. Predictably, Nagaoka Tsuruzō pilloried him for his absence:

When Director Minami came to Ashio at the time of the antipollution measures, he came as a representative of the Japanese government earning 60 yen a month. When he came here as director, it was with an immediate raise to 200 yen a month, so there's no bigger liar than Director Minami. He tells more lies than a prostitute. Three years ago I received a letter of reply from Director Minami. Oh, it was a splendid document, but three years later, nothing has changed. There's only been more and more suffering for the workers. If Director Minami tries to do away with some of the Conditions of Service for Miners at the Ashio Mine, in enforcing his own rules in respect of underground work and other things, he'll be breaking the rules himself.

Then, on 1 February, immediately before the riot, both Minami Sukematsu and Nagaoka Tsuruzō made speeches sharply criticizing Minami Teizō. Nagaoka pointed out, "the director is an unfeeling, cold-blooded man. Once when he was crossing the Hoso o pass in a litter, he ordered the bearers to hurry, and they had to run at top speed all the way without being given a single rest to get their breath! When the world gets such a glimpse of the man, it's not difficult to see the cruel and harsh manner in which he treats Ashio workers!" Minami Sukematsu also focused his attack on the mine director, titling his talk "Showing Three Inches of Steel to Minami Teizō": "If the cruel and arrogant Director Minami does not reconsider his actions now, I shall show him three inches of steel and suggest that he commit seppuku. If that does not make him see the error of his ways, then we shall not refrain from resorting to extraordinary measures."

These public criticisms by Shiseikai leaders, directed at the person of Minami Teizō, drew loud applause from the audiences of mine workers. All left the rally with the firm impression that the chief executive of the Ashio mine had virtually gained his position by "bribery" and was a cold-hearted man lacking in sincerity. Would the wrecking of the underground cabins three days later have led to the attacks on Minami's residence without such criticism from Shiseikai? Obviously, a definitive reply is impossible, but I suspect the answer is no.

A CRITIQUE OF THE ATOMIZED LABOR THEORY

The Idea of the Spontaneous Riot

Organization and Spontaneity

We may now return to the questions posed at the beginning of this chapter concerning the spontaneity theory and the theory of atomized labor. Criticism of the spontaneity theory does not imply a rejection of the concepts of spontaneity or natural occurrence of a riot. The miners' behavior above ground at Honzan on 6 February certainly merits the term *riot,* and there is no reason to believe that it was consciously planned, led, or provoked. The attacks on officials, the destruction of buildings, and acts of arson can only be regarded as spontaneous mob behavior. However, the influence of Shiseikai's very deliberate criticisms of Minami Teizō is hard to deny, and we cannot regard the attacks on the underground cabins at Tsūdō on 4 February, which sparked the riot, as having been entirely spontaneous. There are strong grounds for believing these attacks were planned by some of the lodge bosses. However, most of the miners who actually threw the stones and ignited the dynamite did not do so in the knowledge that they were acting in accordance with a plan. In that sense, a spontaneous element was undeniably part of the attacks.

However much an incident may be planned and organized, an element of spontaneity is inevitably involved when a crowd enacts such an incident. Conversely, if the incident is enacted by a crowd, however spontaneous it may appear, the likelihood is that in the background there will be some form of organization. As David Montgomery has pointed out, "Spontaneity and organization are not mutually exclusive. The two are dialectically indivisible."[207]

Many academic studies to date, however, have tended to use the one word *spontaneous* to account for disputes and riots without further investigation of the causes and characteristics of such events. The result has been that the historical differences between mine riots such as the series of disputes and riots at the Takashima coal mine, the convicts' riot at the Miike coal mine in 1883, and the Ashio riot of 1907 have been ignored, and they have all been subsumed under a blanket description as "acts of spontaneous rebellion by miners who could no longer bear their appalling working conditions."

There are reasons that explain why such a view of events came about and why it has become so widespread. First, these events are poorly documented. In addition to the scarcity of extant documents that reveal anything about the people who took part in disputes and riots, in the documents that do exist we find much evidence of conscious attempts to cover up the facts. This is often the case with court records. Consequently, we must rely on newspaper reports and other reports by outside observers. But outsiders often have trouble figuring out what the dispute or riot is all about; understandably, they see it as something spontaneous. One must critically examine such documents to clarify the mutual relationship between the organized and the spontaneous elements in the various disputes and riots.

Second, when social scientists (especially Japanese labor and social historians) first posed questions of "spontaneity" and "organization," they limited their discussion to organizational forms that were standard in the West, such as trade unions and progressive political parties. They were not interested in traditional or premodern organizational forms. Whenever historians mentioned these organizations, they were not looking to examine concretely their actual function, but rather to hanging dismissive labels on them such as "feudalistic" or "premodern."

The Brotherhoods and the Mine Workers' Movement

We must discuss this problem of "spontaneous" social action in the context of a critique of the atomized labor theory. I am dubious about the value of this theory. I cannot agree with an analysis that directly links the riot and the phenomenon of "atomized labor." Certainly, an important element in the Ashio riot was the "reaction of a workforce exposed to the impact of modernization," but to say the riot broke out because the process of modernization shattered the workers' sense of community goes too far. The leading participants in the riot belonged to brotherhoods, labor organizations akin to craft guilds, which had traditions going back to Tokugawa times. Totally unorganized workers would not have had the strength to start a riot. The miners were able to riot not because they represented a "dissociative" workforce, but, on the contrary, precisely because they were an "associative" workforce.[208] Furthermore, the Ashio riot was neither planned nor executed by the miners themselves who took part in it. What they sought was a wage increase, and they tried, in a very organized fashion, to secure their demand by means of a petition to the mine office.

As we have already seen, the Ashio brotherhoods drew up their twenty-four-article petition immediately before the riot through a highly organized process. That process can be recapitulated as follows:

1. The Tsūdō assemblymen, who had first proposed the petition for a wage increase, pressed the assembly representatives of the other pits to collaborate with them in holding a joint council.

2. All having agreed to consider the proposal, independent discussions followed among the assembly representatives of the four brotherhood organizations at Tsūdō, Honzan, Kodaki, and Sunokobashi.

3. There then followed a marathon meeting of over ten hours of the representatives who had been formally chosen from the assemblies of the four pits.

4. The agreement reached at that meeting was then taken back to each pit, where it was presented and explained to the assembly representatives of the various lodges.

5. The assemblymen then held meetings at their own lodges to gather the men's opinions on the proposed agreement.

6. Having secured their members' approval, a further joint meeting was held of assembly delegates from the four pits to confirm the joint agreement.

7. Only at the end of this process did the proposed joint council finally meet, which resulted in the formal signing of a joint agreement on collaboration.

Of course, one may question the extent to which individuals were really free to express their independent views in the brotherhood, since members were bound by ties of personal obligation to fellow workers either above or below them in status, as well as to the lodge bosses. But from the purely formal organizational viewpoint, the process can only be described as democratic. It was considered extremely important that all the men's opinions be canvassed, and much time was given to the effort to convince the Kodaki assemblymen who had shown little enthusiasm for the petition. This process can in no way be described as the activity of "dissociative" workers.

Also, the actual contents of the petition included clauses that sought to press management to recognize the brotherhoods as organizations that represented the workers' views: "In all cases of unfairness at work in the payment of piecework wages and in the allocation of piecework or of inappropriate rates for ore, assemblymen [are] to have the right to mediate and to investigate the circumstances" and "henceforward, workers [are] to be notified in advance of the announcement of new company regulations affecting them, and the execution of such regulations [is] to be contingent upon agreement [between the company and the workforce]."

Nagaoka Tsuruzō and the Brotherhoods

The significance of the brotherhoods went beyond merely playing an organizational role in the campaign for wage increases. Nagaoka Tsuruzō had played a key role in the two highly "associative" organizations of the Dōshikai and the Shiseikai, and the fact that such an organizer could have emerged from among the ranks of the workers—a rare event at that time— cannot be understood without reference to the brotherhoods. Nagaoka had been a labor organizer since 1893, more than ten years before he arrived at Ashio. In February of that year he led a strike at the Innai silver mine to secure safer working conditions and achieved 70 percent of his demands. From May to December 1893 he fought against the newly imposed miners' tax in Akita prefecture and succeeded in getting the tax abolished. The campaign against the tax was carried on through the organizational agency of the brotherhoods. Nagaoka wrote of it in his autobiography, "A Miner's Life":

In the spring of 1894 [actually 1893] the imposition of a miners' tax was announced in Akita prefecture. I was working at the Innai silver mine at the time, and when the miners there heard of the new tax, they were outraged. Underground the hammers fell silent in the black holes, and after a while the entire mine was filled with the sound of voices shouting their opposition: "No way!"; "We're poor enough already!" Feelings ran high. On 6 May a meeting of miners' leaders was held. . . . Without any bragging or big talk, the whole meeting decided as one to unite in a campaign [against the tax]. Three men were chosen to head the campaign: Takada Tamegorō, Hirakawa Eita, and myself. . . .

Knowing that solidarity would be our key weapon in the campaign, we went on speaking tours round all the mines in the prefecture, and after a while, we organized the Japan Metal Mines' League [Nippon Kōzan Dōmeikai, named in other sources as the Akita Metal Miners' League]. When we established the league, on 14 August we presented a petition in its name calling for the abolition of the miners' tax to the governor of Akita prefecture at his office. We drew his attention to the plight of the miners, but he was not in a position to be able to do anything about it, so we carried on our campaign vigorously, visiting the 36 prefectural assembly members many times. Our efforts were not in vain; on the 19th November the following year [actually December 1893] the prefectural assembly meeting in ordinary session voted to abolish the miners' tax.[209]

What is noteworthy here is the fact that the campaign began with a "meeting" held by the "miners' leaders," by which is probably meant the bosses or *oyabun*. However, since Nagaoka, who was not a lodge boss, was chosen as one of the campaign leaders, we know that this meeting was not restricted to lodge bosses. It must have been a brotherhood assembly. We may also assume that the method of campaigning around all the other mines in the prefecture was based on the brotherhood organizational structure. In a brotherhood it was common practice to invite delegates from neighboring mines to attend induction ceremonies, so exchanges with other mines occurred frequently.

It may seem odd that, given the existence of the brotherhood, a separate organization under the name of the Japan Metal Mines League or the Akita Metal Miners' League should have had to be formed. However, brotherhood rules had never stipulated that they were to be nationwide or even prefecture-wide organizations. Of course, they did maintain connections with brotherhoods in other parts of the country, as indicated by induction certificates and letters of request addressed to "the honorable members of the metal miners' leagues of the Japanese Empire" or "to all the brethren of the metal miners' leagues of the Japanese Empire." The name Japan Metal Mines League or Akita Metal Miners' League was probably chosen because it was felt necessary to have such a formal title when making a case for the abolition of the miners' tax to the governor and the prefectural assembly. The names themselves clearly indicate that the campaign to abolish the tax was conducted on an organizational base of brotherhoods that extended far beyond a single mine. It could well be that Nagaoka's conceptions of the Greater Japan Workers' Association and the Greater Japan Mine Workers' Association had their origins in that autonomous campaign of organization against the miners' tax in 1893.

Moreover, the existence of the brotherhoods played no small part in facilitating Nagaoka's activities at Ashio. It was because he was a brotherhood member that he was able to get into Ashio so easily and to remain there as a union organizer for more than three years. In fact, he spent his first month or so at Ashio in the miners' lodge, thanks to the brotherhood member's right to a night's bed and board. The very fact that a self-confessed trade union organizer like Nagaoka was able to gain employment was also probably due to his being a brotherhood member. It was, after all, a lodge boss's natural duty to recruit workers seeking employment who were brotherhood members. Provided there was a need for new workers, the management did not refuse employment to men who were put forward by the lodge bosses, especially since at that time the company had no training program of its own for miners. Technical training for miners was de facto a matter for the brotherhoods. Bosses and employers could not afford to ignore the brotherhoods and their tradition of "journeyman miners."

Associative Workers and Riots

Two objections can be posed to the conclusions of the foregoing paragraphs. First, one could maintain that the notion of the "dissociative, atomized individual" is used in the sense that the individual avoids any voluntary interaction with his neighbors. In this sense, the term *associative* cannot be used to refer to groups like the brotherhoods, in which people are brought together by the circumstances of their jobs. Second, at the Ashio copper mine, organized union activity could develop only because of the accidental presence there of Nagaoka, a committed labor activist who had contacts with leading socialists. In other words, the situation was exceptional.

In response to the first of these arguments, we may begin by pointing out that face workers or ore diggers did not automatically become brotherhood members; the individual had to decide himself whether he wished to join as a specialist face worker or ore digger, and his decision had to be endorsed. One could not become a member simply by working together with others underground or by sharing the same lodge with them. Candidates for membership had to undergo a formal and involved process of admission. In these induction ceremonies, an individual was bound into a patron-client (*oyabun-kobun*) relationship with a designated regular member, and required to serve an apprenticeship for three years, three months, and ten days, after which he would be recognized as a full-fledged member of the brotherhood. Noteworthy here is the name given to the process of joining the brotherhood: *shussei,* meaning "birth." The term implied that a new member's links with his former life were severed by the induction ceremony; through it he was "reborn" as a skilled miner. In that sense, even if brotherhood members had all originally come from rural villages, they should not be considered to have been simple migrant workers from the countryside.

Two ideas underlie Maruyama Masao's argument that riots are a form of behavior peculiar to "dissociative" workers: first, the idea that "associative" workers are those who form trade unions and engage in collective bargaining with management to determine working conditions; second, the idea that trade unions are groups of purely autonomous, self-motivated, and associative individuals. The pioneer labor economist Ōkōchi Kazuo shared these ideas when he insisted that "trade unions are no more and no less than mass organizations of workers who wish to sell their labor." I question whether the "ideal" trade union would be constituted of such individuals, and I certainly doubt that "actually existing trade unions" can be characterized in this way. By this definition, we are hard-pressed to discover any trade unions in Japan before World War II, and we must consider that most workers in prewar Japan would have been "dissociative." This is obviously a one-sided view of Japan's social history.[210]

Contrary to Maruyama's perspective, we should view industrial laborers as having a generally "associative" attitude or personality in that the production process itself requires individuals to cooperate with each other to develop numerous points of common interest. Managers, of course, are unhappy when workers develop autonomous organizations, and they seek to prevent this. Further, the state's legal and political systems often obstruct workers' efforts to form independent associations. Such opposition has frequently made it impossible for trade unions to exist. Thus, in Japan prior to World War I, for a labor union to exist was an exceptional circumstance. In such a case, it hardly makes sense to point to the absence of trade unions as evidence that worker personalities were "dissociative."

The greatest weakness in Maruyama's paradigm is its monistic assumption that the activity or nonactivity of a mass movement in a given society can be explained by the dominant type of "individual attitudes" or "personality" within that society.[211] Maruyama holds that rioting is allied to "dissociative" and "centripetal" attitudes, but it is not only the attitude of the masses that determines whether or not they express their frustrations by the act of rioting; rather, the manner in which those in authority react to those frustrations is decisive.

This is clearly borne out in the history of U.S. industrial relations, with its many examples of violent disputes involving the destruction of property and even gun battles. According to one account, a conservative estimate of the number of deaths in industrial disputes over the course of U.S. history runs to seven hundred killed and many thousands wounded and injured. The military has been involved in such disputes at least 160 times.[212] Bloodshed during labor disputes was particularly common in the early years of the twentieth century. In just the thirty-three-month period from 1 January 1902 to 30 September 1904, 198 people died and 1966 were wounded in strikes and lockouts.[213]

Could American workers then be said to have been at their most "atomized" during this period? Certainly not. This very period saw unprecedented growth in the unionization of American workers.[214] In 1899, 611,000 workers belonged to trade unions; in the five years to 1904 the number increased by 340 percent to 2,072,000.[215] Most of the violence in these years occurred in connection with the issue of union recognition. In terms of this discussion, it occurred not because workers were "dissociative," but on the contrary, precisely because they were seeking to "associate." The main cause of the violence was not so much the workers' attitudes but rather the capitalists' and owners' unyielding refusal to recognize trade unions and their immediate recourse to heavy-handed action against strikes, action that was invariably supported by the state and federal governments. Similarly, in the series of disputes in the Japanese mining industry in 1907, whether a dispute turned violent or not depended not so much on differences in workers' attitudes, but on differences in the response of managers.

Was Ashio an Exceptional Case?

Turning now to the second possible objection to my critique, it is certainly true that in disputes in other mines, there were no organizers of the caliber of Minami Sukematsu and Nagaoka Tsuruzō, with their extensive contacts with leading socialists. In this regard Ashio may be considered exceptional. But this fact alone does not prove that disputes at all other mines were but the "spasmodic convulsions of hopelessly atomized workers." Strikes, of course, even when they turn to riot, do not suddenly materialize out of nowhere. Every dispute begins with the selection, in some way, of delegates and the drawing up of demands. In the Horonai coal mine riot of April 1907, for example, which followed soon after Ashio, a written demand for higher wages had been presented by miners' and laborers' delegates more than one month before the violence erupted. Even after the demand had been refused, the miners' delegates tried repeatedly to secure a meeting with the mine director at which they could submit their petition, and in the end four hundred workers had to petition en masse for such a meeting. The violence broke out only after this petition too had been refused and the workers' delegates had been sacked.[216] A similar sequence of events unfolded at the Besshi copper mine, where haulers' delegates demanded higher wages on 30 May, followed by miners' delegates on 2 June. Once again managers refused to consider these demands, and the delegates were fired. Violence broke out very soon after.[217]

What, then, was the situation in mining disputes that did not turn violent? Since we find virtually no documentation of such disputes other than newspaper reports, it is difficult to gain an accurate picture of what went on. However, what emerges even from those fragmentary reports is evidence of the unexpectedly organized nature of such disputes and of the positive role played by the brotherhoods. Volume 2 of *Historical Documents of the Japanese Labor Movement* records four industrial disputes in metal mines in the year 1907, apart from the riots at Ashio and Besshi.[218] One of these, at the Asōtsu mine in Wakayama prefecture, was not so much an industrial dispute; rather, it was an instance of strife between miners and the police when the latter attempted to control the gambling that was widespread in the mine. Apart from this, there are reports in the *Osaka Mainichi* and the *Osaka Asahi* newspapers of trouble at three other mines: the Ikuno silver mine in Hyōgo prefecture in July and September, and the Obie and Yoshioka copper mines in Okayama prefecture. Each dispute was led by the local brotherhood. The following are the relevant excerpts from the reports of these disputes:

Ikuno silver mine, July

1. Having made their decision, the mine stewards have been gathering miners' signatures since last night.

2. In addition to the men of the Kanagase and Ōmori pits, the more than 100 miners of the main pit at Wakabayashi joined in too, and a written set of demands was presented to the mine manager on the evening of the 30th.

3. The stewards of the Ōta, Adachi, and Ueki *hanba* at the Kanagase pit decided on joint action with the men of the Ōmori pit, and to this end approached the steward of the Kuwata lodge [at Ōmori]. They are currently meeting to discuss how to coordinate joint action.

4. While sharing the company's strong views on the present difficulties, the police fear a long drawn-out dispute and they spent a whole day calling in company, lodge and stewards' representatives for talks.

5. The stewards are still meeting to find a way forward.

Clearly, at Ikuno the miners' campaign was being organized by the brotherhoods. Each of the three pits, Ōmori, Kanagase, and Wakabayashi (corresponding to Honzan, Kodaki, and Tsūdō at Ashio), had its own brotherhood group. Their method of organizing a joint campaign by meetings between their delegates was identical to that of the Ashio brotherhood.

Obie copper mine

1. At noon yesterday miners at Sakamoto Kinya's Obie mine suddenly appeared at the mine office and demanded in a threatening manner that miners' savings be repaid to them and that they be given second-class refined sake on loan. From nine o'clock in the evening about 150 men gathered at the Kumano shrine on the mountainside, but after choosing a council of 13 men and a negotiating team of 3, they obeyed the police order to disperse and retired without incident.

2. At 10 o'clock this morning the Obie mine manager, Ogawa, ordered personnel officer Satō Aiji and six others to meet Sugita Torakichi and the 13 committee members from the miners' side at the home of lodge boss Yokogawa Ryōzō, as a result of which it was agreed that white rice would be sold at 13 sen per shō (1.8 liters), the average daily wage would be increased to a minimum 90 sen, miners off

sick would be assured of good consideration, and long-serving miners forced to retire through ill-health would be paid an honorarium of a minimum 5 yen. The miners' delegates were well-pleased with the company's unexpected response to their demands, and withdrew after expressing their gratitude. The present dispute would thus, at least for the time being, appear to be at an end.

The role of the brotherhoods in this Obie dispute is not as clear as at Ashio or Ikuno. The terms "negotiating team" and "council" are not normally associated with the brotherhood. It may be that by "council" was meant brotherhood executives. The term "miners' delegates" (*kōfu sōdai*) was used by the brotherhood, but this term in itself does not prove that the brotherhoods were involved. On the other hand, the method of selecting a negotiating team and council certainly is similar to brotherhood procedures. At Obie, the meeting at which brotherhood decisions were made was called the "mine assembly" and all brotherhood members were allowed to attend. Brotherhood officials and stewards were elected at these meetings. It was also normal for brotherhood meetings to be held in the precincts of the local mountain shrine. In short, the behavior of the miners in the Obie dispute would be difficult to explain without reference to what were normal brotherhood customs of holding a mass assembly and electing officials.

Yoshioka copper mine

1. On the evening of the 9th last, a group of 13 or 14 miners' officials met secretly at the Yanai lodge. They decided to present a set of demands to the mine owner regarding their working conditions and resolved to levy a sum of 50 sen per *dōmei* miner to fund their campaign.

2. At first the mine executives were thrown into confusion by the situation, but they quickly recovered and decided on substantial measures. They invited 22 miners' officials to meet with them at the mine office at 5 P.M. on the 12th, where they politely tried to pacify the delegates who, already suspecting a subterfuge, declined at first to declare their intentions. They then revealed that they had planned that their members should stop work when the demands were presented, and if they were not given a hearing, they would resort to their ultimate tactic, whereupon they presented their demands, which the management mostly accepted, and a dangerous situation thus returned to normal.

The use of the term "*dōmei* miner" makes it fairly clear that the brotherhoods (*tomoko dōmei*) were involved in the Yoshioka dispute. The terms "*dōmei* miner" and "*dōmei* brother" were commonly used to denote brotherhood members.

This admittedly small number of examples does show how brotherhoods played a key role in the disputes at the Ikuno, Obie, and Yoshioka metal mines, all of which were settled without violence. The argument that the Ashio workers were somehow exceptional in the degree of their organization, while the disputes in the other mines were "the spasmodic convulsions of hopelessly atomized workers," simply does not stand up.

EPILOGUE: THE BROTHERHOODS AND THE LODGE SYSTEM AFTER THE RIOT

The Abolition of the Assembly Representative System

Thus far I have emphasized the role of the brotherhoods in the mine workers' labor movement, or rather, the need to reappraise that role. This is not to say that the brotherhoods played such a positive role at all times and circumstances. Even trade unions can at times be used by capitalist forces as a means of controlling labor, and it was certainly the case that the patron-client status relationships on which the brotherhoods were based made it easier for the lodge bosses to dominate the workers. The brotherhoods thus frequently served to support such domination by the bosses. Nevertheless, if the bosses preserved their own relative independence vis-à-vis the company whenever there was friction with the company, or, as at Ashio just before the riot, if the ordinary miners' delegates were able to take control of the brotherhood, then the brotherhood became a source of opposition to management. Who was actually leading the brotherhood? The answer to this question determined the relationship between the brotherhood and management.

For this reason, a key question that naturally arose after the riot was what to do with the system of workers' assembly representatives. The question was raised by the boss of lodge No. 1 at Honzan, a man named Yamamoto. On 12 February when the whole mine was in turmoil over the "mass dismissals and selective rehiring," he was the man who advocated the abolition of the assembly representative system.

On receiving Yamamoto's proposal, the Honzan bosses and assembly representatives met a number of times, and at the beginning of March, they finally decided to abolish the assembly system altogether. This sequence of events was noted in the following police reports:

As previously reported, all the Honzan assemblymen today [14 February] met at the same No. 14 lodge and discussed whether to abolish the steward and assembly systems. There followed discussions with each lodge boss, and by 6 P.M. on the 16th the written opinions of the [various] stewards had been returned to No. 14 lodge, whereupon they were handed over to the current steward of the No. 14 lodge and the meeting ended. The opinion of the lodge bosses and of many of the assembly representatives was that the stewards should be retained as before and that the lodge bosses should bear all their costs, while the assembly representatives should be abolished.[219]

At 9 P.M. last night, the 18th [February], there was a meeting of all the 24 Honzan lodge bosses, which, after heated discussion, decided in favor of abolition of the assembly representative system. It was further resolved to inform the assembly representatives of the decision the following day, but to refrain from pressing ahead with abolition if they met with widespread resistance from many of them.[220]

As a result of the previously reported decision to abolish the assembly representatives at Honzan, a meeting of all the lodge bosses last night, the 4th [March], agreed to set up a committee consisting of 5 miners' bosses and 2 hauliers' bosses to deal with any outstanding assembly business to date, and proceeded to elect the members of the committee.[221]

In short, the lodge bosses at Honzan took the authority of the brotherhoods into their own hands by substituting themselves for the assembly representatives. The details of how the matter proceeded at the other pits is not known, but we do know that while this system was abolished at Tsūdō sometime soon after this decision at Honzan, it continued at Kodaki until the middle of September of that year, for on 14 September, the management called a meeting of bosses' delegates at which new "regulations for the use of contractors" were announced. This was noted in a report by Ashio police station chief Tadokoro:

The Mine Office announced the revision of the regulations for the use of lodge bosses. These are currently being discussed all over the mine in view of their provisions that the bosses attached to each pit should be responsible for the rules and regulations in each lodge and should submit these to the pit offices. The standardization of such practices in accordance with those in force at Honzan will no doubt be achieved satisfactorily within the next few days, but the revised provisions with respect to the payment of the lodge charge and the direct payments to independent miners, as well as the obvious abolition of the assemblymen, in line with the spirit of the new regulations, will necessitate some careful surveillance. There may be some argument over the abolition of the assembly representatives at Kodaki, where they have continued to operate. There may also be problems with the miners at Tsūdō who have been hoping that the assembly representatives would be restored there. These matters are under scrutiny and a further report on the current situation will follow in due course. Most of the lodge masters throughout the mine have welcomed the new regulations.[222]

This report makes clear that the assembly representatives were still functioning at Kodaki, while they had been abolished at Tsūdō. It should be noted that clause 4 of the new regulations for contractors stated that "contractors shall represent the said lodge and shall have the duty of belonging to a lodge union." According to the copies of the Regulations of the Honzan Miners' Lodge Unions and the Conditions of Admission to Honzan Miners' Lodges, which were appended to Police Chief Tadokoro's report, although the new compulsory membership of the lodge unions was to be restricted to the lodge bosses only (Union Regulations clause 2), the unions in fact took on the functions of the brotherhood. All the costs of communications and intercourse between miners in different pits and mines would be borne by the lodge unions (Union Regulations clause 12), but the conditions of admission (clauses 5 and 6) recognized that such costs could be collected from the miners in the form of the lodge charge.

One of the aims of the new regulations was no doubt to secure the abolition of the assembly system at Kodaki. Whether they did in fact achieve this is unclear, but judging by the relations among the management, the lodge bosses, and the miners after the riot, it seems likely that the assembly was eventually abolished at Kodaki also.[223]

Thus, the Ashio brotherhoods not only lost their autonomy, in effect being forced to merge with the lodge system; they also ended up serving to reinforce that system. Nevertheless, in 1919 the first genuinely national miners' union was formed around a nucleus of miners from Ashio. This union was rooted in the concept of the brotherhoods, a fact that is testimony to the fundamental strengths of the brotherhoods, with their long history and their widespread organization throughout the country.[224]

The Reform of the Lodge System

The new regulations were not aimed only at the brotherhoods. Management's primary intention was to reform the lodge system. The mine particularly sought to limit the bosses' exploitation of the workers, and to make the miners more independent of the bosses.

Exploitation was tackled by the regulation concerning Conditions of Admission to the Lodge. Clause 4 addressed the lodge charge, a bone of contention between the Tsūdō assemblymen and the bosses, by fixing the monthly amount of the charge at a maximum 1 yen per miner and 70 sen per apprentice. Clause 5 limited the purposes for which the money could be spent on entertainment and lodge costs shared by all the men. The lodge boarding charge, another frequent grievance, was fixed (clause 9) at 6 yen per man per month for the top-rate boarding charge and 5 yen 40 sen for the normal rate.[225] The price of articles sold by the lodge was also brought into line with those loaned by the company. The miners' sense of independence was strengthened by the Regulations for the Use of Lodge Masters. Clause 6 clearly stated: "Lodge Masters shall recognize the right of miners and apprentices who have served more than three months to receive both wages and goods on loan from the company stores directly from the company. Such miners shall be designated independent miners."

Miners had in fact experienced direct supervision by the company prior to the new regulations; for the first three months after being hired, miners were paid directly by the company, but once they got into debt with the lodge bosses, which most did, they were forced to hand over the letters of proxy that authorized the bosses to receive their wages on their behalf. This proxy system had become widespread throughout the mine, but the new regulations put limits on it. Clause 7 stipulated that "balance sheets shall be drawn up listing the wages earned by miners prior to their independence and the amounts owed to their bosses. Written agreements on monthly repayments shall be added to these and signed by both parties. These shall then be submitted to the company." A boss thus needed the company's permission to deduct money owed him from a worker's wages. Also, whereas the boss was previously in a position to receive by proxy all of a worker's wages, depending on how much was owed to him, now he was only allowed to claim a certain amount per month; the rest was to be paid directly to the worker.

The company implemented these reforms of the lodge system because it could no longer afford to ignore the frustrations of the miners which had erupted in the violence of the riot. The reforms also signaled the company's recognition of the need to address the economic situation of the lodge bosses. The mine management realized that the bosses' own low incomes had been a principal cause of their exploitation of the miners through manipulation of the lodge charge and boarding fees. This point was mentioned in a letter of 28 August 1907 from the Ashio mine director to the superintendent at the head office:

The purpose of the changes in the lodge system mentioned above is to rectify abuses in the present state of relations between the lodge masters and the miners, on the one hand by increasing the various allowances paid to lodge masters, thus alleviating their economic difficulties, and on the other hand by affording protection to the miners, freeing them from the yoke of the lodge masters and placing them under the direct supervision of the company. As a result of a recent thorough survey, we discovered that there were a number of other matters which needed attention in addition to those to which we were urgently intending to address ourselves. In short, while the miners' circumstances do indeed require redress, it is currently the straitened circumstances of the lodge masters that require our prior attention. Improvements in the miners' situation will be contingent upon this reform. In addition, we have recognized the need to maintain the authority and prestige of the lodge masters, and after various considerations, we have provided for changes in the regulations for the use of lodge masters and have introduced lodge union rules and a new set of conditions for admission to the lodge, copies of which are appended. These amendments have now been put into effect. Many of them had already existed, but not in written form. This situation has now been rectified.[226]

Ōyama Shigetarō, who discovered this letter, emphasizes on the basis of the latter part of the section quoted above that in the wake of the riot management policy had been "to look after the contractors" and that this had had the effect of "raising the status of the contractors."[227] But this interpretation is too simplistic. The allowances paid to the lodge bosses were indeed raised under the new regulations. A new pit entry commission was established for the bosses, together with a new commission paid to the boss for each new worker he recruited. Also, the pit entry fee paid to the boss for each miner who went down the pit was increased. The boss's pit entry allowance was set at 15 yen per month, but in exchange he was obliged to go down the pit himself for a minimum of fifteen days a month "to supervise the work of his men and keep it up to standard." The recruitment commission was raised to 6 yen: 4 yen were paid after each new miner had worked three months before becoming "independent." A further 1 yen was paid the following month and another 1 yen the month after that. The daily pit entry fee for each individual miner was doubled, from 1 sen 5 rin to 3 sen. Such measures certainly seem to be a policy of "looking after the lodge masters," but they did not necessarily result in an increase in the bosses' status. The power of the bosses vis-à-vis the miners had indeed been strengthened temporarily, but the more fundamental change was a major strengthening of the company's power over the bosses. The lodge system had clearly been weakened.

Ashio's managers still viewed the lodge bosses as necessary to control their workforce and were not yet ready to dispense with them entirely. But the riot had made the managers acutely aware of the contradiction of an autonomous group of lodge masters within the management structure. The mine's attempt to eliminate this contradiction was evident in the 1908 revision of the arrangements for the training of miners, especially in the provision in 1912 of miners' dormitories.[228] But it was not until the labor disputes of 1919, when trade unions demanded that the lodges be abolished, that the lodge system came to an end.

Chapter 2

A Historical Analysis of the Lodge System: A Critique

of the Migrant Labor Theory

The quality of research on the Japanese labor movement has lagged well behind the quantity. The fact that studies in labor movement history only began in earnest after World War II is part of the explanation, accounting for a certain inevitable academic "immaturity" in this field. But a lack of time in itself does not sufficiently explain the low standard. The quality of research into Japan's labor movement history can only be improved, I believe, by reexamining our research methods.[1]

For years Japanese labor histories consisted primarily of chronological reviews or memoirs of labor activists. These presented much interesting material, but little of note in the realm of methodology. In this context, Ōkōchi Kazuo's theory of the migrant labor pattern, which emphasized the distinctive characteristics of the Japanese labor movement and consciously attempted to explain their nature and origins, was a work of great significance. One could say that Ōkōchi's work provided a scientific foundation for studies of Japanese labor movement history, a field that had been devoid of methodology prior to his work.

THE MIGRANT LABOR THEORY AND ITS CRITICS

The major premise behind the theory of migrant labor is straightforward: "the labor movement and labor problems in any one country are fundamentally conditioned by the characteristics (or pattern) of that country's labor force."[2]

The labor force "pattern" is regulated by the underlying economic structure that produces it. That is, the labor force is conditioned by (1) the developmental stage of the capitalist economy, and (2) national and regional differences. Further, national differences lead "over time, to the formation of a characteristically national type of labor force which is a special variant of the uniform standard capitalist model of a labor force, rather than an approxi-

mation to it. This national capitalist economic model constitutes one particular type or form among various categories of economic structure. As long
as this specific capitalist form continues to exist, the national labor force pattern will not disappear into some generalized capitalist labor force pattern."[3]

With these assumptions, Ōkōchi proceeded to define the Japanese labor
force pattern. In the formative period of Japanese capitalism, and even after-
wards, he said, the class of smallholders and peasant farmers continued to
exist, all the while providing industry with its labor supply. This continuity,
he argued, stemmed from the failure to break up the rural class structure
completely and make a clean sweep of the independent smallholders, as had
been the case in England with its enclosure movement. Thus, Japanese
workers inevitably maintained their connections in one way or another with
the premodern agricultural economy. This produced the phenomenon of the
migrant labor pattern (*dekasegi-gata*), using the term *migrant* in its broadest
sense. The migrant labor pattern was itself the Japanese labor force pattern,
Ōkōchi maintains. He argued that it defined the character of all problems of
Japanese labor from the earliest days of Japanese capitalism until at least the
1950s. For example, this pattern of migrant wage labor underlay the problems of low wages, poor working conditions, the lack of a horizontal industrywide labor market, status-based personal relations at work, the company-
based configuration of trade union organizations, the premodern attitudes of
workers even in the postwar era, and the labor movement's lack of stability.

Ōkōchi's argument offered more than a method by which to study the
history of the Japanese labor movement; it comprised a general theory of
Japanese labor, based on his ideas about the labor force and labor supply.
And Ōkōchi went even further. In spite of his assumption that the type of
labor force is conditioned by the developmental stage of the capitalist economy, he argued that the special character of the migrant labor force in Japan
persisted across stages: "it has accompanied the development of Japanese
capitalism throughout the 1870s–1950s without breaking up. Far from dis-
appearing, the migrant labor pattern has consolidated itself and seems to be
evolving as a form of labor organization" according to its own logic.[4] The
migrant labor thesis thus became a means to understand and interpret the
entire history of the Japanese labor movement.

While Ōkōchi's theory exerted great influence on research on Japanese
labor, it was not always well received. Numerous researchers criticized it
severely and put forward a number of counterarguments and revisions.
Detailed examination of the issues raised by his theory must therefore take

account of these criticisms. I should add, however, that most of these critiques themselves remained within the basic logical framework of the migrant labor theory or were based on very general formulaic approaches. Few tackled the theory head-on within the context of the history of the labor movement as a whole.

Virtually all critics point to the migrant theory's deterministic character as one major problem. Here, for example, is Ōtomo Yoshio's criticism of Ōkōchi's argument concerning company-based unions, an integral part of his theory:

"The weakest point of this analysis is that it provides absolutely no hint of an active strategy to overcome the company-based union. The theory simply maintains that a so-called Japanese pattern of wage labor developed due to the structure of Japanese capitalism. . . . If the structure itself does not change, then the Japanese pattern of wage labor is fated to continue, leaving us with an extremely pessimistic view of the working class, those people who ought to take a leading role in changing this structure."[5]

This seems a valid criticism, but it does not advance the argument very far. Ōtomo simply points out that the migrant labor theory is deterministic and serves only to explain the present situation; he does not clarify what makes the theory deterministic. The fundamental difficulty with the migrant labor theory lies in the one-sided nondialectical character of Ōkōchi's concept of the pattern (*kata*). Let us examine what this means in practice.

The first problem is an a priori assumption that underlies Ōkōchi's entire argument; he holds that "the labor movement and labor issues in a particular country are fundamentally determined by characteristics of the labor force peculiar to that country." This assumption straightaway reveals the one-sidedness of the theory. The labor movement does not shadowbox with itself; it struggles with an opponent. The nature of those struggles is determined as much by the opponent as it is by the movement. To explain the character of the labor movement in a particular country only by reference to that country's labor force is therefore inadequate. One must also make clear the character of the opponent, which in this case means the structure of oppression ranging from the labor management policies of a particular company to the use of state power, as well as the structure of industry within that country and the production processes within a particular industry.[6] The character of the labor force is bound up with the character of its opponent. It cannot be understood in isolation.

To be sure, Ōkōchi does not, of course, totally ignore this fact in his analysis of Japanese labor history. In *The Dawn of the Japanese Labor Movement*, for example, he refers to the repressive regulations of the Public Order and Police Law, and in *The Postwar Japanese Labor Movement*, he brings out the significance of the benefits and allowances paid by major companies. The problem is not that he improperly locates these factors in his theory, but that the internal logic of his theory cannot admit their importance.

A further problem, also frequently noted, is that the migrant labor theory makes no allowance whatever for the consciousness or subjectivity of the labor movement. From company-based unions to backward attitudes among the workers, everything is determined in a one-way, mechanistic fashion by the objective factor of the "migrant pattern" of the labor force; the conscious efforts of workers to change their circumstances and even to reform their own movement are overlooked. This is one of the reasons the migrant labor theory can be regarded as a deterministic analysis that holds out no hope for the future.

It is clear then that the main assumption of Ōkōchi's theory—that "the labor movement and labor problems in a particular country are . . . determined by the character of the labor force peculiar to that country"— cannot be accepted as it stands, but should be altered to: the character of the labor force in a particular country is one important element shaping that country's labor movement and labor problems. To determine whether this alteration makes the migrant labor theory more plausible, we must first examine whether or not the migrant labor pattern does indeed account for the special character of the Japanese labor force.

According to Ōkōchi, "the general character" of Japanese wage labor from the early period of industrialization until the 1950s can be defined broadly as "migrant labor." In support of his argument, Ōkōchi presents the following four categories:

1. Multiyear contract labor: female textile and silk factory workers

2. Seasonal labor: fishery workers, construction workers

3. Surplus population labor: the majority of factory workers, who migrate between the towns and the countryside according to fluctuations in the economic climate

4. Commuter workers: those who travel in from outlying suburban villages to work in new industrial areas in the provinces[7]

I have no objection to designating category 2 as migrant labor. Whether the term can also be applied to categories 1 and 4 is open to question, but let us for the moment assume that it can.[8] Namiki Shōkichi has put forward a powerful argument against designating category 3, surplus population labor (mostly male workers in factories, mines, and transport), as migrant labor. On the basis of exhaustive analysis of national census on the movements of village populations (in villages of fewer than 5000 people), he was able to clearly establish the following facts.[9]

From 1920 until the 1950s the number of people permanently leaving their villages to move to towns has been roughly equal to the natural increase in village population. The proportion of this "surplus population" leaving the villages has remained more or less constant in good economic times and bad. Adequate data for the period prior to 1920 are lacking, but it would seem reasonable to assume that the same basic scenario has prevailed since the 1880s.

Of course, this is not to deny that when the economy faltered some workers returned to their villages temporarily. But the statistics do show that, on the whole, very few workers did so even when the economic climate was bad and despite the fact that they had originally been farmers. In short, in the case of male workers in factories, mines, and transport, the only way to salvage the concept of "migrant labor" is to redefine it as all those who left farming villages permanently or temporarily.

Even if these objections are put aside, the claim that migrant labor is the characteristic pattern of Japanese labor would still be problematic. It characterizes the labor force solely in terms of the labor market, and while this is certainly one factor that influences the labor force, it is by no means the only one.

Another major determining factor is none other than the productive process itself. The character of the labor force is shaped by the productive process, which is controlled by capital. For example, there are great differences between the attitudes and lifestyles of printing industry workers such as typesetters and compositors, whose jobs require a fair degree of education, and those of coal miners engaged in heavy manual labor in underground pits. Even within a single industry, such as shipbuilding, some men work indoors in the highly skilled job of engine construction, which calls for great precision and technical know-how, and other men perform heavy manual labor outdoors in the shipyards, actually putting the ships together. And even within a single production department, the character of the labor force frequently will undergo changes as new technologies are introduced or new production methods adopted.

In general, we can say that however premodern in character a labor force may be when first recruited to industry, the technical and social training required by modern production processes turns this body of workers into a modern workforce. By ignoring this important fact, the migrant labor theory becomes all the more deterministic.

Problems for Analysis

While the discussion thus far has clarified the major flaws of the migrant labor theory, our critique is not yet complete. The crucial fact remains that, despite many valid objections, this theory continued to exert a major influence on Japanese labor studies. The theory addressed itself to the contemporary Japanese situation of the 1950s, and offered an effective, if one-dimensional, analysis of that situation. In contrast, most critics of the theory went no further than criticizing and amending its methodology. It remains for critics of the migrant labor theory to develop a superior methodology, a theory that can better account for the situation of Japanese labor, past and present. By analyzing the Ashio riot of 1907, this short chapter offers one attempt to do this.

I shall begin by considering how Ōkōchi evaluated the series of industrial disputes in the metal mining industry in 1907, which began with the Ashio riot. He touched on these disputes at various places in his book *The Dawn of the Japanese Labor Movement* as follows:

The main characteristic [of the Ashio riot] was that a powerful mode of control based on harsh, primitive labor relations and a slave-like lodging system provoked a re-action in the form of the riot which no labor union was able to control. [In fact,] all the large-scale disputes in the period 1907–17 in coal mines, metal mines, shipyards and arsenals had their origins in the same kind of social relations as did the riot at Ashio. . . .

Demands for wage hikes were a common feature of all these disputes. There was a sudden upsurge of demands for increases in wages that had been held down during the [Russo-Japanese] war, demands to which the workers were probably impelled by their strengthened position in the wake of postwar layoffs and rationalization. . . .

Apart from the disputes in the coal mines, the many conspicuously large-scale strikes in the copper mines were the result of the workers' reaction to their suffering under a weighty double burden of constant demands for increased production to supply the military and the oppressive feudal regime of mine management. . . .

None of the disputes developed in a normal fashion; each was a spontaneous outburst. These were not strikes called because a labor union's demands had been refused; they were a kind of spontaneous combustion, ignited by sparks of pent-up frustration over harsh working conditions and the constraints of status-bound relations at work.[10]

We can sum up this view of the 1907 mining disputes as follows:

1. They were caused by the "pent-up frustration" of the workers at the "powerful mode of control based on harsh, primitive labor relations and the slave-like lodging system."

2. Since labor union organization was suppressed, opposition could only take the form of "spontaneous outbursts" that frequently turned violent.

3. The sudden spate of industrial disputes and demands for wage hikes in 1907 occurred because wages had been held down during the Russo-Japanese War and because postwar personnel cuts and rationalization programs had intensified the work regime.

There are several dubious aspects to such a position, but in this chapter I will focus mainly on the second of the two purported foundations of the "powerful control" over workers that supposedly provoked the riot: "harsh, primitive labor relations and the slave-like lodging system."[11]

The first factor, "harsh, primitive labor relations," has not only been variously applied by different scholars, but Ōkōchi himself used it to mean so many different things at different times that we cannot define it with any clarity. Here it appears to mean excessive working hours and low wages, so let us first consider what Ōkōchi means by this.[12]

In the mining industry, he maintains, the lodging system forced workers to endure extremely long working hours and low wages, leading to a great accumulation of frustration and resentment. When this frustration eventually became unsupportable, it erupted in the form of strikes and riots.

Ōkōchi's argument does indeed explain one aspect of the disputes in the mining industry. The lodging system imposed extremely intensive labor on the workers through premodern, patron-client personal relations, thereby adding intermediary exploitation by the lodge bosses to exploitation by mine capital. This certainly greatly exacerbated the workers' frustrations. However, we must recognize that the lodge system from its inception had the control and domination of the workforce as one of its main functions. If the lodge system was as powerful as Ōkōchi asserts, how could the workers have risen to challenge it, no matter how dire their economic circumstances? Would not the workers' "pent-up frustrations" at least have been resolved in some other way than by an open resort to violence? Looked at in this light, can we not argue that the strikes and disputes of 1907 occurred not because of the continuing "strong controlling force of the lodge system," but rather because the "lodge system had weakened"?

In fact, the circumstances of the Ashio riot confirm this hypothesis. As we saw in chapter 1, those at the head of the riot were the underground miners, the key workers at the mine, while the principal objects of their wrath were not the lodge bosses but the company officials, from the mine director down to the lower-ranking supervisory staff. The important point for us is that immediately prior to the outbreak of the riot the miners had openly confronted the lodge bosses over leadership of the campaign for a wage hike and over restricting exploitation by the lodge bosses. Furthermore, the miners organized into their brotherhood had put the lodge bosses on the defensive. There are good reasons to suspect that the riot was planned and provoked by the bosses to extricate themselves from this situation forced upon them by the brotherhood. In any case, it is clear that the miners emerged the winners from their head-to-head confrontation with the bosses. Their victory, no matter how short-lived, proves that the authority of the lodge bosses was in fact weakening at that time.

How and why did that weakening of the lodge system occur? This chapter will examine the validity of the migrant labor theory by attempting to answer this question. In so doing, we must not make simplistic assumptions that the lodge system was characterized by slave-like oppression, the shackles of status relations, or primitive labor relations. Instead, we must trace the concrete historical circumstances and development of the system.

DEFINITION OF THE LODGE SYSTEM

The Functions of the Lodge System

Our first task is to define the *lodge system* (*hanba seido* in Japanese, literally, "eating place system").[13] The term originated in popular, not academic, discourse and has for this reason been interpreted variously by different scholars. In such a context, any study of the system's history must first define what we mean by *lodge*. To this end, we will first consider the common functions of the lodge system as outlined in the first comprehensive nation-wide survey into the circumstances of mine workers in Japan ("Kōfu taigū jirei" [Mine workers' working conditions]). The survey, conducted in 1906 by the Mining Department of the Ministry of Agriculture and Commerce, looked at metal mines and coal mines with over five hundred workers. The report's first section, titled "The Supervision of Mine Workers: Direct Control and the Lodge System," includes the following passage:

the duties of the lodge boss under the lodge system in general terms include the following:

1. Taking care of all matters concerning the hiring of mineworkers

2. Representing mine workers' interests to the mine owner

3. Providing new mine workers with accommodations and supplying them with provisions, eating and cooking utensils, fuel, items of furniture and materials necessary in the performance of their duties

4. Lodging unmarried mine workers in the lodge, providing them with food and drink and taking all precautions for their welfare

5. Getting the mine workers under their charge to their place of work, allocating them their duties, and carrying out supervision of their performance of those duties

6. Providing appropriate treatment and compensation in cases of death, injury and illness among mine workers under their charge

7. Overseeing mine workers' daily conduct and preventing escapes

8. Ensuring that work contracted for is carried out by the mine workers under their charge

9. Providing the mine workers under their charge with all their daily necessities

10. Receiving wages for the mine workers under their charge in a lump sum and paying each mine worker

11. Mediating in disputes between mine workers and settling any such disputes amicably

12. Communicating information from the mine office to the mine workers, and representing mine workers' views to the mine owners.[14]

From this rather unsystematic list, we can identify the following four aspects of the lodge boss's responsibility:

1. Labor supply procurement (1, 2, 7)
2. Work subcontracting (5, 8)
3. Handling of wages (10)
4. Off-the-job supervision of workers (3, 4, 6, 9, 11, 12)

Labor Supply Procurement

Given the extremely poor work conditions and the remote location of many mines, securing and maintaining a stable labor supply was the most serious problem facing mine managers in this period. The lodge system was above all a means to deal with this problem. Lodge bosses would recruit men through family or community connections, sometimes resorting to "methods that almost amounted to kidnapping." Once employed, the men were ensnared by advance payments or else their personal possessions were placed in the custody of the boss, thus restricting their freedom of movement. Those attempting to escape without having repaid their debts were subjected to harsh physical punishments.[15] The point to note here is that in most cases, the boss's role was not limited to recruiting. He retained ongoing responsibility, with the right in practice to hire and fire those miners he recruited, who became "his men." The boss was thus able to maintain a degree of independence vis-à-vis the mine owner.

Work Subcontracting

In connection with this point, it is worth quoting from a highly detailed "Survey Report into Mining Methods" drawn up by Takahashi Yūji, an engineer with the Superintendant of Mines Office, following visits in 1906 to twenty mines, mostly in the Tohoku region of northern Japan. We will also return to this quotation later, in examining the history of the lodge system.

Three categories of miners can be distinguished: the large lodge miners, the small lodge miners, and the miners in the direct employ of the company. The system of large lodges is the traditional one. It is still employed in two or three of the larger mines and in most of the smaller ones; it is the system most open to abuse. The large lodge system generally operates in one of two ways. One mode takes miners from the whole mine or a large section of the mine. In this system, the mine owner simply has the right of ownership; he needs no knowledge or experience of mining operations, nor does he need to provide any of the capital required to begin such operations. The contractor handles all these matters, and also supplies the labor and materials and manages all aspects of the operation. In return for the right to work the mine, he supplies the owner with a certain predetermined amount of ore or coal or else a share in the profits accrued from its sale. . . . In such a large lodge system, the contractor is the master lodge boss, and under him are the bosses of smaller lodges. These bosses possess practical, if imperfect, experience of actual mining operations. Each boss has control over from eight or nine up to several dozen miners. This is the normal practice among the lower orders of society. . . . There are a number of variations on this large lodge system; in the Tohoku region (northeast Japan), the so-called dressed-ore purchase system is in operation. This is virtually the same as the Kyushu system, except that the mine owner needs some knowledge of the industry and must provide some capital to work the mine. The extraction process throughout the whole mine or in a large part of it is contracted out. The contractors select the ore to be dug, and sell it to the owner in accordance with the terms of the contract with respect to the quality and quantity of the ore. In some mines, contracting extends only to the extraction process; in others, the contract also covers refining. . . . Despite these variations, there is no difference whatsoever between such systems in the relationships that obtain between the contractors and their miners. However, in the case of the small lodge system, we see differences in that, first, contracting is used for less extensive operations and for shorter periods. Second, the contractors and the mine owner or his officials work out their own estimates for the terms and the price of a certain job, and then determine an overall general estimate. The contract is then offered to those contractors who offer the lowest estimates, an arrangement similar to the so-called tender system. Accordingly, contracts may be awarded not just to one contractor but to several or even a great many. The number of miners working under one of these contractors is roughly the same as the number who work under one of the bosses attached to the large lodges under the large lodge system.[16]

Several different types of contracting systems are described here. In the first, the contractor provides for all his own costs and insurance, and receives from the mine owner the right to work the whole or a part of the mine. In the second type, the mine owner undertakes to buy ore or refined gold, silver, or copper at a fixed price, and again the contractor receives the right to work the whole or part of the mine. In the third case, the mine owner is directly responsible for the management of the mine, but temporarily contracts out certain operations such as the opening up of new pits and ore extraction.

Clearly, in 1906 the first two types of contracting were in use in only "two or three of the larger mines and in most of the smaller ones," and these constituted "the traditional system[s]" that were in decline. Thus, the form of the lodge system contracting that concerns us is the third, the small lodge system. In fact, after introducing the large and small lodge systems, the actual accounts in "Mine Workers' Working Conditions" focus exclusively on the small lodge system.[17]

Contracts under this system were short-term and limited to certain operations such as the opening up of new pits and ore extraction. The lodge bosses themselves apportioned the work among their men and supervised and directed the work, or else they selected some of their men to do so. Because the bosses' contracts were partial and short-term, however, their powers of supervision and direction were not absolute; the basic overall direction of operations lay with the company, and the lodge bosses had to take direction from company officials.

Handling of Wages

Contracting work out to the lodge bosses inevitably gave the bosses the right to handle their men's wages. These were paid in a lump sum to the bosses, who then paid them out to the miners. The system allowed the bosses to recover, with interest, the recruiting advances they had paid to new miners, as well as the men's boarding fees, bedding fees, and any loans the men might have taken out for other daily necessities. It also enabled the bosses to rake off the men's wages easily under various pretexts.

The practice of work subcontracting had major significance for wage determination. The boss was in practice able to fix the amount of each man's wage at will. Of course, the ore extractors' wages were paid on a piece-rate basis, and the criteria for determining rates were often set by the mine owner. But such extraction piece rates were inevitably affected by the condition of the ore face—the quality of the lodes, the relative hardness of the base rock, and so on—and such conditions were constantly changing. The imbalances caused by these variations were rectified and adjusted by periodic inspections, but the imbalances could not be eliminated entirely. The bosses' control over allocating work sites allowed them in practice to determine each man's wage level, and this control was a powerful factor in the bosses' domination of the workers. The use of naked violence has often been cited as the basis of the bosses' power, but the power to determine wages (and issue loans) was far more important.

Off-the-Job Supervision of Workers

We need not consider this aspect in great detail; it is a well-known feature of the lodge system. However, we must not overlook the loans for board and daily necessities, items 3 and 9 in the 1906 listing of lodge boss functions. Along with the obligation to repay his recruiting advance, these loans were a significant extra burden on the new miner; in effect, they restricted his freedom of movement. In addition, we must note the bosses' significant role as intermediary (item 12). The bosses acted as a kind of buffer between management and workers, facilitating management control of the workforce and acting as a safety valve to prevent workers' frustrations from breaking out into open defiance.

De Facto Employers

Their relatively independent authority to hire and fire, allot work schedules, direct operations, and handle wages conveyed the impression to outsiders, no less than to the bosses themselves, that the lodge bosses were the de facto employers of the miners. These forms of authority were the foundation for the powerful control of the lodge system over the miners. But the role of bosses as the miners' employers was more apparent than real, a subjective understanding shared only by the bosses. The main means of production were all in the hands of the company; the bosses possessed only a few simple items of equipment. Although mine owners contracted out work of various sorts to a number of bosses, they retained control over the overall management and direction of the mine's operation. Even the bosses' ability to manipulate wages was only possible within a framework of rates laid down by the company. In sum, the fundamental claim to the surplus labor of the miners lay with the owners. The bosses' exploitation of the miners was only that of middlemen; the company was the real employer. The bosses were not genuine contractors able to carry out the whole job with their own equipment, or even contractors who did the job with equipment hired from independent wholesalers. To put it another way, the lodge system was a form of contracting entirely controlled by industrial capital. The bosses retained virtually independent authority in the realm of "labor management" and a degree of autonomy in the production process, but they were fundamentally dependent on capital.

THE MINE MASTER SYSTEM

The historical roots of the lodge system can be traced to the *yamashi* form of mining organization typical in the premodern era. We shall translate this as the *mine master system.*

In the premodern era, all mines were owned by feudal lords, who worked them either directly under the supervision of appointed magistrates or bailiffs, or indirectly through contracting merchants who paid the lord a fixed rate for the ore extracted. The contractors (*ukenushi*) were similar to today's mine-lot contractors. However, neither the lord's bailiffs nor the contracting merchants were involved in the actual mining operation itself; that was left to the so-called mine masters.

Each mine master contracted to work either one, two, or three sectors of the mine. He was a completely independent operator who provided all his own equipment and employed all the labor—miners, haulers, shorers, and refiners—to carry out all operations from extraction to refining. The responsibilities of the bailiffs and merchants were for the most part limited to transporting and distributing the refined ores. They were in the position of buyers who had a monopoly over the purchase of the refined ore.[18] This system is clearly comparable to the large lodge system described above.

This method of organizing mine production was dictated above all by the low level of mining technology in the period. Methods of extraction had advanced from the raccoon-digging methods of the earliest times to methods using tunnels and the sinking of shafts, but the lack of technological development in drilling, pumping, and ventilation usually made deep mining impossible. Operations were restricted to the irregular extraction of ore from rich veins close to the surface. This necessitated the opening of a number of pits on the surface even to exploit a single lode, so that one mine was in effect simply a collection of several independent pits. In such circumstances, it was difficult for either a bailiff or a contracting merchant to control production directly and oversee an integrated mining operation. Instead, they divided the mine into its constituent pits and subcontracted production at each pit to the mine masters, while they themselves looked after the transport and distribution end of the operation. In this fashion, the state of premodern technology shaped the mine master system.

However, in certain sections of the largest mines, when these mines were in their heyday, the bailiffs and merchants did control production directly by overseeing the digging of large-scale pits and shafts for drainage and ventilation. In such cases, extraction, refining, and transport operations were subcontracted out to skilled miners (called *kanako*). These men normally contracted to work from one to three faces, employing their own miners and haulers where necessary. *Kanako* differed from the mine masters (*yamashi*) in that their duties were limited to extraction, refining, and transport; they had no authority over a pit and were in no sense managers. Clearly, the *kanako* system was an embryonic form of the lodge system that is the concern of this chapter. But this does not mean that the *kanako* over time evolved into lodge bosses; rather, these are two versions of a single type of mine operation in two eras.

THE GROWTH OF THE LODGE SYSTEM

Subcontractors

Our next task is to examine the transition from the mine master system just described to the lodge system of the early 1900s, using the Ashio copper mine as our case study.

Copper was first discovered at Ashio in 1550, and by the 1680s the mine was renowned as the most productive in Japan. Its annual output was almost 1500 tons. But Ashio declined thereafter, and was on the verge of closing by the end of the Edo period (1603–1867). Not much more is known about the mine in the Edo era, but we can be certain that when Furukawa Ichibei took over the mine in 1877, the mine master system was still in operation.

When I began this research in the 1950s my sources painted a picture of the mine master as a powerful figure. As *The Life of Furukawa Ichibei* records: "When Furukawa took over, more than 250 pits had been dug into outcrops of ore, and 74 sites were being worked, at which operations were contracted out among 38 different contractors."[19] Further, "Ashio at that time in effect belonged to the contractors; the owner merely supplied them with rice and miso and bought up the ore they produced."[20] A 1937 biography of one Ashio mine manager, Kimura Chōbei, claims: "Some contractors would run short of money and would apply for the loan of various items from the company office, but most were powerful men of authority who carried out all operations in the pits for which they had contracted. The company merely bought up the raw copper which the contractors had extracted and refined."[21] These accounts reveal that the "contractors" of the 1870s were in fact the mine masters described above. They contracted to work the pits, extracting and refining ore. Each pit was worked by a different contractor, who were in practical charge of all operations. Furukawa seems to have played the limited role of supplying rice and miso, extending loans where necessary, and buying up the ore.

Recently, however, the Furukawa Mining Company published a commemorative "100-Year History of the Furukawa Company," and this offers new documentation that changes our view considerably, such as reports on the numbers of men employed by the contractors at the time of the company's takeover of the mine. Eighteen of the thirty-three contractors employed only one miner, and six employed just two miners. This is hardly an image of "powerful men of authority." The strongest of the contractors was one Kamiyama Seiya, but even he only employed 19 miners, 6 haulers, 8 surface workers, and 8 female ore dressers, for a total of 41 workers. The second largest employer was Saitō Hachirō, with 14 workers: 6 miners, 2 haulers, 2 surface workers, and 4 female ore dressers. Thus, most of the contractors must have been the skilled miners described above (*kanako*), rather than so-called mountain masters.

Unified Pit Operations

With the mine's operations divided up among so many small-scale contractors, the long-standing problems of pumping and drainage, which had caused the mine to decline, could not be addressed. Neither could the mine's output be increased to allow competition with U.S. mines, which were then rapidly expanding production and cutting costs. The only way to meet these two challenges, which faced all of Japan's copper mines, was to thoroughly modernize the entire technology of the mine: prospecting, pit blasting, ore extraction, transport, and drainage. State-owned mines were better able to do this, by introducing the latest foreign machinery and equipment.

The stumbling block was the owner's need to eliminate the contractor's exclusive right to work a particular face before implementing such changes. Modernizing a mine's technology required an integrated plan for the entire mine, so the mine owner needed direct control over operations in the different pits. State-owned mines were able to achieve this control using the literal force of state authority against the contractors. Private mines such as Ashio were not in a position to change so rapidly. The process took time and required a certain amount of compromise. *The Life of Furukawa Ichibei* has this to say:

Furukawa's early challenge at Ashio was to bring the contractors under a unified command so that prospecting and extraction could be carried out according to his plans. The comment of pit manager Asano that "bad practices are even worse than they are generally rumored to be" suggests to us how many bad habits had become entrenched over the years. In addition . . . a number of contractors hostile to the new management were secretly planning to apply to the government for licenses to work those portions of the mine for which Furukawa had no operating rights. Although Furukawa actually took over at Ashio in March 1877, he was unable to proceed straightaway to reform the managerial regime. . . .

[Furukawa's strategy] to conquer these bad habits of the past and establish a new regime of direct control by the mine owner was to begin by taking control over new pits, and then gradually take into his own hands those pits that had been worked by the contractors, eventually bringing the entire mine under unified management. As a first step, in January 1878 . . . he opened new pits to be managed directly by the company, at [eight sites on the mountain].[22]

To exploit these new pits, Furukawa brought in skilled miners from the Furukawa copper mine at Kusakura. This allowed him to expand the sphere of his direct control rapidly and cut back the number of pits worked by subcontractors. By January 1881, the total output of the Ashio mine operation was 56,250 kilograms, of which the subcontractors produced only 12,375 kilograms (21 percent).[23] While expanding the company's direct management, Furukawa progressively bought out the contractors' rights to work their pits, including the Takanosu, Ashio's main pit, where an extremely rich lode had been discovered in August 1881.

Furukawa had thus established the preconditions for a fully unified management of the mine.[24] In 1885 he bought the Ani and Innai mines, and having secured in 1888 an agreement to sell his copper to an international copper syndicate which gave him access to powerful financial and technological resources, he was able to invest massively in the acquisition of the latest technology, with which he soon turned Ashio into a world-class copper mine.[25] How did these changes affect the contracting system?

The Abolition of the Contracting System

The first change was for the company to take over the ore-dressing and refining operations. Previously, the contractors had charge of all operations from extraction to refining, and had then sold the refined copper to the company, but after this change their only job was extraction. In other words, to use the terms of a 1907 "Survey Report on Mining Methods," contracting at Ashio in the late 1880s shifted from the first to the second type of "large lodge" system.[26]

The next step was gradually to restrict and ultimately to remove the contractors' customary monopoly rights to work certain pits. Furukawa did this by extending loans to the contractors and by supplying them with any necessary labor. The company also moved to buy up the more productive pits. Gradually the contractors were enveloped and ensnared by the company.

I am virtually certain that the mode of organizing production that resulted from these changes was in fact the lodge system. But unfortunately, almost no extant documents give a picture of the lodge system in the 1890s. All we have is the simple account of the situation in 1906 contained in "Mine Workers' Working Conditions":

Ashio copper mine: The lodge system operates at this mine, with lodge bosses in charge of miners, shorers, drill operators, and underground transport workers, and gang leaders in charge of workers of other jobs. The duties of these bosses are to recruit new workers, to provide their men with food, drink, and other daily necessities, to receive the men's wages on their behalf and to distribute those wages (three months after recruitment, miners can become independent of their bosses and receive their provisions and wages themselves), and to look after the miners' welfare. The bosses are paid an allowance by the company and also a commission for each miner they send down the pit. In addition, the bosses are paid once a month for the number of times the independent miners they have recruited go down the pit.[27]

Supervision of the work of the miners directly employed by the company is carried out by company officials, lodge bosses, and gang leaders, whereas Category 2 miners working under the contractors are supervised by their bosses and thus only indirectly by the company officials.[28]

This report shows that two types of lodge system were in operation at Ashio at the time of the riot. In the first, key workers such as miners, shorers, drill operators, and underground transport workers were known as category 1 workers, and they were directly employed by the company. The lodge bosses appear to be unable to bid for the contracts to carry out the work done by such men; their main responsibilities were limited to recruitment and supervision of the workers' daily needs and behavior, but they still did handle and pay out the miners' wages. In the second system, the various grades of laborers such as haulers and carters (category 2 workers) had no direct relationship with the company. They were employed by the gang bosses to do work for which the bosses had contracted, and they worked under the supervision of their bosses.

Even in 1906, then, some work was still being contracted out, and the fact that workers directly employed by the company were nevertheless paid through the lodge bosses shows that Furukawa's abolition of the subcontracting system after his takeover of the mine was incomplete. Certain elements of that system were clearly still in place.

But an important question remains. Did any contracting take place for the digging of new pits and the extracting of ore? That is, did the lodge bosses have no rights at all to contract for the work done by category 1 workers?

The following passage sheds some light on the matter. It is from the "Outline of Operations at the Ashio Copper Mine" published in 1897: "Twice a month, a contracted operation commonly known as the 'major assessment' is carried out. The width of veins, the quality of ore, and the likely ease of extraction are appraised, and extraction targets are assigned to men chosen either by designation or by lot." Further, "An Inspection Report on the Ashio Copper Mine, Tochigi Prefecture" in the August 1886 *Bulletin of the Japanese Mining Industry Association* reports that "[ore] extraction is subcontracted," and the March 1887 number of the same journal carries a "Report from the Ashio Copper Mine" which notes that "much of the opening up of new pits and of ore extraction is carried out by the contracting method." This evidence suggests that up to 1897 at least, contracting took place even in the actual mining process.

When and under what circumstances, then, was contracting in the mining process finally done away with? The question is obviously extremely important in explaining the riot of 1907, because the principal agents in the riot were none other than category 1 workers such as miners and shorers, and also because the weakening of the lodge system, which I have argued was the factor that made the riot possible, resulted directly from the bosses' loss of their role as contractors in the mining process. Unfortunately, there are hardly any sources available that conclusively show us when and how contracting ceased to be. To gain some insight into the process, we must examine how the lodge system came into being, and in particular, how contracting was able to continue in the mining process.

THE PERSISTENCE OF THE LODGE SYSTEM

The Lodge System and the Migrant Labor Theory

How could a premodern form of labor management such as the lodge system emerge under a modern capitalist managerial regime? Ōkōchi Kazuo gave the following answer:

1. "The persistence of a peculiarly Japanese configuration of labor, namely the restricted, slave-like pattern of labor relations common in the Meiji period, can only be understood as a result of the peculiarity of the process of the formation of wage labor." This "peculiarity" is for Ōkōchi, of course, the migrant labor pattern, by means of which "the feudal nature and structure of village life and of the rural family, governed by a status-bound hierarchical ethos and permeating personal relations and all aspects of rural labor . . . were carried over into the industrial realm, and the result was that the labor-management relationship assumed a feudal and hierarchical character."[29]

2. Further, "the fundamental factor inhibiting the creation of a unified labor market was migratory quality of the labor supply and the consequent scarcity of any settled reserves of labor. Also as a result [of the migrant pattern], the recruiting of workers could not take place through a broad, horizontal labor market, but had to be

carried out on the basis of personal relations. The fact that the recruiting of a labor supply did not take place in a rational fashion through a labor market of some breadth, but took place entirely on the basis of personal relations, led to deterioration in working conditions, the restriction of labor relations within a system of status-bound hierarchy, the growth of gang-boss systems and other forms of exploitation of the supply of labor."[30]

Ōkōchi's argument certainly accounts for part of the problem. That most miners came from rural villages is attested to by many sources. Ashio was no exception; its labor force was drawn largely from the four northern prefectures of Toyama, Niigata, Fukui, and Ishikawa. This is one of the reasons mine workers so readily acquiesced to the premodern regime of the lodge bosses. Also, the recruiting of workers through native-place and family connections, rather than through an impersonal labor market, did have the effect of lowering working conditions and of facilitating hierarchical control on a personal basis.[31]

The Continuation of Contract Labor in the Mining Process

Nevertheless, these explanations do not suffice to explain the persistence of the lodge system. Ōkōchi's argument does not take into consideration the fact that the lodge system was more than a means of recruiting and guaranteeing the supply of labor; it was also a form of contracting for mining and refining operations themselves. The character of the Japanese labor market was indeed one of the factors that made possible, or that facilitated, the emergence of the lodge system, but it did not make it inevitable. The premodern character of the labor force continued to exist within the capitalist structure as long as it enabled capitalist managers to exploit their workers effectively, and it was used by management only as long as it did not contradict that purpose. In general, however premodern the character of labor market relations, the technology of modern industrial processes requires technical training and socialization, which ultimately creates a modern workforce. The persistence of the lodge system and its role in production cannot be understood simply as a function of labor market or labor force characteristics. Rather, it was intimately connected to the character of the production process in the mining industry at that time.

The links between the production process and the lodge system can be seen by examining the details of operations at Ashio, the mine using the most modern technology of any comparable operation in Japan at the time.

Most noteworthy of all are technologies for ore dressing and refining. Steam-powered crushers and trommeles were quickly introduced into the ore-dressing process. The methods employed at Ashio—smelting with water jacket furnaces, refining with Bessemer converters, using electricity in the refining process—were all of the highest contemporary international standard.[32]

The hydroelectric power station built at Ashio in 1890 was the first of its kind in Japan. Installed only eight years after the construction of the world's first such power station for commercial use was built in Appleton, Wisconsin, it ensured a steady supply of power for drainage and for the transport of ore both underground and outside the pits.

Begun in 1885 and completed in 1896, the Daitsūdō main underground tunnel extended for over 3000 meters, enabling the many previously separate underground tunnels to be linked up and facilitating not only ventilation and drainage but also the mechanization of the transport system.

Already before the turn of the century, then, Ashio was the most advanced mine in Japan and a world-class mining operation employing the very latest technology. However, technological problems remained in actually extracting the ore, which, after all, is the heart of the mining process. Here the company was slow to mechanize. This is not to say that there was no progress at all. In the latter half of the nineteenth century one technical advance was the use of black gunpowder and dynamite for blasting new pits and extracting ore. These explosives enabled the rapid extension of tunnels deep underground, and they temporarily solved the age-old problems of drainage and ventilation. They also resulted in a greatly increased output of ore. The resurgence of this industry, which had reached a peak in the sixteenth and seventeenth centuries only to decline in the eighteenth and early nineteenth centuries, was due largely to the use of these explosives.

The new explosives did not, however, alter the nonmechanized character of the extraction process itself. The drilling and placing (mortizing) of the explosives continued to be done by hammer and chisel. In 1885 the first power drills arrived at Ashio from the Ani copper mine, just bought by the Furukawa Company from the government. But these drills were expensive to operate and were too large and unwieldy to use at the faces. Of little value for extraction, their main use was in digging new tunnels at the main pits and shafts.[33]

Ashio's extraction methods were described in a report of the Japan Mining Industry Association in 1885: "There has been some effort to learn from Western methods of extraction, first digging lower tunnels, and connecting them with upper ones where appropriate. When a vein is met, digging expands out from it to left and right; the method is very similar to overhand stoping. When the veins are soft, hammers and chisels are used to extract the ore, and the surrounding rock is blasted with gunpowder. If the rock is very hard or water bursts occur which make it difficult to use gunpowder, the recourse is to dynamite."[34]

This report makes clear that already in 1885 the latest method of extraction, overhand stoping, seems to have been in use at Ashio, but in fact, the similarity to the overhand stoping method extended only as far as the opening up of pits prior to actual extraction (this process is described in detail in Figure 2.1 below). Thereafter, the traditional raccoon-digging method was used. An account of this method was given in the "Outline of Operations at the Ashio Copper Mine" (1897): "There are currently few places where the stoping method of extraction is in operation. The so-called 'raccoon-digging' method is used to exploit the whole width of the vein." Raccoon digging produced only very rich ore from veins that were easy to dig. This method left behind very uneven and irregular trails, and made the working space extremely narrow and cramped.

It was therefore very difficult to mechanize the extraction and the transport of ore from the faces to the main tunnels. Electric trams and lifts were operating in the main tunnels, and powerful automatic pumps dealt with drainage, but at the faces, men were still using hammers and chisels. The extracted ore was selected at the face and put into sacks which haulers carried on their backs to service tunnels; from there they were taken by hand cart to the main tunnels. This inefficient process was being gradually modernized throughout the Japanese mining industry at the time, but it was precisely this transitional phase that allowed a premodern form of labor management such as the lodge system to exist and survive within a modern capitalist industry.

The efficiency of extraction largely depended on the effort of the individual worker. This was not simply because of the manual nature of the job, for this dependence did not change with the introduction of pneumatic drills.

The miner at the face was further pressured by the mechanization of ore transport from the face. For the first time, the speed of the machinery put direct pressure on the workers.

There were only two ways of improving efficiency of extraction in these circumstances: implementing piecework wages "by which the quality and strength of the work [could] be controlled by the wage regime itself,"[35] or tightening up workplace supervision. Piecework wages "laid the basis for a system of class-based exploitation and oppression."[36] That is,

on the one hand [they] facilitate the introduction of a parasitic element, the sub-contractor, into the relationship between the capitalist and the wage laborer. This intermediary's profit results entirely from the difference between what the capitalist is prepared to pay for the work and how much the intermediary actually hands over to the workers. . . . On the other hand, piecework enables capitalists and certain leading workers to enter into agreements as to how much a job is worth, and then those leading workers themselves recruit and pay men to work under them at that rate, in which case, the exploitation of workers by capitalists is carried on through the intermediate exploitation of workers by other workers.[37]

Furthermore, unlike normal piecework, which was based on the individual worker and his output, the job of ore extraction was assessed "according to the width of the veins and the relative hardness of the surrounding rock"; "different rates were fixed for each place." This was a group-based system in which the face, not the individual worker, was the unit of assessment.

Piecework wages did not of themselves inevitably produce the lodge system in the mining industry. They merely facilitated that process. What did inevitably involve the lodge bosses in production was the difficulty of increasing supervision of the work underground so as to boost efficiency. The workplace, that is, the faces, were scattered over a large area in accord with the location and quality of the veins. Although they were linked by a network of horizontal tunnels and vertical shafts, the dispersion, the three-dimensional nature, and the relative isolation of the faces meant that the underground workplace was in no way comparable to a workplace in an ordinary factory. To get around from face to face, miners had to squeeze one-by-one through very narrow tunnels, climb up slippery ladders, and walk carefully up and down logs carved into steps. No light from outside shone down the pits, of course, and a miner at the face had to rely on the feeble illumination of lanterns. For a mine owner to supervise and direct the underground workers effectively under such conditions, he would have needed as many overseers as miners.

This situation is what drew lodge boss subcontracting into the production process, leading to "the exploitation of workers by capitalists . . . through the intermediate exploitation of workers by other workers." As "Mine Workers' Working Conditions" clearly indicates, one of "the main ways in which [the company] profits from the lodge system" is that the system "supervises the miners' attendance, puts them to work and allocates their jobs, thus saving the mine owner a great deal of trouble and keeping down the number of officials he has to employ." In short, the lodge system was less a response to features of the Japanese labor market or labor force than a response to a particular stage of technological development in the Japanese mining industry. Only such an interpretation allows us to holistically and historically understand the lodge system.

DEVELOPMENTS IN EXTRACTION METHODS

From "Raccoon Digging" to the Overhand Stoping Method

The lodge system was rooted in the technology of the early stage of the industrial revolution in Japan's mining industry. At this stage, while the mechanization of transport, drainage, ore dressing, and refining proceeded apace, extraction technologies remained at the primitive level of "raccoon digging" with hammers and chisels. The logic of this situation thus suggests that further technological developments, especially in the area of ore extraction, would eventually lead to the end of the lodge system. We must therefore examine changes in the technology of digging to explain the abolition of subcontracting in the production process.

We will first consider the type of equipment used in ore extraction. Put simply, there was no change at all throughout the period. Pneumatic drills came into use at the faces only after 1910; until then hammers and chisels were the miner's only means of extracting ore. But if the tools did not change, the extraction method did. Ashio miners shifted from so-called raccoon digging to the overhand stoping method.

With raccoon digging, only the richest ore could be mined. The amount of ore extracted was high relative to the amount of ore-bearing rock dug, and its quality high as well. Less transport was needed to carry the ore because smaller amounts were dug, and ore dressing was likewise a simple operation. This in turn meant that only low levels of investment were needed for transport and ore-dressing facilities, and the return on this investment (the value of copper produces) was high. Especially when capital resources were restricted, this was an advantageous situation that resisted change.[38]

Yet significant disadvantages accompanied the benefits of raccoon digging. First, by following the various ore veins to get at the richest ore, tunnels became very narrow and irregular. This in turn lowered the efficiency of the underground transport system and made ventilation progressively more difficult. Second, because piece-rate wages were pegged to the amount and quality of ore produced, miners engaged in so-called rough digging, by which they would avoid digging in difficult spots where rocks were hard. This inevitably shortened the life of a mine. Third, low-grade ore was abandoned at the face, and this became a source of water pollution. Fourth, mechanization of the extraction process and of transport at the faces was impossible.

In the mine's early years of operation, when Furukawa's capital resources were limited, there was neither means nor motive to address these problems. But by the late 1890s, as transport, drainage, ore-dressing, and refining facilities were fully mechanized, the mine management gradually recognized the need to tackle these issues. The facts that copper output peaked in 1891 and that severe pollution damage affected the lower reaches of the Watarase River moved the matter of change in extraction method to the top of the mine's agenda. A letter of December 1893 addressed to Furukawa Ichibei by Ashio's mine director, Kimura Chōshichi, is the first sign of this new policy: "In 1894 output is estimated to reach 10,000 tons. We will implement overhand stoping extraction, and we will build a big ore-dressing plant."[39] However, it is clear from the 1897 "Outline of Operations at the Ashio Copper Mine" that new methods were being adopted very slowly: "the overhand stoping method of extraction has to date been introduced in only a few places in the mine . . . the aim is to shift over gradually to overhand stoping, and because this will necessitate an increase in the scale of ore-dressing operations to the point where 600 tons can be processed every 24 hours. We plan to complete this expansion within two years. But to achieve this target, we must use hydroelectric power and install triple-phase power generators."

The mine's goal was thus to change over completely to overhand stoping by the end of the 1890s. But exactly when the changeover was in fact completed is not clear; raccoon digging was definitely still going on at Sunokobashi in 1907. One clue to the progress of the changeover is the fact that in 1903 there was a sudden sharp drop in the quality of ore mined at Ashio.[40] The fact that overhand stoping inevitably required the mining of lower-grade ore suggests that by 1903 this method was in use throughout almost all of the mine.

Overhand Stoping and Eliminating Contract Labor

That production contracting came to an end just as the changeover to overhand stoping took place around the turn of the century was no coincidence. While no available sources document the connection between these two events at Ashio, one document throws some light on their intimate relationship at the Besshi copper mine.

While new facilities were being installed throughout the mine, the opportunity was taken in 1906 to rationalize mining methods, a step that was both necessary and pressing. The production department implemented a major change in the lodge system to purge the abuses and bad habits to which the system was prone. . . . In September 1906 the production department issued new regulations controlling the lodges; three new lodges were created, bringing the total to twelve, and each lodge was limited to 120 men; inadequate lodge bosses were dismissed, and new ones were chosen by the production department. Whereas previously the department had sub-contracted the actual work of ore extraction to the lodge bosses, had not demarcated the mining areas underground in any detailed way, and had allowed the bosses to extract ore over a relatively wide area at their discretion, the department now introduced a system of allotting faces or sectors and also introduced the overhand stoping method. The lodge bosses' assignments to various sectors were determined by lottery. On 1 April 1907 the lodge charge, collected by the lodge boss from the men in his lodge, was abolished. A new system was instituted whereby the production department paid an equivalent sum directly to the lodge bosses. This system was enforced with great seriousness and authority. The changes improved the atmosphere of the whole mine. The majority of good mine workers were protected, the previous unsystematic and indiscriminate extraction methods were avoided, and efficiency of copper production greatly increased.[41]

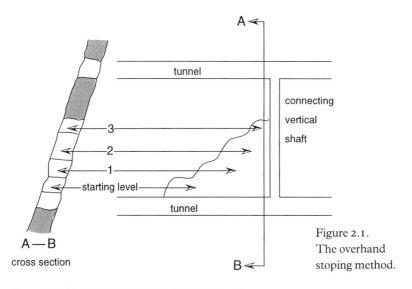

A —B
cross section

Figure 2.1.
The overhand
stoping method.

Source: Terui Takeo, Textbook of Mining, vol. 3, no.12
(Tokyo Hakuashobō, 1955).

To understand why the introduction of the overhand stoping method led inevitably to the end of production contracting, we must examine what this method involved (see Figure 2.1).

In overhand stoping, parallel tunnels were first dug above and below the ore-bearing rock, and these tunnels were connected by vertical shafts sunk at regular intervals. A section of rock between the tunnels, of a fixed height and width, was then demarcated and gradually dug into at different levels. With this method both lumps of ore and of the surrounding rock were extracted; to that extent it was inferior to raccoon digging, which extracted only lumps of rich ore. However, since the stoping method also dug the low-grade ore avoided by raccoon digging, it left nothing behind and at the same time made underground transport, ventilation, and shoring a lot easier. It thus overcame most of the disadvantages of raccoon digging.

The role of the lodge boss changed significantly with the new method. With raccoon digging a miner followed the vein, digging only the richest ore. This required skill and experience, for the miner had to recognize the different types of rock and use his chisels accordingly. The lodge boss, who could direct the work on the basis of his own experience as a skilled miner, was needed to supervise this extraction process. But the needs of overhand stoping were different. The work could not be directed and supervised simply on the basis of such experience. Variations in the type of vein meant that the steps or levels had to be dug differently, and transport to take away the ore also had to be arranged accordingly. Overseeing such work required an increased amount of technical, "scientific" skill. The lodge bosses, limited to their former underground skills, were clearly not equal to the task. This was the main reason the introduction of the overhand stoping method meant the end of contracting in the production process. In addition, with overhand stoping the faces were grouped and reordered, greatly facilitating direct supervision of the miners and reducing the need for the lodge boss as intermediary.

The following two sources confirm that this change in the lodge system was going on not only at Ashio and Besshi in the early 1900s, but in many of the larger mines throughout the country:

Although the overhand and underhand stoping methods were being used increasingly in the years 1890 to 1895, even in those mines which were in good order many miners were still able to dig as they pleased, or else the determination of wages was based on the quantity or quality of the ore dug, which led to innumerable abuses. Chasing after profits, miners dug only the richest and softest veins of ore. Unable to break out of old habits, they simply avoided any harder veins, irrespective of whether or not they might contain good ore . . . 34 (80 percent) of the 41 largest mines had introduced the [overhand] stoping method by 1903.[42]

It is extremely rare for lodge bosses to possess all the powers described above; in only two or three mines is this the case. Most mines supply workers with what they need for work every day and do not allow lodge bosses to receive workers' wages on their behalf. Contracting for production work is also forbidden, and the duties of lodge bosses extend to no more than providing accommodation, food, drink and other daily provisions for unmarried workers.[43]

CHANGES IN THE LODGE SYSTEM

When the mine ceased to contract with lodge bosses for production, what was the effect on the lodge system? Until this point, the lodge bosses had maintained independent authority over recruiting and dismissing miners and setting and paying wages. This authority was the basis of their tight control over the miners, and their position as contractors in the production process was its foundation. When the mine abolished the system of contracting with lodge bosses for ore production, the bosses lost more than one of several varied functions; this change led inevitably to change in other aspects of the lodge system.

The main function of the lodge bosses continued to be that of securing labor for the mine. Especially with the loss of other functions, recruiting workers and holding onto them by means of advance loans became the lodge system's most important function, although the mine came to place wide-ranging restraints on the bosses' ability to hire and fire at will. This much is clear from the Furukawa Ashio Copper Mine Miners' Service Regulations, introduced around 1900, which laid down different procedures for the hiring of category 1 workers such as miners and shorers, who were under the company's direct employ, and category 2 workers, such as carters and haulers, who were employed by the lodge bosses. With the clause "category 2 workers are those employed indirectly through the contractors," the company recognized the right of the bosses to control the workers in this particular group. In contrast, category 1 workers were to apply directly to the company: "those desirous of requesting employment are to present their request through an intermediary from one of the lodges." Since only the lodge bosses could in fact "introduce" a worker to the company under this rule, they retained a measure of de facto hiring authority, but the company had final authority over hiring these miners. Company regulations stated that "those seeking employment will be examined as to their background and, if judged appropriate, candidates will take the test for category 1 workers, a successful result in which will secure them employment, in which case, they are to provide at least two reliable guarantors from the same lodge and sign a contract to be drawn up in the appropriate manner." In other words, as the company terminated production contracting it also took over from the lodge bosses the power to hire and fire and made this clear in written regulations.

The most critical change to affect the lodge bosses at this time was of course a change in their second major function, that of intermediary in the production process. In terminating the bosses' role as production contractors, the company did not immediately exclude them from all aspects of the production. Lodge bosses were still responsible for ensuring that miners got to work, and for a time they retained responsibility for supervising the work of their men. But in this role they were in fact no more than "assistants" to company officials, and their supervisory role gradually declined as the company strengthened its direct supervision of work. The situation during this transition period is reflected in a section of the company service regulations mentioned above: "Those contractors experiencing difficulties in performing the contractor's duties should apply to the relevant department and abide by the department's decision to grant them a fixed or an indefinite period of release from their work."

The bosses' third main function—the administration of wages—could hardly remain unaffected in this context. Their de facto power to set wages by assigning rock faces to their men naturally disappeared when the company terminated contracting and took over work assignments. However, the bosses managed to retain a middleman role in actually distributing wages from company to worker. While most mining companies implemented new regulations and sought to eliminate this intermediate exploitation as much as possible when they abolished subcontracting, so long as the miners continued to accept recruiting advances repaid from wages, or paid for their lodgings and daily necessities, the lodge bosses were able to maintain some control over pay distribution.

The bosses' fourth main function was to supervise the daily lives of the miners. This role did not change in substance, but with the loss or restriction of the bosses' other roles, this function increased in relative importance. In particular, because the bosses could make up for the income lost because of the elimination of contracting by raising the prices of accommodations and provisions or other assessments, the significance of this function increased sharply.

A wide array of changes in the lodge system thus weakened the lodge boss's direct control over his workers. That control had rested on the boss's unimpeded authority to hire and fire workers and to fix their wages. To all outward appearances, the bosses had been the mine workers' employers. But the termination of production contracting largely deprived them of this authority. They no longer appeared as de facto employers, but were shown to be no more than the intermediate exploiters of the workers under their control.

To be sure, the bosses did not lose all power over hiring, firing, and wage setting. The miner seeking employment first had to be introduced to the company by a lodge boss, and on the miner's securing employment, that boss became his guarantor. This power should not be underestimated. However, this situation was allowed to continue only to the extent that it facilitated the company's control of the workforce. Whenever there was a clash between the interests of the bosses and those of the owner, the company made clear the restrictions on the bosses' room to maneuver. At Ashio, the bosses continued to distribute wages to their men, thus retaining some ability to manipulate wage levels, but as the bosses were no longer contracting for production and were even losing their role as work supervisors, the basis for this role was entirely undermined. The bosses' only compensation for the loss of their contracting privileges was a commission they received for each miner sent down the pits, and as this was whittled away in real terms by inflation, the lodge bosses compensated with increased lodge charges and other levies. The miners viewed the bosses' actions as unjust and parasitic and felt their exploitation ever more keenly.

As Ōkōchi indicated, the series of mine workers' riots and disputes in 1907 all had "the same social foundation as that of the Ashio copper mine riot." But this "social foundation" was not at all "the powerful control of the slave-like lodge system" that he claimed it to be. It was in fact the opposite. The social foundation of the riot was the weakening of the lodge system, a process unfolding in major mines up and down the country at the turn of the century. The migrant labor theorists failed to perceive this fact because they limited their concern to characteristics of the labor supply and the labor market. They believed these to be at the root of all the problems of the Japanese labor movement and of Japanese labor issues in general, from the earliest days of wage labor until the present. They overlooked the centrality to any consideration of labor issues of the workplace itself, the site where the productive process is controlled by capital. They forgot that "the bourgeoisie cannot exist without constantly revolutionizing the instruments of production, and thereby the relations of production, and with them the whole relations of society."[44]

Conclusions:

The Significance of Ashio

In this book I have sought to challenge two widely held assumptions that have powerfully influenced the study of Japanese labor history since the 1950s. The first is the thesis of the atomized worker, the second is the theory of the migrant labor pattern. I pursued a historical analysis of the Ashio riot of 1907, and its background, as a means to make this challenge. As a consequence of this strategy, I have not summarized the historical significance of the riot itself, and have only touched briefly on its impact and on developments in the mining industry and the labor movement after 1907. Full treatment of these subjects would require more than this brief concluding chapter, but in this space I do wish to review the causes of the riot and discuss its consequences. Finally, I will build on the book's argument to draw some broader conclusions and suggest an agenda for future research in Japanese labor history.

THE CAUSES OF THE RIOT

Chapter 1 examined the direct causes of the riot. The second chapter set forth the reasons why the situation of the lodge bosses not only rendered them unable to suppress the miners' wage demands, but indeed invited worker resistance. (Chapter 3—of the original Japanese edition—explored changes in both working conditions and technology that formed the background to the workers' wage demands.) It remains, however, to clarify the relationship among these various factors.

The Demand for Higher Wages

The main reason for the pit miners' demand for higher wages was the significant decline in their real wages relative to those of other workers at Ashio. That decline had two sources. First, and most specifically, it stemmed from the post-1897 shift in the Furukawa Company's strategy, away from aggressive expansion toward "consolidation" in order to guarantee steady profits over the long term. Second, and more generally, the decline can be attributed in part to the effects of severe price inflation in the wake of the Russo-Japanese War of 1904–5.

The company's founder, Furukawa Ichibei, had consistently pursued a policy of increasing the company's market share. He had therefore used profits from Ashio to acquire more and more mines, while increasing his investment in these mines and paying the workers comparatively high wages to stimulate greater production. But under the leadership of his adopted son, Junkichi, who took over effective control of the company after the crisis of the Pollution Prevention Order in 1897, the company shifted to a policy of retrenchment and consolidation. In addition to reining back regular investment, Junkichi made cuts in operating costs in several areas. These cuts included a freeze imposed in 1897 on pit miners' wages, which represented a large proportion of the cost of refined copper. In contrast to the pit miners, the wages of refinery workers had been sharply reduced with the introduction of Western-style furnaces in the late 1880s and early 1890s. By the 1900s, a seniority-style wage structure, based on length of service, was in place for these men. Meanwhile, wages for unskilled workers at Ashio had followed national trends and increased modestly over these years. By the early 1900s, the nominal wages of miners were still higher than these other groups of workers, but because of the wage freeze they had begun to decline sharply both relatively and in absolute terms.

To cover the 2 billion yen cost of the Russo-Japanese War, the government raised indirect taxes, tightened its monopoly on tobacco, imposed a new monopoly on salt production and sales, and borrowed money abroad. The new salt monopoly hit ordinary people particularly hard. It not only raised the price of salt itself, it also drove up the price of staples such as miso and soy sauce, which have salt as a major ingredient.

The conventional explanation for the simultaneous outburst of labor riots nationwide in 1907 looks to the effects of the economic recession of that year, but this view simply does not bear scrutiny. The stock market decline in January 1907 was certainly evidence of a coming recession, but the economy did not show any serious effects until the autumn of 1907. In the first half of the year the feverish industrial expansion of the second half of 1906 in fact continued. This expansion resulted in serious labor shortages in the mining industry, and this—not a recession—contributed to the surge of strikes of these months.[1] Most of the strikes in mining and other industries as well were marked not by opposition to wage cuts and layoffs, but by demands for higher wages.

The other reason the miners led the campaign for a wage hike is found in the customs of the miners themselves. They were, after all, workers accustomed to meeting with their fellows on a regular basis, choosing their representatives, having their views endorsed as the general will of all miners, and acting in unison accordingly. These practices had been in place since the emergence of autonomous miners' brotherhoods in the eighteenth century. Nor was this the only significance of the brotherhoods. The Shiseikai union led by Nagaoka Tsuruzō and Minami Sukematsu played a major role in the wage campaign, and the brotherhood tradition enabled such labor leaders to emerge from within the ranks of the miners. That Nagaoka conceived of a national labor union and was able to carry out his organizing activities cannot be understood without reference to the brotherhoods. Further, brotherhoods were active in all the areas in which disputes took place in metal mines and coal mines in 1907 (see Table C.1 in next section).

Immediate Causes of the Riot

The next question concerns the immediate causes of the riot that erupted on 4 February 1907. Why did the attack on the Tsūdō supervisors' cabins take place? There are strong grounds for suspecting that the lodge bosses deliberately set up the attack to discredit the Shiseikai union, out of fear that the miners' demand for the restoration of control over brotherhood funds (the treasury box) would undermine their own shaky control over the miners. The brotherhood assembly representatives, under the influence of Shiseikai, had openly demanded the return of the box, and on 5 February, the bosses reluctantly complied. Behind the miners' aggressive attitude lay their constantly worsening relations with the lodge bosses. As chapter 2 has shown, the bosses antagonized the miners by increasing various levies on the miners to boost the bosses' income following the loss of their subcontracting rights, a loss that in itself had weakened their control over the miners.

After the attack on the underground cabins, company officials were assaulted and their living quarters destroyed. These acts were clearly the result of the miners' "pent-up frustrations" over their treatment at the hands of the lower-ranking officials who had become accustomed to demanding bribes when assessing wages. Such bribery had become commonplace because wage assessments were made at Ashio on the basis of projected estimates of extracted ore from a particular face. Much was thus left to the discretion of the on-the-spot supervisors, whose own wages without such bribes were lower than those of the miners. In fact, customs of bribery permeated Ashio's entire organization, from top to bottom. Further, supervisors were referred to as "officials" (*yakuin*), a discriminatory term that signified all too plainly the difference in status between workers and staff. I shall return to this point later.

That the violence spread from assaults on lower-level supervisors to attacks on "officials" in general was connected to the fact that Ashio's chief executive at the time was an archetypal "wicked emperor." Minami Teizō was a former government bureaucrat, the man who had signed the Pollution Prevention Order that had threatened Ashio's very existence, who everyone knew could only have got the job of mine director through bribery and who, moreover, had been a stickler for regulations since the moment of his appointment, threatening anyone who displeased him with penalties of all kinds. Such a man was ideally suited to play the role of Ashio's very own archvillain. Ranged squarely against him in the eyes of many miners stood Shiseikai, the "friends of justice," whose champion, Minami Sukematsu, ironically had the same family name as the villain of the piece and was unsparing in his public criticisms of the mine director.

THE IMPACT OF THE RIOT

Impact on the Workers

The first major effect of the Ashio riot was to catalyze a number of other strikes and riots, in particular in the coal and metal mining industries. According to the "Survey of Strikes," a somewhat inaccurate report issued by the Ministry of Agriculture and Commerce, there were sixty industrial actions in 1907.[2] Fifty-four of these involved a total of 11,483 workers (figures are unavailable for the other six), the highest number of strikes and strike participants for any year prior to World War I. Disputes in the mining industry accounted for sixteen of the sixty (27 percent), and twelve of those sixteen disputes drew in a total of 2471 workers, 22 percent of all participants in these fifty-four strikes.

Figures for the remaining four disputes in the mining industry can be surmised from "Mining Industry Trends in 1907," also issued by the Ministry. That publication lists numbers of workers involved and working days lost in the riots at Ashio, Horonai, and Besshi, as well as the mine names, the numbers involved, and the days lost in all sixteen strikes in the mining industry in 1907. The total number of workers involved is listed as 3923, meaning that an additional 1452 workers joined the four remaining disputes. The total of 3923 workers represents 30.3 percent of the strike participants enumerated in the Ministry's "Survey of Strikes."

While the percentage of mining strikers would be slightly lower if the participants in the two remaining nonmining strikes were added to the total, the huge disputes at the Ashio, Horonai, and Besshi mines are completely omitted from these surveys because they were considered riots, not 'strikes.' Indeed, Table C.1 reveals that numerous mining industry disputes are missing from the survey.[3] If these are included, then a total of 10,000 strike participants in mining industry disputes is very conservative. The gaps in information on both mining and nonmining disputes in the Ministry's "Survey of Strikes" prevent any firm conclusions concerning the absolute numbers and relative mining industry proportions of disputes and participants. But Table C.1 lists ten more mining disputes than are found in the comprehensive "Chronology of the Japanese Labor Movement" compiled by Aoki Kōji (which records a total of 238 disputes in all industries in 1907). I estimate that the mining industry accounted for roughly 20 percent of all disputes and 40 to 50 percent of all participants in strikes in 1907.

This table shows that the Ashio riot in February, the Horonai riot in May, and the Besshi riot in June acted as catalysts for a series of disputes throughout the mining industry from February through March, May through June, and in July. The situation only began to ease in August, when the disputes quickly tailed off. This suggests that the riots, or rather reports about the riots, did indeed spark other miners to vent their "pent-up frustrations." Miners in almost all these strikes and riots demanded higher wages or else demanded the abolition or return of "reserve funds" confiscated from pay as a sort of forced savings to discourage job-hopping or quitting.

That so many took part in these incidents nationwide was probably the result of several factors: first, the fact that other mine workers, like those at

Ashio, were suffering from similar conditions of inflation and a decline in real wages; second, that the Ashio riot initiated a chain reaction, with anger at these conditions surfacing at other mines; and third, that the mining brotherhoods played an active role in many mines. In addition to the mines shown in the table, there were probably others where the owners, fearing that their workers might respond by imitating those at Ashio and Besshi, accepted demands for higher wages without reporting that they were faced with a strike.

Newspaper reports were a key factor in the spread of the disputes. The daily reports of events at Ashio and Besshi incited workers at other mines. Although all the papers criticized socialist "agitators" for provoking disputes and "riot," a number sympathized with the workers' plight and criticized the mine owners, officials, and lodge bosses. News made its way to other mines not only by means of newspapers, but also by the more direct route of oral reports from mine workers who had been laid off or who, with the help of fellow brotherhood members, had made their way to other mines after quitting their former mines. Such reports obviously would have had a more direct effect on their hearers. Finally, illustrated magazines and even films about the Ashio riot appeared, though what effect these might have had is difficult to judge.[4]

Finally, how did the "riots" or disputes affect the wage levels of the miners? Tables C.2 and C.3 show the changes in average wage levels from 1906 to 1908 at the mines where disputes occurred. Apart from Besshi, wages in all mines rose in 1907, especially in those mines where they had previously been relatively low. At the Yamagata Toki mine in Akita prefecture, where the first major dispute of the year occurred, wages actually doubled in its wake. Whether these increases resulted directly from disputes or whether they reflected the fact that the labor market had become a seller's market is still unclear. For the moment, we may note that apart from the Besshi mine, where managers responded to the riot by actually cutting wages, the pay of miners nationwide tended to converge from 1907 to 1908.

Impact on the Shiseikai

The riotous conclusion to the Ashio workers' campaign for higher wages had disastrous consequences for their organization. The breakup of the Ashio branch of the Shiseikai spelled the end of the series of efforts to

Table C.1. Labor Disputes in Mining, 1907

Date[1]	Name of mine[2]	Major product	Workers involved				Main demands
			Prefecture	Type of job	Number	Workers' actions	
1.19	Toki	copper	Akita	hand-digger	700	strike	wage raise, anti-forced saving
2. 4	Ashio	copper	Tochigi	hand-digger	2000	riot	wage raise
2. 6	Ikuno	silver	Hyōgo	hand-digger	500+	strike	wage raise
2. 6	Miike	coal	Fukuoka	miner		strike	wage raise
2.15	Yūsenji	copper	Ishikawa	miner		strike	wage raise, abolish savings plan
2.16	Fukui	coal	Nagasaki	hand-digger		strike	wage raise, refund savings
2.21	Takane	copper	Gifu	hand-digger	1000+	unrest	wage raise
2.23	Yūbari	coal	Hokkaidō			strike	wage raise
2.24	Makimine	copper	Miyazaki	electrician	30	strike	wage raise
3. 1	Ikuno	silver	Hyōgo			strike	wage raise
3. 2	Yūbari	coal	Hokkaidō	porter	700	strike	wage raise
3. 6	Ikushunbetu	coal	Hokkaidō	hand-digger	500+	strike	wage raise
3. 8	Ohya-quarry	stone	Tochigi	stonecutter	600+	strike plan	wage raise
3.10	Higashiyama	oil	Niigata		400	demand	wage raise
3.22	Horonai	coal	Hokkaidō			demand	wage raise
3.26	Ebisawa	?	Fukushima	miner	50	destroy office	wage raise
3. –	Nabeyama	lime	Tochigi			strike	wage raise
4.26	Makimine	copper	Miyazaki	hand-digger	170	strike	wage raise
4.28	Horonai	coal	Hokkaidō	hand-digger	300	riot	wage raise
5. 1	Yūbari	coal	Hokkaidō	porter	45	strike	wage raise
5. 3	Utashinai	coal	Hokkaidō			unrest	wage raise
5. 3	Kamui	coal	Hokkaidō			unrest	wage raise
5. 3	Monju	coal	Hokkaidō			unrest	wage raise
5. 9	Shiomachi	?	Hyōgo	hand-digger	36	assaulted police station	release of the arrested
5.10	Iimori	iron	Wakayama	miner		strike	wage raise
5. –	Ani	copper	Akita		300	strike	wage raise

Date	Place	Mineral	Prefecture	Worker	Number	Event	Demand
6. 2	Besshi	copper	Ehime	miner	1000	riot	wage raise
6. 8	Abukawa	?	Akita	hand-digger	21	strike	wage raise
6.10	Ishikari	sulfur	Hokkaidō	hand-digger	40+	demand	wage raise
6.12	Mitsumori	sulfur	Hokkaidō	hand-digger		demand	wage raise
6.30	Obie	copper	Okayama	hand-digger	25	strike	wage raise, lower rice price
6. –	Amemasugawa	?	Hokkaidō	hand-digger	600	unrest	wage raise
7. 1	Fukiya	copper	Okayama	hand-digger	400	strike	wage raise
7. 1	Yūbari	coal	Hokkaidō	hand-digger	50	strike	wage raise
7. 6	Osarizawa	copper	Akita	miner	100+	strike	wage raise
7. 7	Yusenji	copper	Ishikawa	women workers	16	strike	wage raise
7.11	Nishinokawa	copper	Ehime	porter	2800	strike	wage raise
7.11	Yoshioka	copper	Okayama	miner	150	strike	wage raise
7.13	Oiwake	coke	Hokkaidō	operative	400	strike	wage raise
7.14	Ikuno	silver	Hyōgo	hand-digger	30+	unrest	wage raise
7.14	Funaoka	?	Kyoto	hand-digger	2000	strike	wage raise
7.15	Yūbari	coal	Hokkaidō	hand-digger	40	strike	improvement of working conditions
7.16	Yamatoya	?	Kyoto	hand-digger	1000	strike	wage raise
7.21	Utashinai	coal	Hokkaidō	hand-digger		strike	
7.28	Usami	coal	Ibaraki	hand-digger	38	strike	wage raise
7. –	Iimori	iron	Wakayama			unrest	
7. –	Shinyūbari	coal	Hokkaidō			strike?	
8.30	Ikuno	silver	Hyōgo	miner	250	strike	wage raise
8. –	Kamiji	?	Wakayama		52	strike	lower rice price
8. –	Sasu	zinc	Nagasaki		20	strike	
9. 1	Kosaka	copper	Akita	smelter		riot plan	
10.12	Hoshu	coal	Fukuoka	hand-digger	900	strike	

Notes: 1. All dates for newspaper reports are of 1907. 2. Many place names were incorrect in newspaper reports; they have been corrected by referring to *Honpō kōgyō ippan* (An outline of our nation's mining industry).

Sources: Hirokawa Sadahide, *Honpō kōgyō no sūsei: 1907* (Trends in our nation's mining industry: 1907), 224, and *Nihon kōzan sōran* (Survey of Japanese mines). Hirokawa Sadahide, "Hokkaidō ni okeru tankō rōdōsha no keisei to 1907 nen no hokutan sōgi" (Coal miners in Hokkaidō and the Hokutan mine strike of 1907), *Nihon shi kenkyū* (Japanese historical studies), no. 114.

Tomono Sotokichi, *Horonai kōzan bōdō shimatsu* (The Horonai coal mine riot) (Tokyo: Miyama Shobō, 1975).

Table C.2. Wage Change, Metal Mines Involved in Disputes in 1907

year[1]	Miners					Refinery Workers				
	1906	1907		1908		1906	1907		1908	
Name of Mine	wage[2]	wage	(change)	wage	(change)	wage	wage	(change)	wage	(change)
	sen	sen	%	sen	%	sen	sen	%	sen	%
Toki[3]	45.0	88.2	(196.0)	83.3	(94.4)	40.0	44.7	(111.8)	64.9	(145.2)
Ashio	72.5	85.7	(118.2)	84.5	(98.6)	44.6	49.0	(109.9)	50.0	(102.0)
Yūsenji	68.4	69.5	(101.6)	79.6	(114.5)	37.5	44.0	(117.3)	41.3	(93.9)
Takane	80.0	96.0	(120.0)	85.0	(88.5)	50.0	51.0	(102.0)	51.0	(100.0)
Makimine	59.5	70.0	(117.6)	71.1	(101.6)	39.4	44.7	(113.5)	46.1	(103.1)
Ani	44.9	64.0	(142.5)	60.0	(93.8)	40.0	39.0	(97.5)	44.0	(112.8)
Besshi	83.3	80.6	(96.2)	79.8	(99.0)	66.8	67.5	(101.0)	67.2	(99.6)
Obie	59.4	69.6	(117.2)	67.5	(97.0)	52.5	45.2	(86.1)	46.0	(101.8)
Osarizawa	63.9	73.7	(115.3)	74.0	(100.4)	44.0	44.2	(100.5)	44.4	(100.5)

Notes: 1. Yearly figures are for the end of June. 2. Average daily wage; 100 sen = 1 yen. 3. Toki mine sold all its raw ore and therefore had no refinery workers; the figures relate to underground haulage workers

Source: Nōshōmushō, kōzan kyoku (Ministry of Agriculture and Commerce Mining Bureau) Honpo kōgyō ippan (Trends of Japanese Mining) (Tokyo: Nōshōmushō, 1907–9)

Table C.3. Wage Change, Coal Mines Involved in Disputes in 1907

year[1]	Miners					Underground Haulers				
	1906	1907	(change)	1908	(change)	1906	1907	(change)	1908	(change)
Name of Mine	wage[2]	wage	%	wage	%	wage	wage	%	wage	%
	sen	sen		sen		sen	sen		sen	
Ikushunbetsu	99.9	108.2	(108.3)	104.0	(96.1)	61.1	78.0	(127.7)	66.0	(84.6)
Horonai	100.2	109.3	(109.1)	110.0	(100.6)	61.9	76.1	(122.9)	68.0	(89.4)
Yūbari-No. 1	134.3	135.0	(100.5)	151.3	(112.1)	87.7	97.6	(111.3)	117.3	(120.2)
Hōshu	70.0	105.0	(150.0)	104.0	(99.1)	47.0	46.5	(98.9)	46.5	(100.0)

Notes: 1. Yearly figures are for the end of June. 2. Average daily wage; 100 sen = 1 yen.

Source: Nōshōmushō, kōzan kyoku (Ministry of Agriculture and Commerce, Mining Bureau) *Honpo kōgyō ippan* (Trends of Japanese Mining) (Tokyo: Nōshōmusho, 1907–9).

unionize the workforce that had been led by Nagaoka Tsuruzō and Minami Sukematsu. The brotherhoods fell under the control of the lodge bosses and their autonomy was seriously weakened.

Further, while the mine's managers thoroughly investigated the riot and learned a number of valuable lessons, with the collapse of the Shiseikai the workers had no organization in which they might accumulate similar knowledge. The Shiseikai activists, including Minami and Nagaoka, had few experiences of reviewing a past struggle, nor had they been trained to do so. Most of the activists were thrown into jail after their arrest and later put on trial on charges of inciting civil disorder. Those lucky enough not to be arrested were chased out of Ashio and went their separate ways. The Utsunomiya District Court declared the leading Shiseikai activists—Minami, Nagaoka, Imori Shingo, Hayashi Kotarō, Yamamoto Riichirō—innocent; only Ōnishi Saichi was found guilty. The public prosecutor appealed these verdicts, but his appeals were rejected by both the High Court and the Supreme Court.[5]

After his release, Nagaoka went to work for the *Shakai shinbun*, a newspaper run by the leading socialist, Katayama Sen. He also took part in speaking tours, but his calls for the formation of a national miners' union were not heeded. Until the riot, Nagaoka and the other activists had been able to remain in Ashio and continue their work, even after the order restricting his activities had been issued in May 1905. But after the riot, they were constantly followed about by the police from the moment they set foot in the town, and the company fired any workers who were seen fraternizing with them. A police box was erected in front of the shop owned by the parents of the activist Hayashi Kotarō, and all the shop's customers were questioned by police as they went in or out. Such surveillance was not restricted to Ashio. Imori Shingo moved to the Ikuno mine and tried to continue his organizing work there, but he was blacklisted and could not get a job.[6] In fact, none of the Ashio activists were able to make direct use of their experience in the months and years after the riot.

And yet, the work of the Shiseikai activists was not entirely fruitless. When more sustained union activities emerged in Japan just over a decade after the riot, strong organizations sprang up not only in shipyards and arsenals, but at mines all across the nation, beginning with the Ashio copper mine and the Yūbari coal mine. In the autumn of 1919 three unions emerged to represent the interests of miners: the All-Japan Mine Workers' League

(Dai Nippon Kōzan Rōdō Dōmeikai; hereafter AJML), the National Miners' Union (Zenkoku Kōfu Kumiai), and the mining section of the Friendly Society (Yūaikai). Of these, the AJML established a strong base at Ashio and Kamaishi and claimed six thousand members at its peak. It played the leading role in the Ashio strike of 1919 in which demands were pressed for higher wages, the abolition of the lodge system, and the right of collective bargaining. The second of these unions, the National Miners' Union, was formed by the members of the Shinjinkai of Tokyo University with the intention of transforming the mining brotherhoods into a thoroughly modern trade union. This union also drew its main support from Ashio, as well as the Yūbari coal mine. Its membership reached some two thousand men in twenty-one branches nationwide at its peak.[7] The third of these groups, the miners' section of the Yūaikai, was centered at Jōban coal field, with branches at the Hitachi and Ogoya metal mines and the Tagawa coal mine. Its influence was strongest among machinists at the mines rather than miners. In October 1920 these three unions amalgamated to form the All-Japan General Mine Workers' Federation (Zen Nihon Kōfu Sōrengō kai; hereafter AJGMF), one of the industrywide labor unions in existence in Japan before World War II. The AJGMF spearheaded major disputes at Ashio, Yūbari, Ogoya, and Besshi, and conducted bitter struggles during the economic depression that hit the metal mining industry in 1920. Like the National Miners' Union, its main organizational bases were Ashio and Yūbari.

It hardly seems a coincidence that Ashio and Yūbari, the two mines where Nagaoka Tsuruzō and Minami Sukematsu had been most active, emerged as the strongholds of union organizing after World War I. While the evidence is fragmentary, it does suggest that the organizing activity of these two men was connected with the postwar movement. For example, the founder of the AJML, Matsuba Kōju, had been a boss at a lodge for day laborers at Tsūdō and his name appears on the wage hike petition put forward by the lodge bosses in 1907. Surely his experience of the riot had some impact on his decision to found the AJML and fight for the abolition of the lodge system. And without question, activists in the postwar organizing movement understood themselves to be building on the legacy of the earlier era. Yasuda Tametarō first joined the National Miners' Union, then served as chairman of the Yūbari branch of the AJGMF, and in the 1920s joined the Nankatsu Labor Association.[8] He spoke in public about his own experiences at Ashio at the time of the riot and declared: "the cause of that great struggle between workers and capitalists was the violence perpetrated by the management."[9] The AJGMF magazine, *Kōzan rōdōsha* (Mine worker), carried an article of memoirs by a former activist who had been a hauler at Ashio at the time of the riot.[10] He describes how management stirred up the violence once the dispute was underway and proudly states that Ashio was "the birthplace of the labor movement in the Japanese metal mining industry." Other evidence comes from Taguchi Kamezō, a former Ashio worker (though not a miner) who later became a prominent labor leader as chairman of the Kantō Metal Workers Union in the General Federation of Labor of Japan (Sōdōmei), and served as chairman of the Kantō Labor League at the time of the Sōdōmei split in 1925. He was a worker in the engineering workshops at Ashio who witnessed the riot, and he later claimed, "that was when I resolved to become a labor leader."[11]

Approaching the question of legacies from another angle, would the Ashio branch of Shiseikai have sustained itself if the 1907 call for a wage increase had not ended as it did? If so, what effect would that have had on the postwar development of union organization in the metal mining industry? Even supposing that the wage campaign had succeeded without violence, it is highly unlikely that Shiseikai could have survived until the end of World War I. Nevertheless, the joint action of the Shiseikai and the mining brotherhood is a rare example in Japanese history of the potential for a traditional trade organization of workers to develop into a modern labor union. As such, these connections merit further examination.

The Japan Socialist Party (Nihon shakaitō)

When the Ashio branch of Shiseikai collapsed, there existed one organization that greatly valued the efforts of the Ashio rioters and argued they had shown a direction that the socialist movement ought to take. This was the Japan Socialist Party (Nihon shakaitō), to which Nagaoka Tsuruzō, Minami Sukematsu, Hayashi Kotarō, Kishi Kiyoshi, and Takeda Seinosuke all belonged.[12] Its response to the riot shed light on the organization's character. On 17 February 1907, coincidentally just ten days after the riot ended, the party held its second annual convention in Tokyo. Over sixty delegates from around the country attended. At the start of the meeting Ishikawa Sanshirō urgently moved that a telegram be sent in the name of the conference to comrades Minami, Nagaoka, and Nishikawa, at that moment in jail on charges stemming from the riot. The proposal was met with spontaneous applause by the whole conference. Later, article 1 of the party's bylaws was revised from "the party shall promote socialism in accord with the laws of the land" to "the party aims at the realization of socialism." A debate followed on a resolution put forward by Sakai Toshihiko on behalf of the executive council. The main speakers were Kōtoku Shusui and Tazoe Tetsuji. The debate marked the first time that the Japanese socialist movement had debated its principles in public.

Kōtoku argued for the principle of "direct action" to replace the existing policy of "parliamentary action." He supported his position by invoking the Ashio riot. He compared its impact to that of the charismatic Tanaka Shōzō, who had been campaigning for years against the Ashio owners, demanding redress for the immense damage to farmland from the mine's polluted runoff waters.

Old Tanaka Shōzō is a man worthy of the greatest respect. In the next ten years or so, we are likely to see half a dozen of his caliber in the Diet. But what has actually resulted from 20 years of Tanaka Shōzō raising his voice over there? None of you were able to even shake a finger at Furukawa's Ashio copper mine. But look what the workers of Ashio were able to achieve in just three days! They sent shivers down the spines of the entire ruling class! (applause) Yes, violence is evil, but we must recognize that what could not be achieved in twenty years was achieved by just three days of direct action. I am not saying that we should all go out on strike right away, but the working class must build up its strength through solidarity and experience.[13]

Kōtoku, Tazoe, and the convention participants were united in their support of the clause in the resolution that read, "the party shall champion the class aims of working people, and shall serve those aims in solidarity with the working class," but Kōtoku had no conception of the patience and forbearance that were required to champion those class aims. He stressed the fact that the Ashio riot had frightened the ruling class and praised the "effectiveness" of the workers' action. What Kōtoku and those who applauded his speech at the convention did not know was that Shiseikai activists like Nagaoka Tsuruzō, who knew the meaning of poverty and oppression and had been working to "champion the class aims of working people" in constant solidarity with them, even to the point of sacrificing their own families' welfare, had actually been striving desperately to prevent the workers from resorting to violence.[14] Further, the convention-goers did not understand that the riot itself had, in a sense, taken place only as the result of determined and stubborn efforts of organizers like Nagaoka to nurture the solidarity of the workers.

Instead, Kōtoku emphasized and praised what he saw as the spontaneous nature of the riot. He argued that "when it comes to the public takeover of capitalists' assets, the self-awareness and discipline of the workers will enable this to be achieved without leaders. Riots are undesirable, but, as in the streetcar riots, the riots over the peace treaty, and this Ashio riot, they happen without leaders.[15] The [Ashio] men have no leaders. They simply resorted to direct action." Kōtoku was unaware that during the weeks and months before the riot, the membership of Shiseikai had increased dramatically through the efforts of "leaders" like Minami Sukematsu, who had set aside the old-style mutual aid organization of the Metal Workers' Union a decade before in favor of an organization that raised and vigorously pursued specific demands for higher wages and the removal of Chinese rice. Not only Kōtoku but his supporters and opponents alike were debating the "awareness and discipline of the working class" with scarcely any knowledge of the workers' situation or any effort to acquire such knowledge directly. They were even unaware of the work of organizers at Ashio who were members of their own party! The Japan Socialist Party at that time was in fact hardly more than a philosophical movement of intellectuals, by intellectuals, and for intellectuals.

The Impact on Management

Those who learned most from the riot were the Ashio managers, as might be expected given their superior resources of money, personnel, and organization. They displayed their new knowledge clearly in a document titled "Report on the Ashio Riot," compiled in the wake of the incident by the mine office staff. After describing the course of the riot, the report takes up its "direct" and "indirect" impact. Direct effects include wage hikes and revision of the regulations concerning worker illness and accident benefits. Although the increase did not approach the 60 percent raise sought by miners and lodge bosses, wages did rise by an average of nearly 20 percent. The improvement in accident benefits and sick pay probably reflected an awareness of Nagaoka's constant efforts to raise the issue of injured workers.

The report neglected to mention, however, the most significant direct effect of the riot; the reorganization of the brotherhoods and the lodging system. The main points were as follows. After the riot the Ashio miners' brotherhoods were forced to abolish the assembly system of representation, and the brotherhoods were incorporated into the lodge system as a part of the labor management apparatus. But the brotherhoods did not lose their autonomy altogether; in the union movement that emerged after World War I, the National Miners' Union based predominantly at Ashio and Yūbari had some success in organizing along the lines of the brotherhood structure.

In addition, the lodge system itself came under tighter management control. Of particular importance was an increase in the autonomy of the miners via further encroachment on the exploitative intermediary role of the lodge bosses. The rules were changed so that three months after hiring, a mine worker was regarded as "independent." He was able to receive his wages directly from the mine office and could buy food and supplies himself from the company stores. Further, individual lodge bosses had been able to exploit their men by charging high prices for goods and loans obtained through the lodge, but this possibility was removed by the company's new stipulation that price increases within the lodge first had to be agreed upon by a "lodge union" consisting of all the lodge bosses. At the same time, the bosses' allowance was increased to compensate them for their loss of income. Together, these measures significantly weakened the lodge bosses in their relationship to management.

But the more interesting portion of the report on the riot was the section dealing with its "indirect" effects:

The social impact of the Ashio riot has been considerable, and space allows us to cite only the main points of that impact. (1) At just this one company, a force of over 50 special constables was required to maintain order among the workers after the riot had been suppressed. (2) This 50-man plus increase at the Ashio local police station created an imbalance with other stations, and the Ashio station consequently was elevated to the status of a central station. (3) Low-ranking officials in direct contact with the workers were in the habit of treating them badly, but whether they are sincere in this change or not, the riot has in any case forced them to mend their ways and respect the character [*jinkaku*] of their subordinates more. (4) Officials have come to harmonize their thinking with some of the more influential miners. (5) The company has begun to pay serious attention to the wishes of the workers. (6) Managers have realized that the workers are as important a resource as capital in the management of the enterprise, and the workers' status has consequently been improved. (7) After the Ashio riot, workers nationwide took similar action to press their claims, causing great alarm among employers and financiers. (8) Society as a whole has learned how dangerous the combination of simple-minded, ignorant workers and ultra-radical socialists can be. Whatever the causes of the riot, buildings were in fact destroyed, people wounded, and the prefectural authorities powerless to stop the violence. In the end, the hellish situation at the mine created by the mindless fury of the workers could only be dealt with by recourse to the full powers of the state. All this can only be deplored in the strongest possible terms.[16]

What is most striking about this report is the reference to the officials having to show greater respect for the character (*jinkaku*) of the workers.[17] This is less the report writer's self-criticism than it is a general criticism of the way officials treated workers. While recognizing that the officials' change of heart may not have been genuine, he notes that they "have come to harmonize their thinking with some of the more influential miners," that "the company has begun to pay serious attention to the wishes of the workers," and that "managers have realized that the workers are as important a resource as capital in the management of the enterprise."

After World War I, recognition of worker "dignity" or "character" (*jinkaku*) was one of the union movement's principal demands. In addition, a key slogan of management policy at that time was "harmonizing the thinking of workers and staff." This slogan was reflected in new labor-management policies which set up factory councils and company unions in response to the union movement at many companies. That Ashio's managers were so quick, indeed prescient, in recognizing this situation is significant, as is their concrete response to this recognition in the form of new policies, albeit partial ones. One such response was the inauguration in May 1913 of a monthly magazine for Ashio workers, *Ashio dōzan kōfu no tomo* (The Ashio mine workers' friend).[18] In addition to essays that were little more than sermons, it carried letters and articles by workers as well as information on the finances of the mutual aid council. This information can be seen as a response to the demand for publication of this council's budget, one of the twenty-four demands put forward by the brotherhoods just before the riot.

The company's magazine deserves special mention, because it was a concrete sign that Japanese employers were moving away from the old notion of workers as a "labor force" supplied by and controlled through the lodge bosses, themselves workers, and instead were beginning to think in terms of workers as regular employees under the direct control of the company.

Impact on the State

The Ashio riot sparked a series of strikes and riots across the country, the largest number of industrial actions of any year before World War I. Troops were needed to quell the riots at the Sumitomo Besshi mine, run by the prime minister's brother, and the Ashio mine, under the effective control of the home minister, Hara Kei. On each of these occasions, the home minister reported on the extent of the rioting and the measures taken to deal with it in an audience with the emperor.[19] Despite all this, after the events of that tumultuous year the labor policies of the state did not noticeably change. It is not clear why this is the case. I suspect that Hara and other government officials really believed the rioting was simply the result of socialist agitation, so that measures to deal with socialism were more important than new labor policies. In addition, with the Public Order and Police Law already in force, government leaders felt no need for new legislation.[20]

Nevertheless, in the face of the string of riots at Ashio, Horonai, and Besshi, the government was not entirely bereft of policy. A number of new steps were taken at the administrative level. One concerned the policing of mines, as reported in the *Osaka asahi shimbun* of 13 June 1907:

Authorities Clamp Down on Miners

Since the recent mine riots the authorities have been paying closer attention to enforcing mining laws and regulations, and tighter policing of the mines. Every mine now usually has mine police underground keeping an eye on the workers. The police are thoroughly informed as to every aspect of relations between mine owners, miners, and other workers, and between mine officials, miners and other workers, and they are determined to prevent a recurrence of riotous behavior.

What the Home Ministry had in mind by "tighter policing" and enforcement of regulations was not at all the enforcement of mine safety that Nagaoka Tsuruzō had constantly called for.[21] Rather, their new "policing" reflected the Ministry's recognition that during the riot, the police had been unable to enter the dark underground labyrinth of the pits. The Ministry sought to rectify this situation with regular underground police patrols.

At the same time, the police also moved to restrict the mobility of so-called traveling miners. Such efforts stemmed from awareness that the movement of these men from mine to mine, mediated by the brotherhoods, played a role in the spread of the rioting. Soon after the Besshi riot the *Osaka asahi shimbun* carried the following report:

Miners' Movements Restricted

Since the riots at the Ashio and Besshi copper mines and the Horonai coal mine, authorities have been anxiously seeking ways of controlling the situation. All agree that the policing of mines should be more rigorous and that the first requirement is for police officers to be better informed about the situation in mining. But actually achieving this goal is no simple matter; a great many factors have to be taken into consideration. It is extremely difficult to implement normal instructions thoroughly. There must be the fullest cooperation with the superior officer responsible for the policing of a particular mine. The most urgent requirement at present is to control so-called traveling miners, but although mine owners agree not to employ men who have been ejected from other mines for some impropriety or other, in practice this agreement cannot be enforced easily. Nevertheless, it is clear that all subsequent disturbances since the Ashio riot have been caused by the agitators of these "travelers." The Ashio riot itself was not unrelated to the violence at the Yūbari mine of last year [1906], and the strictest measures ought to have been taken at that time to prevent Yūbari miners from coming to Ashio.[22]

How the authorities intended to enforce restrictions on miners' movements is not clear. As long as they could not train new workers themselves, mine owners were dependent on the brotherhoods for the training of miners and were thus in no position to stop employing miners from other mines. Even at Ashio, managers first began planning to train their own miners only after the riot. But from this time on, the police began to investigate all those arriving at the mine seeking employment, and this was certainly part of a policy to restrict labor movement organizing. Shiseikai members and all those with a history of labor movement activity were blacklisted by management, refused employment, and forced to leave town by the police, even if they had committed no specific offense.

As a result of requests made by the Furukawa Company, Ashio received special attention in the form of increased police surveillance. On 5 March, only a month after the riot, the number of "requested constables" on duty was suddenly increased from five to forty-five.[23] Six police boxes were erected at Honzan, Tsūdō, and Kodaki, and eighteen, nine, and eleven officers, respectively, were posted to them. This brought the total police strength at Ashio to sixty-two. The status of the Ashio station was raised from a branch of the Nikkō constabulary to that of a full station in its own right. The first police chief of the new Ashio station was Tadokoro Tanemi, who had been at the forefront of the authorities' suppression of the riot. The superior officer in charge at the time of the riot, Fujiyama Sainosuke, had to resign to take responsibility for the riot, but he soon found a job with the Furukawa Company.

SUBJECTS FOR FUTURE RESEARCH

In closing, I would like to address a few more general issues related to the specific findings of this study and suggest some directions for future research. My points here are less conclusions than interim suggestions, for my method in this book has not been to develop a general theory but to begin with the claims of other scholars, examine them in a new light, and point out the limits or defects in existing theories. I have found that in this process of comparing my findings to those of previous researchers, rejecting old explanations that cannot make sense of the evidence and contriving new explanations in their place, the solution to one problem would often throw up a new one which then demanded my attention. My hope in this book has been that readers might gain something not only from the rather limited interim conclusions to follow, but also from following this process of investigation and rethinking old paradigms.

Economism in Japanese Labor Studies

Throughout this book, I have argued that studies of labor-capital relations and the labor movement as developed by scholars of modern Japanese history and Japanese capitalism have been extremely and excessively economistic. I mean this in the following two senses.

First, scholars have largely ignored the historical, social, and cultural environment in which labor-capital relations are embedded. In particular, there has been little consideration of one factor vital for understanding the labor movement: the subjectivity of the workers themselves—how they lived, worked, thought, and felt. By now it is commonplace to assert that the formation and development of the labor movement does not simply or directly result from the increasing impoverishment of workers, but most Japanese histories of modern Japan and the Japanese labor movement have yet to adopt this perspective. This may be a strong statement, but we can certainly say that very few concrete studies of the labor movement have incorporated such a perspective. The labor histories of other nations in recent years, especially the advanced nations in Europe and North America, have sought to understand the subjective formation of the labor movement in historical perspective, but comparable examination of the history of the working class in Japan has not taken place. The main reason for this is the status of labor history as a relatively late-developing field of inquiry.

The second point is also related to the tendency to ignore or treat lightly the subjective dimension. Academic studies of workers' conditions, especially workers' conditions before World War II, have been excessively economistic. Academic understanding of what "poverty" meant to workers has been far too simplistic. For this reason, whatever industry or occupation is being discussed, low wages and long working hours are taken for granted, and working conditions are invariably described with set phrases such as *slavery, unbelievably wretched, harsh, extremely poor.* There is no detailed analysis of the workers' conditions, no attempt at a comprehensive grasp of their situation.

Such an approach invariably leads scholars to explain disputes and riots as "spontaneous outbursts of opposition" to economic privation. The atomized labor force theory is not simply an economistic explanation; it owes much to the discipline of sociology. But the lengthy quote at the start of chapter 1 that presents this theory reveals that a simplistic economism is implicit in it, or rather forms a premise of it.

I am not denying here that hunger is a factor in labor disputes and riots. The actions of 1907 were clearly related to the inflation of that year. Yet not all workers who may be enduring "unbelievably wretched conditions" undertake collective actions to defend themselves. We can find numerous examples of people who, though starving, did not organize a movement to resist their oppression. Is it not in fact the case that, in the history of human-ity, examples where those suffering from starvation took mass action to improve their situation are in the minority? Economic factors alone are simply insufficient to account for labor disputes and riots.

Our analysis of the Ashio riot revealed that those who led the campaign for higher wages were the underground miners, the highest paid of Ashio's workers. Of course they were poor in the overall context of Japanese society at that time, but theirs was not the poverty of hunger and near-starvation. Their problem was that they could remember a time in the recent past when they had been relatively "better off" compared to other workers at Ashio and to workers in other industries. Violence broke out, in response to a pre-cipitating factor, at the historical moment when they had lost that relative affluence or seemed about to lose it.

The actual spark may indeed have been a random attack on a super-visor by a miner fed up with the arrogance of mine "officials." But in a broader sense there were also important outside influences: the constant calls to action from labor activists such as Minami Sukematsu and Nagaoka Tsuruzō and the news of violence at other mines. At the same time, in order to respond to such outside influences and develop a "movement," some kind of organization was necessary. Mine workers were a significant force in the pre–World War I labor movement because the mining industry con-centrated large numbers of male workers in a single place and a single enter-prise, but in addition, we cannot explain the mine workers' role without reference to their brotherhood organizations. Whether in assemblies of the whole, or meetings of miners' representatives from the various lodges, miners were accustomed to gathering on a regular basis to exchange views, elect representatives, and pass resolutions duly adopted as the general will of all miners and considered binding on them. Through the medium of the brotherhoods, they were accustomed to collective action; this was a critical factor enabling their mass actions in the twentieth century.

That the most militant workers were not the poorest but the more affluent was a phenomenon true at Ashio and all the major mines that had expanded rapidly in the decade or so before 1907. The other mines that experienced rioting that year—Besshi, Yūbari, and Horonai—were all relatively "high-wage" mines. Why, then, did their workers riot? Although circumstances in each mine differed somewhat, it appears to me that all these mines had the following factors in common.

First, well before the riots, output rose substantially at each mine due to the discovery of rich new ore lodes or coal seams. This produced a demand for labor greater than the local supply. To attract labor from further afield, these mines therefore paid higher wages than elsewhere; the high quality of output from the new lodes and seams enabled the companies to pay these wages. However, once a sufficient number of workers had been secured, the mines sought to limit further wage increases. The metal mining industry in particular faced sharp fluctuations in world market prices, and low prices put pressure on mines to reduce wages. Yet once workers were accustomed to a higher standard of living, it was difficult for management to simply cut wages. Meanwhile, the exploitative lodge system took shape in these same years premised on these relatively high wage levels, but the system remained in place even if the wage levels fell, and workers felt the squeeze. When inflation compounded the problem, miner households faced the choice of going into debt or cutting back their standard of living. Often they did both. Workers in this situation were attracted to the labor movement. Further, while the mines employed large numbers of workers, managers did not control them directly and were thus unable to grasp or address the extensive worker frustrations. Instead, the companies sought to maintain discipline with various rules, regulations, and penalties, which only angered the workers further.

Similar clashes took place in large companies outside the mining industry. The engineers' strike of 1898 at the Japan Railway Company, for example, was one of the most famous strikes in the history of the Japanese labor movement. The wages of the locomotive engineers were already among the highest in Japan at the time, but the men went on strike for still higher wages because "after the late 1880s, and especially following the severe inflation of the period after the Sino-Japanese War (1894–95), most workers' nominal wages rose, whereas their own wages did not."[24] A comparable situation led to the dispute at the naval arsenal at Kure in August 1906: "while workers had been able to earn high wages during the [Russo-Japanese] war due to overtime work and night shifts, work schedules were cut back after the war and night shifts were canceled. Wages thus dropped considerably, and on top of this, today's inflation has made life even more difficult. What finally stirred ordinary workers to rise up in anger was the arbitrariness and petty despotism of foreman and bosses with regard to promotions."[25] In both these examples, poverty was one factor in the disputes, but this was clearly not the sort of poverty one associates with "working conditions akin to slavery." I will not offer further examples here, but one can find a number of similar disputes in the years after World War I as well.

Workers' Consciousness

As mentioned in the introduction, since 1971 I have been arguing that detailed case studies of labor disputes are both significant and necessary undertakings for labor historians. Through analysis of workers' actions in moments of struggle, we gain insight into the consciousness and ideas of workers, both leaders and the rank and file, who rarely leave behind documentary accounts of their thinking. In addition, by investigating the "abnormal circumstances" of a moment of dispute, one can discover information about the "normal circumstances" of working-class existence that in "normal" times are taken for granted and not recorded. I began to articulate this position at more or less the same time that the fields of social and labor history in the West were rapidly expanding, and scholars were beginning to stress the importance of "mentalité" and "consciousness" and discuss methods of studying these phenomena.

Has this examination of the Ashio riot yielded fruits that validate my claims on behalf of "dispute research"? The reader must ultimately decide, but let me suggest a few insights of this study.

First, examination of the riots has made clear how profoundly the mine workers resented discriminatory treatment. Their strong support for the Shiseikai's call to "eliminate Nanking rice" reflected the workers' anger that officials could buy Japanese rice while they could not. The course of the "riot" itself, with its attacks on mine supervisors, makes this anger all the more evident. Pressing the point somewhat, one could even call the Ashio riot an act of judgment and revenge on the officials. Of particular note, this violence targeted university-educated staff less than the lower-level officials promoted from among the workers, probably because the latter worked closely with the miners every day and demanded bribes in the course of setting wages. Despite sharing common origins with the workers, the supervisors and overseers tended to put on airs once promoted and look down on their former comrades. Accumulated frustration and resentment at such "status discrimination" moved these men to violence during the riot. To make sense of the particular features and the historical evolution of Japan's labor-capital relations, we must pay attention to the structure of the relationship between production workers and company staff, and changes in that relationship, in other cases as well.

Past studies of incidents such as the Ashio riot or other labor disputes have ignored or underemphasized the significance of worker violence against officials, seeing it as something purely emotional, lacking any "conscious" motivation. At the same time, past studies have been equally inclined to jump to the conclusion that any dispute is a sign of the heightened class consciousness of the working class. Both these perspectives overlook a point essential to a full understanding of Japanese workers: anger at discrimination was by no means limited to disputes and riots in the early industrial era. Although there are differences in extent, we can find similar rage in many of the major labor disputes of both the pre–World War II and immediate postwar periods. To define this anger simply as a sign of greater working-class consciousness is to lose sight of a central characteristic of the mentality of Japanese workers.

The strike just mentioned of the Japan Railway Company locomotive engineers is an excellent example of anger at discrimination motivating a major dispute. The engineers demanded that their status be raised to the level of the office staff and that their job title be changed from *kikankata,* a term reminiscent of the "horse-drawn carriage masters" of old, to *kikanshu* (locomotive engineer). They insisted they were technicians, not mere workers or laborers, and that they therefore deserved to be treated as staff employees and paid accordingly. They were particularly angry that the company barred them from promotion to the post of station master. Of course, for these men as for the workers at the Kure naval arsenal, a wage increase was an important objective. But their motivation was not only economic; it also reflected a desire for greater social recognition and respect for their worth as human beings. Thus, it is significant that the railway workers described their protest as a demand for "better treatment" and named their organization the Grand Alliance for Better Treatment. "Better treatment," of course, had two meanings: improved conditions in the form of higher wages, and higher status.

To be sure, troubled relations between workers and staff employees, especially those who themselves had been former workers, are by no means unique to Japan. Yet such tensions were arguably of particular importance in Japan because of the nature of the changes brought about by the Meiji

Restoration of 1868. The new Meiji government abolished the social order in which status was rigidly defined. The new equality among the four feudal-era classes of samurai, peasant, artisan, and merchant was more than nominal; substantial social changes did ensue.[26] But literal equality was not achieved in post-Restoration society; social distinctions based on occupation remained. Because labor in new occupations in factories and mines was undertaken by people whose economic deprivation left them no other choice, the rest of society scorned these workers as members of "lower-stratum society." Factory workers were considered to occupy an even lower rung on the social ladder than farmers, craftsmen, or merchants, whose social ranking had roots in the old order. The power of this older value system is also revealed by the fact that factory workers disliked the neologism *shokkō* (factory hand) and spoke of themselves as *shokunin,* an old word for artisan.

Workers had to endure not only such discrimination in society at large, but discrimination in the workplace as well. Modern industrial processes required a division of labor, and it was only natural that people whose mentality had been molded by experience within a feudal social structure would interpret the job categories of the new industrial order in terms of the status divisions of the old order. Industrial workers were by no means opposed to status difference as such, but they failed to see why they should be regarded as members of a "lower stratum" or why they should be relegated to the bottom of the company pecking order simply because they were workers. They did not share the sentiment common among British workers of the same period that a worker's son should of course become a worker, or the British workers' pride in belonging to the working class. To the contrary, Japanese factory workers and miners were unwilling members of the working class who would have preferred not to be workers at all. For them, higher social status was an important goal. Given this goal, we can understand why workers who were promoted to "official" rank believed they had taken the first step on the road out of the working class and thus tended to look down on their former comrades. We can equally well understand that their former comrades harbored bitter resentment against such "officials."

Although workers in Japan were very sensitive to "discrimination" and felt a strong emotional demand for the treatment accorded "normal people," they did not oppose differentiation in general. They did not object to high status for a person with superior talents, but they resented the higher status of those with indifferent ability. In corporations of the prewar era, it was primarily educational background and secondarily personal connections that decided one's place in the company hierarchy. While educational attainment reflected ability to an extent, a family's wealth was a factor as well. The quality of elementary education did not differ by social background, in contrast to the case in England, as the children of landlords and tenants sat next to each other in class and were ranked in accord with their ability; however, only a child with financial resources could go beyond the elementary level. Not a few Japanese labor leaders before the 1950s joined the labor movement out of frustration that, because of their family's meager resources, they had been unable to go on to higher education. They had to watch while others, richer but less gifted than they, had gone on to higher education and become members of the elite. Another reason, then, why the relatively well-paid, and not the poorest, workers led the labor protest was that they felt this kind of discrimination most keenly.

Japanese workers, who believed that ranking in accord with individual achievement was only right and proper, were unlikely to accept a basic principle of unions in the West, especially traditional craft unions, which sought to eliminate competition among workers. For example, organized workers in Japan have hardly ever mounted protests against piece-rate work as such. Notwithstanding the fact that bribery was so widespread at Ashio precisely because of piece-rate wages, not a single voice was raised against the system. Although union platforms today might deny this, is a deeply rooted willingness to accept competition among workers not still present? Rather than objecting to status differences based on merit, union members object above all to treatment that fails to recognize their ability.

To pursue this matter of worker ideas about ability and status further, cross-national comparisons are useful, indeed necessary.[27] Unfortunately, I fear I have not been sufficiently comparative in this study. For example, in discussing the subcontracting system in chapter 2, I said that it was only natural that a piece-rate system should have developed for underground work where centralized managerial supervision was obviously more difficult than in factories. However, when I later studied the history of mining in other countries, I discovered that although subcontracting systems (such as tutwork, tribute systems, and butty systems) and piece-rate wages were indeed common among underground miners, fixed daily wages were in fact the norm for miners in the western United States. And in fact, one American miners' union, the Western Federation of Miners, campaigned for the principle of a fixed rate for all underground workers, regardless of job category or skill level.[28] In other words, in the logic of capital, piece-rate work was necessary given the difficulty of supervising and directing men underground, but whether or not such a system was imposed depended on the response of the workers and on the balance of power between workers and capital. Why then, in contrast to miners in the western United States, did Japanese miners not oppose piece-rate systems? In the following section, I suggest that the answer to this question stems from different traditions of craft unions and craft guilds, but a firm conclusion requires a good deal more research.

Premodern Legacies

The matter of traditions inherited from premodern society has been virtually ignored by the economistic scholarship of Japanese labor historians, but any serious study of worker subjectivity must pay attention to this issue. I have dwelled at length on the important role played by the mining brotherhoods that originated in the Tokugawa era in the strikes and riots of the early twentieth century. Any discussion of the labor movement among miners in twentieth-century Japan must take into account these brotherhoods as well as the customs of comradeship and mutual aid among miners of the Tokugawa period. The monthly rotation and shared responsibilities of the brotherhood executive committee membership (the ōtōban) and the practice of decision making by unanimous vote of all brotherhood members were social practices common to many organizations of the Tokugawa era.

The role of the brotherhoods was not the only aspect of the Ashio riot in which behavior and values common to popular movements of early modern society were manifest. In the attack on the residence of the mine director, Minami Teizō, the leader told the men with him to "eat and drink all you like; smash the place thoroughly, but no looting." Such an attitude was typical of the peasants' riots of the Edo period. Also, at moments of labor dispute in Japan, workers have consistently tended to demand human "sincerity" of management and officials, as well as raise economic demands. In a society where the claim to leadership by those of superior status is made on the basis of higher moral and human qualities as well as on ability, to lack "sincerity" or humane feelings is to place one's legitimacy as a leader in jeopardy.

Further, in labor disputes of the modern era, rather than seek to clarify points of conflict between labor and management to arrive at a compromise, both parties have tended to stick to their position and finally participate in an emotional moment of reconciliation that in fact leaves the points of contention obscured. In the case of the Ashio riot, before resuming work, workers and mine company representatives together prayed at the mine's guardian shrine to "purify the mountain from the defilement caused by the riot" in a typically symbolic and very Japanese way of bringing a conflict to an end. Such behavior may not be unique to Japan, but I have rarely seen evidence of it in the labor history of the West.

In pursuing areas of connection to the early modern past, we must take note of the fact that Japanese labor leaders before World War I often sought to legitimize their claims in terms of positive law. Nagaoka Tsuruzō did just this in his speeches on the eve of the riot, which referred to the Mining Industry Law, the Mining Industry Police Ordinances, and even Article 17 of the Public Order and Police Law. In framing their demands in this fashion, workers were affirming that they too were subjects of the Japanese Empire, who bore a heavy burden in building a "rich country and a strong army."[29] Thus, to build a labor movement in the face of severe government repression, workers appealed to state ideology and sought to appropriate for their own purposes the notion at the heart of the *modern* emperor system of *ikkun bammin* ("the whole nation under the emperor," literally "one lord, ten thousand people"). And yet, despite this appeal to the ideology of the modern state, labor leaders rarely made their claims in the name of individual human rights or natural law, and these concepts did not sink deep roots.[30] Why was this so? I do not believe it is possible to answer this long-debated question, as so many have done, by pointing to the premodern character of state and society in modern Japan stemming from an incomplete bourgeois revolution. Rather, answers must be sought in the nature of early modern society.[31]

Historical studies of modern Japan, however, have shown very little concern with such links to premodern society. This is particularly true of labor movement history. Most studies in modern labor history begin after the Meiji Restoration (1868), usually in fact after the Sino-Japanese War (1894–95). Hardly any Japanese scholars have investigated how or even whether preindustrial working practices, forms of organization, or popular values influenced worker organizations and the labor movement of the industrial era. Even those few scholars who have posited important connections to the past have tended, as with the migrant labor theory, to frame the question as one of "semifeudal" legacies or "premodern backwardness." In such interpretations, the mining brotherhoods have long been regarded as negative impediments to labor organizing.

We must go beyond such negative interpretative perspectives. During the early years of industrialization, artisans formed the nucleus of the nation's pool of skilled workers. Relations between artisan organizations with origins even before the Edo era, and the Tokugawa or domain authorities, artisan values and working practices, and the connection of these to the evolution of working-class organizations and values in the industrial era—all are important problems demanding further study. Also, from a different perspective than that of the migrant labor theory, we must investigate the influence on industrial society of the working practices, organizational forms, and values of rural communities that later provided much of the nation's industrial labor force.

For several decades now, scholars of labor history in the West have been demonstrating that artisans rather than wage laborers in factories were the major actors in the early labor movements in Europe and the United States.[32] In Japan, by contrast, that factory workers created the labor movement has been an unquestioned "natural" premise. In part, this reflects the fact that, unlike in the West, skilled craftsmen such as carpenters, masons, and plasterers played minor roles in Japan's early labor movement. I believe that the reason for this lies in the absence in early modern Japan of Western-style guilds. As is well known, European guilds maintained long-established customs of controlling the labor supply and safeguarding working conditions by applying their strict rules of entry to apprenticeship and by setting limits on their members' working hours and jobs. By comparison, the rules on entry to a trade of early modern worker organizations in Japan were very weak. In fact, "weak" does not convey the situation well. In the well-known case of the Osaka carpenters guild late in the Tokugawa period, the elders who ran the guild ordered unlicensed Osaka area carpenters to obtain licenses so as to lighten the burden of guild obligations on each member.[33] In the case of the mining brotherhoods, the apprenticeship period of three years, three months, and ten days is thought to have functioned as a means of controlling entry, but it was hardly effective since there was no provision for penalties against those who moved on before serving the full term. I have discovered no instance of mine owners or engineers complaining that the brotherhoods obstructed efforts to increase the supply of skilled miners.[34] Although Japanese artisanal guilds did seek to regulate wages and working hours through formal agreements, the workers themselves were far from zealous in seeking to enforce such agreements, and neither the Tokugawa authorities nor society approved of them.

Determined efforts of European and American trade unions to oppose mechanization and rationalization and restrict entry to a trade are well known. We find almost no parallel endeavors in Japan, apart from the movement of rickshaw drivers against the introduction of trains or streetcars. In the western United States, miners campaigned against the use of dynamite, but no such movement emerged in Japan.[35] In the Ashio copper mine, the introduction of Western furnaces was a fatal blow to the livelihood of traditional Japanese furnace masters, but they made no attempt to block the use of the new technology either during or after the initial, experimental stage.

Why did European and American craft unions adopt such a militant stance, and why were their tactics successful to an extent? The answer must be sought in the practices and values of the preindustrial guilds. At the very basis of the guild was the attempt to limit competition between workers by controlling workers' output and wages. Such behavior was sanctioned not only by producers but by society at large. By contrast, social approval of limits on production did not develop in Tokugawa-period Japan. Why is this so? I suspect that the absence of a guild tradition is related to the strong meritocratic element in Japanese society, the belief that those with ability should be accorded high status and high financial rewards. Could it not be said that Japanese workers have demanded equality of opportunity rather than equality of result, as in the West? This entire question—the lack of a guild tradition, the meritocratic orientation of workers—is by no means irrelevant to the contemporary labor scene. It is related to the character of modern Japanese labor unions, typically organized by enterprise and consisting of blue- and white-collar regular employees only. A detailed examination of this subject lies beyond the scope of this book, but it deserves to be taken up in the future.[36]

Epilogue:

Japanese Miners in Comparative Perspective

In this epilogue, I compare the Japanese labor movement and labor-management relationship to those of other countries, with particular reference to the Ashio uprising. Given my limited reading on international labor movements and labor relations in English and limited knowledge of research on collective violence in other countries, I employ this comparative method mainly to clarify distinctive characteristics of Japanese labor relations.

SIMILARITIES

The Kerr and Siegel Thesis

A significant body of comparative research stresses the common character of labor and labor movements in the mining industry worldwide. Scholars have noted in particular that in all countries, miners are more prone to go on strike than workers in any other industry. Early industrial Japan, up to the 1910s, is no exception. Numerous labor conflicts took place in the mines, including some violent battles.[1]

One of the most influential works to analyze the propensity of miners to strike was an article published over forty years ago by Clark Kerr and Abraham Siegel. They conducted a comparative statistical study of various industries in eleven countries for which good statistical data were available—eight European nations, the United States, Australia, and New Zealand. They found that the highest propensity to strike in all countries was in mining, maritime, and longshore occupations.[2] They examined the commonalities behind this inclination to strike in these several industries, and did not focus on the mining industry in particular. But this article has been of particular interest to students of the history and sociology of mining labor. It has become an indispensable jumping-off point for the study of transnational mining labor movements and labor relations.

The key concept in the Kerr and Siegel study was the *isolated mass*. They argued that common to all strike-prone industries was the presence of *socially isolated masses:*

> The miners, the sailors, the longshoremen, the loggers . . . form isolated masses, almost a "race apart." They live in their own separate communities. . . . There are few neutrals in them to mediate the conflicts and dilute the mass. . . . The employees form a largely homogenous, undifferentiated mass. . . . Here you do not have the occupational stratification of the metal or building crafts, of the hotel or restaurant, or of the government bureau. In these communities there are not the myriad of voluntary associations with mixed memberships which characterize the multi-industry town. The employer is usually an absentee owner who . . . exhausts a mine and moves on. . . .
>
>   The worker is as detached from the employer as from the community at large. The strike for this isolated mass is a kind of colonial revolt against a far-removed authority, an outlet for accumulated tensions, and a substitute for occupational and social mobility.[3]

In addition, they suggested that characteristics of the jobs in question were related to the strike-happy behavior of these workers:

> The second hypothesis is that the inherent nature of the job determines, by selection and conditioning, the kinds of workers employed and their attitudes, and these workers, in turn, cause conflict or peace. If the job is physically difficult and unpleasant, unskilled or semi-skilled, and casual or seasonal, and fosters an independent spirit, it will draw tough, inconstant, combative and virile workers, and they are inclined to strike.[4]

Furthermore, to shore up these two hypotheses they compared industries with particularly high and low strike propensities and concluded: "The polar cases then may be described as follows: (1) an isolated mass of persons doing unpleasant work and (2) dispersed individuals doing pleasant work."[5]

Critiques of Kerr and Siegel

The theory of the isolated mass was extremely well received at the outset. Before long, however, sociologists and historians specializing in mining raised a variety of criticisms. Today few would support the original, unmodified thesis. The objections of sociologists tend to focus on methodological points, while historians, using studies of specific regions and times, have demonstrated that miners constituted neither a clearly isolated mass nor a particularly homogeneous society.

P. K. Edwards undertook the most comprehensive criticism of the Kerr and Siegel thesis.[6] He examined the isolated mass thesis in its method, its logic, and its evidence, and he was painfully sharp in pointing out its errors. The heart of his criticisms, which he developed as follows, addressed the logic of the thesis:

1. "Isolated mass" implies a typology along two axes, one running from *individual* to *mass* and another from *isolated* to *integrated*. But Kerr and Siegel seem unclear on this point. Therefore they draw on indices of "lack of occupational differentiation," "low opportunities for social mobility," and "separation from employers and the public," but nowhere do they articulate a method for comparing the degree of "massness" among different groups of laborers.

2. Kerr and Siegel present the character of the workforce as an "isolated mass" as the chief cause of strikes, so they cannot theoretically acknowledge that political and economic factors in a particular industry can influence the strike rate. Yet they do argue that, under specific conditions, other factors can influence the rate of strikes.

3. It is not necessarily the case, as Kerr and Siegel claim, that when laborers have grievances, socially neutral people will come forward as mediators. Nor is it necessarily the case that a fierce conflict will arise within a socially isolated mass.

4. Overall, Kerr and Siegel do not clearly show the logical link between the isolated mass and strike activity.

5. The Kerr and Siegel thesis is a static argument that cannot account for changes over time.

Among the many historians who have undertaken criticism of the Kerr and Siegel thesis,[7] the work of Alan B. Campbell stands out. In comparing two coal fields in Scotland's Lanarkshire, he proved that colliers were not necessarily isolated from "normal" society. He spent one chapter in particular on the Kerr and Siegel thesis and explained the meaning of coal mining in the region's cultural heritage.[8]

I agree with most of these logical criticisms of Kerr and Siegel. Their argument has many evidentiary and logical weaknesses. In the final analysis, the isolated mass argument was a provocative theory without empirical support. Its sociological method is problematic, for it attributes a timeless propensity to strike to particular industries without investigating historical changes. For example, it seems obvious that the influence of the working environment on labor must have changed profoundly even within mining, as the industry moved from placer mining to underground mining to today's dominant open-cut strip mining. The Ashio case has demonstrated that even within a single company, technological changes have a substantial effect on labor-management relations.

The Rimlinger Thesis

In the midst of this river of criticism, however, the initial question put forward by Kerr and Siegel was forgotten. Are there any truly global factors explaining the frequency of strikes in certain industries, particularly mining?

In this book I examined a Japanese mine riot in the early twentieth century, not the interwar era studied by Kerr and Siegel. So here I would like to move their problem back in time a bit, and consider the reasons why the mining industries in so many countries experienced violent disputes during the early stages of industrialization.

To this end, one very useful source is the work of G. V. Rimlinger. Early on he took note of the criticisms of Kerr and Siegel, and he studied the strike behavior of coal miners in England, the United States, Germany, and France.[9] He made three main points. First, through analysis of strike statistics for the four countries, he discovered distinctive features. In the ratio of strikes to the size of the workforce and in the total of working days lost, England and the United States were quite high compared to France and Germany, particularly the Saar territory. Rimlinger showed that the French and German miners were as capable as their American and English counterparts of staging long and large strikes, but that they did so less frequently. Not all miners, then, shared the tendency toward frequent strikes. Second, he articulates some common characteristics of coal mining labor across national boundaries that do withstand scrutiny. Third, he examines some particular features of each country's sociocultural context. Most relevant here is his second point, the presentation of commonalities among mine laborers. Does the Japanese evidence fit his thesis?

Rimlinger looked at the effect of the coal mining environment on workers from two angles. First he addressed the effect of the production environment on the *mentality* of the laborers and made several points. He argued that the following characteristics of mine work place the laborer under constant strain and produce various dissatisfactions: the nature of heavy manual labor at the unpleasantly hot and humid rock face; the variation in earnings based on factors beyond individual control, including but not limited to the quality of the rock face, the labors of prior shifts, and the quality of teamwork with colleagues; dangerous work in a dark tunnel; and the possibility of meeting with great disaster at any time. He also noted that miners lived with a constant and widespread feeling of job insecurity, because they worked in an industry where labor costs were a high proportion of production costs and the price of the product varied widely. Further, in many countries the number of mine jobs had declined steadily over time. Finally, he claimed mutual understanding between management and labor was more difficult than in factories because mine work sites were underground and otherwise quite isolated.

Second, Rimlinger examined the influence of the mining environment on the miners' *actions* such as organizing labor organizations or protesting violently, which they undertook as a result of these discontents. He describes the miners' "separatism" that arises as the geographic isolation and occupational traits of mine labor create a distinctive social grouping. Both outsiders and the miners themselves recognize this. Compared to workers in other industries, miners have a strong consciousness of themselves as sharing a common fate. He also notes the need and habit of mutual aid and cooperation. The miners' productive groups are built on a basis of mutual trust and dependence, and miners show a strong sense of group responsibility. The close human relationships and pride of craftsmanship "reinforce their separateness and their cohesion." Finally, he looks at individual or collective acts of violence in the mines. He argues that it results from the psychological weight of highly dangerous, back-breaking work. Miners look down on people who accumulate money, seeing it as inadequate compensation for their hazardous and harrowing labors. In this light, it is easy to see why they resent outsiders, whether from management or labor organizations, who try to control them or exercise power over them.

This study of Ashio makes it clear that the characteristics and causal factors identified by Rimlinger are common to the Japanese mining industry. Rimlinger looked only at coal mining, but his argument could apply to all underground mining, metal mining included. At the risk of oversimplifying, one may conclude that dark, dangerous, unpleasant, and grueling underground labor is the hallmark of mining, a common stamp that marks mine labor similarly across national boundaries.

Yet while recognizing the contributions of Rimlinger's work, there are several points that he ignores or passes over too lightly. First, he stresses the psychological aspects of the danger of mining and the tension imposed on the miners. While this is certainly important, the political aspects of this danger must also be stressed. In the early industrial era safety often became a point of conflict between management and labor. In the mining industry, devoted to the collection of limited natural resources, operators tried to avoid safety-related expenditures wherever possible, since these were extra costs that would not increase productivity. The dangerous conditions that resulted created a daily accumulating resentment on the part of the miners against the operators. Safety issues frequently became points of contention, particularly when a disaster or accident occurred. Also, victims of workplace accidents were sometimes transformed by the experience into labor movement activists.[10]

Second, greater attention should be given to the fact that, in addition to gas explosions and cave-ins, the common occupational disease of silicosis (black lung) among miners forced many to stop working at a relatively young age. The shared uncertainty about when a workplace injury or occupational disease would force miners to stop working was a condition that gave birth to labor organizations focused on mutual aid. These came into existence all over the world: the *tomoko dōmei* in Japan, the *Knappshaften* in Germany, the *Friendly Society* in England. Mutual aid groups became a useful tool when the workers held a common complaint and it came time to take group action against a common opponent.[11] In the case of the Ashio uprising, the *tomoko dōmei* mutual aid society clearly played an important role.

Third, the piecework pay system rivaled unsafe conditions as a cause of conflict between management and labor in mining, one not addressed in depth by Rimlinger. Piecework has been widely used in mining operations all over the world.[12] Direct supervision is extremely difficult in a mine, compared to a factory, because the workplace is deep within dark tunnels. So mine operators generally turned to piecework, a system in which "the pay structure itself regulated the quality and intensity of labor."[13] An important difference between piecework in factories and mines is that a great deal of leeway exists in a mine for subjectivity on the part of the assessor. For example, to assess piecework wages in mining, one must not only weigh the collected ore but assess the difficulty of processing the rocks or powder. Moreover, differences in location can mean that the same labor will produce different results. The position of the rock face affects the transit time to and from the face, and therefore the time available to actually work it. The working environment differs depending on the ambient temperature, water sources, the hardness of the rock around the vein, and ventilation. All of these, of course, can reduce the ability of a miner to collect ore. Under these conditions, it is almost inevitable that the ore assessor or the official in charge of job assignments will make arbitrary judgments and seek or accept bribes.[14] This happened in Japan, and it was a profound grievance of miners the world over.

Fourth, Rimlinger describes the isolated underground workplace as an obstacle to mutual understanding between management and labor. That is one way to look at the matter. But at the same time, group labor in a place difficult to supervise contributed to the autonomy of mining work groups. Isolation can be seen as an advantage in creating self-directed worker organizations.[15]

Fifth, the truck system, as is well known, was also a frequent source of confrontation that must be factored into the analysis of a common miner's condition.[16] At many mines, because of their location, the company distributed daily necessities, and the miners had no choice but to rely on the company for what they needed. In a sense it was only natural that profit-seeking operators sought to maximize their gains from their control of the distribution system and sold low-quality goods at high prices. Moreover, as was true at Ashio, distribution of goods could serve as a means of labor management, for instance to control attendance. These practices increased the dissatisfaction of the workers.

Rimlinger makes one further important point when he argues that combativeness and unity among miners can, under certain social conditions, be used by the mine operators to strengthen their control. This tendency can be seen in the case of Japanese miners. True, in the spirited 1907 conflict and others, the existence of the *tomoko dōmei,* at Ashio as well as at many other mines, worked to encourage labor conflict. However, at the same time, at small mines the *tomoko dōmei* could be and was used by operators as a tool to control workers. Even at Ashio, after the violence was over, the operators reconfigured the *tomoko dōmei* into an organization of labor control. In this sense, Rimlinger's argument is important.

DIFFERENCES

The cross-national commonality of mine labor is thus considerable, not only in terms of social psychology but in common systems of economic and social organization, institutions of solidarity, and the politics of contention with mine operators. Yet characteristic features distinguish various national contexts. Drawing on Ashio as well as more general evidence from Japan, I close by discussing some distinctive traits in Japan and their sources.

Differences in the Quality of Violence

One huge difference between the Ashio uprising and similar mine disputes in the United States at about the same time is the number of deaths that resulted. According to Price V. Fishback, from 1890 to 1909 the number of dead from mining strikes in the United States reached 163, an average annual death rate per 10,000 workers of 12.8, 21.3 times greater than in the manufacturing industries.[17] During the Ashio uprising, there was a single death, a worker who burned to death while drunk on stolen liquor, not a victim of malice or murder. Why did this sort of difference develop between the mine disputes of Japan and the United States?

The first point to make is that the high death toll in the United States is probably more distinctive than the low count in Japan. For example, even in the food riots of England from the eighteenth to nineteenth centuries, there were extremely few people killed by the "mobs."[18] In the United States, on the other hand, even in the relatively calmer nonmining fields, in the twenty years after 1890, historians count 130 people killed in strike-related incidents.[19]

As a nonspecialist, I cannot produce a satisfactory explanation of this violence in U.S. labor history with any confidence. But I cannot help but think that the constitutional "right to bear arms" and the use of racial conflict as a strike-breaking technique were crucial factors behind the high death tolls.

Melvyn Dubofsky describes mining disputes in the turn-of-the-century American west as follows: "During the ten years from 1894 to 1904, Western miners literally waged armed war with their capitalist adversaries. Miners' unions sometimes purchased and stocked rifles and ammunition, drilled in military fashion, and prepared, if all else failed, to achieve their objectives with rifle, torch, and dynamite stick."[20]

U.S. labor disputes, particularly mining disputes, saw both laborers and operators preparing weapons for "self-defense." Disputes could become shootouts at almost any provocation, and they often looked more like feuds and vendettas than strikes. As far as racial tension is concerned, black strike-breakers were occasionally brought into mines picketed by white miners, which could certainly have contributed to the ease with which shooting erupted.[21]

On the other hand, why were there so few fatalities in Japanese labor disputes? Of course, the populace had no right to carry and use guns, and it is probably relevant that for many years the wearing of swords was prohibited to all but the samurai class. In the Ashio disturbance, although the "mob" had access to the powerful weapon of dynamite, they never used it against people but instead blew up an unoccupied "foremen's cabin." Punishment or revenge directed at the "officials," the targets of their grievances, was chiefly carried out with sticks or fists. The intent to restrain their activities and avoid murder can be seen concretely in the accounts of the "mob" action against Mine Director Minami. Also, the governor who was responsible for calling out the police to put down the riot ordered them "under no circumstances to draw your swords." This certainly must have had a large impact. Because of this order, even when the police were surrounded by the "mob" they did not use their sabers. Also, the army divisions involved in the final suppression did not use real bullets at all, but only fired blank warning shots.

Adversarial Relations and "Harmonious" Relations

Behind these differences lie each country's historical, social, and cultural traditions. Most important among these are the differences between Japan and the United States in the way people think about labor-management relations.

Common wisdom in the United States holds that the relationship between labor and management is at base an adversarial one. Not only do workers and managers believe this, but the actions of federal and state governments and the courts reflect this understanding. To avoid conflicts that escalate into violence, the government introduced systems of collective bargaining and labor contracts, attempting to deal with labor problems through fixed rules. In other words, adversarialism is the foundation of the U.S. labor relations system.[22]

On the other hand, in Japan both labor and management, as well as the government and society at large, consider the basic principle of labor relations to be "the preservation of a mutual, cooperative relationship." Of course, one can find plenty of cases of outright confrontation between workers and employers, when both labor and management speak in adversarial terms. However, both sides tend to consider these instances to be exceptions to a much more desirable state of cooperation. Management looks at these confrontations as a failure of labor to share a mutual understanding, while workers tend to think of problems as being rooted in the poor character of individual managers, a failure of compassion on their part toward the workers.[23]

For example, a song written by Nagaoka Tsuruzō, the Ashio labor movement leader, says, "Is Furukawa [Junkichi] our master? Hey, hey, not a bit: he trods on us weaker ones, a devil who knows neither duty nor pity." Implicit in these lyrics is the image of the preferred employer, an individual who does know "duty" and "pity" and treats workers as human beings. This is stated even more clearly in Nagaoka's autobiography. Here he gives the name of Furukawa Ichibei, the company founder, as an example of an "ideal businessman," offers three specific examples of his care and consideration of the workers, and writes, "the miners thought of Ichibei as a parent or a god."

Us and Them

The powerfully rooted "us and them" class consciousness of the British working class is relevant to this Japanese-U.S. distinction. This consciousness was probably shared by early American workers, who, after all, were immigrants from Britain, and it likely contributed to adversarial labor relations.

The "us and them" consciousness of blue-collar workers reflects their anger at disdainful treatment by other classes. One finds a similar "resentment against unfair discrimination" among Japanese blue-collar workers who reacted to the disparaging regard for the "lower classes" among people of so-called general society.[24] But in sharp contrast to the Japanese, the British working class did not demand that both "us" and "them" be recognized as members of a common society. Instead they created a relatively autonomous society—a world of "us," with a distinctive lifestyle, social customs, and language—and shut themselves into it.

British blue-collar workers took this course not simply, as common wisdom suggests, because of great pride at being a member of the working class. In addition, other classes, particularly the lower middle class, which was not so clearly superior in income to the better-off members of the working class, strove to mark themselves off from the blue-collar class by consciously preserving a distinctive middle-class lifestyle, customs, and language. One eloquent witness to the chasm between these classes was George Orwell, a member of the lower middle class, who, as an opponent of the class structure, described working-class life.[25]

Blue-collar workers in Japan, on the other hand, like Japanese capitalists, managers, and white-collar employees, did not come to view such an adversarial labor relationship as desirable. Japanese blue-collar workers did not seek to create an "us only" world. They continually demanded recognition that workers were full members of the so-called general society. Blue-collar workers strongly argued with managers that they were as indispensable to the company as their white-collar colleagues.[26]

The Japanese labor movement in its early years reflected this worker perspective. Those groups that succeeded in organizing workers, such as the Yūaikai and the Rōdō Kumiai Kiseikai, shared the goal of raising the social position of workers. As leaders of these groups were demanding the recognition of blue-collar workers as full members of society, they simultaneously were calling on the workers to become worthy of social acceptance by self-cultivation, by improving their skills, and by generally "endeavoring to become human beings who deserved respect."

At its peak during World War I and the "Taishō Democracy"[27] period, the labor movement focused more on demanding that society "first, recognize our humanity" than on their own self-improvement. But in any event, the Japanese labor union movement was from the start marked by a concern to do more than maintain and improve working conditions. It was sensitive to the position of the worker in society and continually demanded "the acceptance of blue-collar workers as human beings by society as a whole and by individual companies." And in the aftermath of World War II, when the labor union movement grew at lightning pace, this sensitivity was a decisive factor leading blue-collar and white-collar workers to form unions jointly.

One feature of present-day Japanese labor relations that differs greatly from other countries is the "white-collarization" of blue-collar workers. That is, blue-collar workers in Japan are not paid hourly or daily wages, but receive a monthly salary, and they take home bonuses at the same rate as their white-collar colleagues. Even in the area of job advancement there is no fundamental difference between treatment of blue- and white-collar workers.[28] The existence of the "mixed white- and blue-collar unions" has been an important force leading the treatment of blue-collar workers to approach that of white-collar employees. These joint unions were born when the democratization program of the postwar American Occupation took specific shape at the workplace in the form of demands for the "elimination of status distinctions based on trade." The distinctive institution of joint labor unions emerged in a context of long years of worker resentment at status discrimination and demands to eliminate this not by creating an autonomous society but by winning acceptance as full members within corporate society. At the same time, both managers and state bureaucrats saw independent blue-collar labor unions as part of a disharmonious structure of class conflict, and they promoted policies to integrate workers into general society as much as possible. Of course, it required a moment of almost revolutionary change in the form of democratization after defeat in war to realize these changes. But the fact remains that the context in which joint unions emerged included a social and cultural gap between white-collar and blue-collar workers far shallower than in Britain.

The Tradition of Craft Unionism

An important factor contributed to such differences between Western and Japanese labor relations: the weakness of craft unions. In preindustrial Japan, strong independent guilds, which could have been the base for craft unions, hardly existed. Or, one could state the issue conversely: a tradition of guilds and craft unionism was a formative element in Euro-American labor history. I believe this issue is fundamental to any effective international historical comparison in labor history.

The basic function of guilds is to monopolize work within a particular trade and to deny work to nonmembers. Also, while they control the increase in membership through the apprentice system, guilds independently regulate their working hours and workload and thereby control competition within their ranks. The craft union of early industrial Europe was clearly established on this historical foundation. The basic policies of craft unions—the control of the labor market through an apprentice system, refusing to work with nonmembers, unilateral control of wages, and resistance to the introduction of new technology—were identical to those of the guilds. In the background of these positions is a general social acceptance of this sort of market regulation. In the United States, which lacked a guild tradition, and in the strong craft unions of England, and even in factories without labor unions, there existed the concept of a "stint" by which the workers controlled their own rate of production.[29] Even in the piecework-pay world of coal mining the union movement sought self-regulated output.[30] Underlying these efforts was certainly a general societal acknowledgment of their legitimacy.

To be sure, in Japan one can find craft-union-like organizations among workers in some occupations. Many artisans, especially carpenters and stonemasons in the construction trade, had their own trade organizations. One of the strongest of these was the miners' brotherhood, discussed at length in this book. Among the brotherhood regulations was a requirement for a three-year, three-month, ten-day apprenticeship before one could enter the organization. However, nonmembers were in practice able to work as miners, and the brotherhood did not control the labor market. Also, this apprenticeship system existed in form more than substance. Many individuals fled their masters during their apprenticeship and went to work elsewhere as full-fledged miners. In addition, there are no known cases in which the mining brotherhoods opposed the introduction of new technologies, including dynamite, blasting powder, and power drills, which lowered the value of their skill. Neither did the brotherhoods oppose the piecework system, which forced workers to compete with each other. Rather, they strongly believed that the most skilled and effective would naturally bring home the most pay. Such characteristics are not unique to the miners, but can be seen in other Japanese craft organizations as well.

To understand why craft organizations took on distinctive characters, one must turn to the historical context. Japanese cities before the Meiji Restoration (1868) differed from the cities of Europe, with their traditions of independence reaching to the Middle Ages. The vast majority of Japan's cities, after the establishment of the Tokugawa order in the 1600s, were castle towns under the direct supervision and control of their lords. Mining towns also were controlled by agents of the shogunate or domain lord.

In these cities, autonomous groups of citizens did not flourish, and merchant organizations independent of the ruler's authority could not be established. Of course, traders and artisans did form occupationally based groups and sought to protect the common interests of members, but the feudal authorities gave greatest priority to ease of control, in some cases outlawing these groups and in others ordering their formation. In the first decades of the Tokugawa era (1600–1867), the shogunate in principle did not recognize "guilds" formed by traders or artisans. But in the mid–seventeenth century, it did begin to recognize Osaka-based guilds of shippers, money-changers, lumber and oil dealers, and some others. Further, in the 1720s, to change a situation of declining rice prices (the primary source of tax revenue) and soaring prices of consumer goods in the cities, the Tokugawa rulers commanded artisans and traders to form trade associations. Over a century later, in 1841, the Tokugawa issued an order outlawing and dismantling these groups, but ten years after that it once more ordered the formation of guilds. The organizations of traders and artisans in late feudal and early modern Japan were thus bodies under the arbitrary control of authorities. Rather than defend the interests of members through autonomous institutions of self-rule, these groups sought to defend themselves by relying on the authority or regulatory power of the Tokugawa and domain rulers. It appears to me that the situation in Japan today, where the United States and others criticize various government regulations that constitute informal, nontariff barriers to trade, is related to this history. In any case, in Tokugawa Japan it was not possible to establish socially accepted customs by which occupational organizations undertook autonomous self-regulation, as in European cities. Although traders and artisans tried to use their guilds, when they existed, to set prices and regulate wage levels, neither their customers nor the society as a whole recognized these efforts as fair or just.

These differences in historical traditions surrounding the relationship between state authorities and organizations of traders or artisans, beginning with the difference in the guild tradition, have influenced labor-management relations of the industrial era in various ways. For example, consider the vagueness of the concept of an occupation or vocation in Japan. This is an important factor in creating the potential for the so-called flexibility of present-day Japanese labor relations, and it is also indivisible from the historical precedents. In clarifying the boundaries between their organizations, European craft guilds and craft unions were also clarifying the boundaries between occupations. But in Japan this sort of demarcation almost never took place. In the West, the division between skilled and unskilled labor, or even between skilled and semiskilled labor, was clearly drawn, and it was accompanied by a substantial status gap. In Japan, the boundary between skilled and semiskilled labor was and remains decidedly unclear. The foundation of the "flexibility" in Japanese labor relations is the relative lack of resistance on the part of workers to crossing job categories. It is widely known that Japanese employees today are more company-oriented than occupation-oriented. The present-day organization of Japanese worker unions along largely company lines can be traced back to this lack of a craft tradition, in addition to the blurred distinction between blue-collar and white-collar workers related above.

It would take another book to argue this point properly. Here I can only close with an opinion grounded in the study of labor at the far eastern tip of Asia that the tradition of craft unionism must surely be considered a major factor in the history of labor relations and the labor movement in the West.

Notes

ABBREVIATIONS

NRUS   Rōdō undō shiryō iinkai, ed., *Nihon rōdō undō shiryō* (Historical documents of the Japanese labor movement) (Tokyo: Rōdō undō shiryō iinkai, 1959–75)

TKS   Tochigi Prefecture, ed., *Tochigi ken shi: Shiryō hen, kingendai, 2* (The history of Tochigi Prefecture: Document ed., modern era, vol. 2) (Tokyo: Tochigi Prefecture, 1977)

EDITOR'S PREFACE

1. All Japanese names in this book are presented in the Japanese style, with family name first and given name second.

2. These works include the following early examples: Aoki Masahisa, "Nittetsu kikankata sōgi kenkyū" (A study of the locomotive engineers' strike at Japan Railway Company), *Rōdō undō shi kenkyū* (Studies in labor movement history) no. 62 (1979); Miyake Akimasa, "Daiichiji taisengo no jūkōgyō daikeiei rōdōsha undō" (The workers movement before and after the Russo-Japanese War), *Shakai keizai shigaku* (Social and economic history) 44, no. 5 (March 1979); Nishinarita Yutaka, "Nichirō sensōgo ni okeru zaibatsu zōsen kigyō no keiei kikō to rōshi kankei: Mitsubishi zōsenjo no bunseki" (Labor relations and management structure in *zaibatsu* shipbuilding firms after the Russo-Japanese War: Analysis of the Mitsubishi Shipyard), *Ryūkoku daigaku keizai keiei ronshū* (Ryūkoku University Economic and Management Studies) 18, nos. 1–4 (June 1978–March 1979).

3. Some of the best are collected in Yamamoto Kiyoshi, ed., *Nihon no rōdō sōgi, 1945–1985* (Japan's labor disputes, 1945–1985) (Tokyo: Tokyo University Press, 1991).

NOTES TO AUTHOR'S INTRODUCTION

1. Maruyama's interpretation gained a wide readership in the English-speaking world because it appeared first in English. See Masao Maruyama, "Patterns of Individuation and the Case of Japan: A Conceptual Scheme," in *Changing Japanese Attitudes toward Modernization,* ed. Marius B. Jansen (Princeton: Princeton Univer-

sity Press, 1965), 491 for this quote. The discussion of Ashio can be found on pp. 513–14.

2. The term is taken from the title of the founding texts of this school, the so-called *kōza* (or lectures) school analysis, first published in *Nihon shihonshugi hattatsu shi kōza* (Lectures on the historical development of Japanese capitalism) (Tokyo: Iwanami shoten, 1932), 7 vols.

3. The great extent of the influence of lecture interpretations such as Yamada Moritarō's *Analysis of Japanese Capitalism* on Japanese social and historical science in the first three decades after World War II is hard to imagine today. The leading scholars in postwar Japanese social science, not only Marxists but also their critics such as Maruyama, all felt the impact of the *kōza* school in one way or another. Although one discerns little or no theoretical common ground between Maruyama's work and that of the *kōza-ha* scholars. Maruyama claimed that when he read the *Lectures on the Historical Development of Japanese Capitalism*, "In terms of the scientific analysis of Japanese capitalism it was as though the scales had fallen from my eyes." See Mainichi shinbun, ed., *Shōwa shisōshi e no shōgen* (Testimony on the intellectual history of the Shōwa era) (Tokyo: Mainichi Shinbunsha, 1968), 44–45.

4. For English-language discussions of the pollution incidents, see "Symposium: The Ashio Copper Mine Pollution Incident," articles by Kenneth B. Pyle, F. G. Notehelfer, and Alan Stone, *Journal of Japanese Studies* 1, no. 2 (spring 1975): 347–407, and Jun Ui, ed., *Industrial Pollution in Japan* (Tokyo: United Nations University, 1992).

5. These documents were published by Hōsei University Press in 204 volumes. The series title was *Fukkoku shiriizu: Nihon shakai undō shiryō* (Republication series: Historical documents of the Japanese social movement).

6. Matsuzawa's pioneering work was published as Matsuzawa Hiroaki, *Nihon shakaishugi no shisō* (Socialist thought in Japan) (Tokyo: Chikuma shobō, 1973).

7. Rōdō mondai bunken kenkyūkai (Labor Studies Bibliographic Research Group), ed., *Bunken kenkyū: Nihon no rōdō mondai, zōhoban* (Bibliographic studies of Japanese labor issues, expanded ed.) (Tokyo: Sōgō rōdō kenkyū jo, 1971), 300–302. The quote from Ōkōchi is from his *Shakai seisaku 40 nen* (Forty years of social policy) (Tokyo: Tokyo University Press, 1970), 416–17.

8. Originally published as Nakanishi Yō, "Nihon ni okeru 'shakai seisaku, rōdō mondai' kenkyū no gen jiten," in *Keizaigaku ronshū* 37, no. 3 (October 1971). Also published as part of Nakanishi Yō, *Nihon ni okeru "shakai seisaku, rōdō mondai" kenkyū* (Tokyo: Tokyo University Press, 1979).

9. Nakanishi Yō, *Nihon ni okeru "shakai seisaku, rōdō mondai" kenkyū*, 181–83.

10. Kurita Ken, comment on "Miyake Akimasa 'Senkan ki Nihon rōdō undō no hōhō' ni tsuite" (Miyake Akimasa's report on research methods on interwar Japan's labor history), *Rōdō undō kenkyū kai kaihō*, no. 4 (December 1982): 6.

NOTES TO PROLOGUE

1. There was a silver mine on the small island of Tsushima, located in the sea between Kyushu and the Korean Peninsula, which was worked in the seventh century. Also, in midwestern Honshu—including present-day Okayama and Hyogo prefectures—it is said that copper mines were discovered and worked from the eighth to the early ninth centuries.

2. According to the calculations of Yamaguchi Keiji, the populations of the chief mining towns were as follows: Sado-Aikawa gold mine, 80,000; Iwami silver mine, 150,000–200,000; Ikuno silver mine, 15,000–20,000; Nobesawa silver mine, 28,000; Innai silver mine, 7,000–10,000. Nagahara Keiji and Yamaguchi Keiji, *Kōza: Nihon gijutsu no shakaishi—saikō to yakin* (Lectures on the social history of technology in Japan, vol. 5: Extraction and refining) (Tokyo: Nihon hyōronsha, 1983), 193.

3. The chief mines operated by each *zaibatsu* were Mitsui *zaibatsu:* Miike coal mine, Kamioka mine; Mitsubishi *zaibatsu:* Takashima coal mine and copper mines at Arakawa, Ikuno, Osarizawa, and Yoshioka; Sumitomo *zaibatsu:* Besshi copper mine; Furukawa *zaibatsu:* Ashio copper mine, Ani copper mine; Kuhara *zaibatsu:* Hitachi copper mine; Fujita *zaibatsu:* Kosaka mine.

4. Nimura Kazuo, "Genchiku-ki ni okeru kōzan rōdōsha sū: Meiji zenki sangyō tōkei no ginmi" (The number of mine laborers in the era of primitive accumulation: Scrutiny of early Meiji industrial statistics), parts 1 and 2, *Kenkyū shiryō geppō* (Research Documents Monthly Report), Hōsei University, Ōhara Social Research Institute, nos. 289–290 (September–October 1982).

5. Kenneth Strong, *Ox against the Storm: A Biography of Tanaka Shōzō* (Victoria: University of British Columbia Press, 1977).

6. Mutsu Munemitsu (1844–1897) was a career politician who served as ambassador to the United States and the minister of agriculture and foreign affairs. He is credited with renegotiating the unequal treaties with the British in 1894. He became acquainted with Furukawa Ichibei during the latter's Ono group days, when Mutsu was an officer of the Finance Ministry. In 1873 his second son, Junkichi, was promised to be adopted into the Furukawa household. Hara Kei (1856–1921) began his career as a newspaper reporter, then entered the Foreign Ministry and worked as the Paris secretary for Consul Amazu, where he was noticed by Mutsu Munemitsu. When Mutsu became agriculture minister and then foreign minister, Hara moved with him, advancing to the post of deputy foreign minister. In 1902 he was elected to the Diet, and served as home minister and posts and communications minister before earning the sobriquet "the commoner prime minister," when he led the Seiyūkai in forming Japan's first party cabinet in 1918.

7. The 1897 pay regulations provided for the following monthly minimum rates for company officials: Grade 1, ¥300; Grade 2, ¥200; Grade 3, ¥100; Grade 4, ¥70;

Grade 5, ¥50; Grade 6, ¥30; Grade 7, ¥20; Grade 8, ¥10. Daily minimum rates for Grades 9 and 10 were over ¥1 and 40 sen. Higher technical school graduates were straightaway taken on at the Grade 6 pay level. See Hoshino Riichirō, ed., *Nikkō denki seidōjo shi* (A history of Nikko Electrical Copper Refining Co.), vol. 1, pt. 2 (Nikkō: Nikkō Electric Refinery Co., 1951), 45, and Nakata Takayoshi, "Furukawa kōgyō kaisha waikanishite shain o saiyō suru ka" (How does the Furukawa Company hire its employees?), *Jitsugyō no Nippon* (Business Japan), 15 July 1907.

8. Tanaka Naoki, *Kindai Nihon tankō rōdō shi kenkyū* (Historical studies of coal mine labor in modern Japan) (Tokyo: Sofūkan, 1987), 130. Although the percentage dropped in the 1930s, the practice continued until the government promulgated regulations in 1933 forbidding women from pit work.

9. Aside from these employees, the Ashio mining office paid the expenses of five policemen stationed at the Ashio branch station. After the riots, this number was increased to fifty.

10. Kenkon Ichihoi (pen name of Matsubara Iwagorō), *Shakai hyaku hōmen* (One hundred realms of society) (Tokyo: Minyūsha, 1897), 73–75.

11. The terms for "master" and "apprentice" in Japanese are *oyakata* and *totei,* which literally translate as "parent status" and "younger brother follower," respectively.

12. This sort of ritual greeting survives today among gangsters (*yakuza*) and some itinerant tradesmen. It has been made familiar to contemporary Japanese by gangster movies and by the hero of the popular film series, *Otoko wa tsurai yo* (It's tough being a man).

13. Although these brotherhoods originated among metal miners, *tomoko dōmei* also came to be formed in coal mines, such as those in Hokkaidō and Jōban, where many of the workers were former metal miners.

14. This document ("Ashio kōzan kōfu ippan kisoku jōrei") is located in the archive of the Tokyo University Economics Faculty Library.

15. Article 51 states, "The member(s) responsible for the box for the period of one month shall receive an honorarium of five yen from the reserve fund," and article 52 states, "The monthly rotation order will be changed after a full two years by the drawing of lots." The fact that more than two *ōtōban* served at one time is illustrated by article 29, which states, "Two *ōtōban* shall be chosen for collection and observation duty." At Kodaki, where there were twenty-three lodges, it appears that each lodge had a period of responsibility for the box during the course of a two-year rotation. See TKS, 764.

NOTES TO CHAPTER 1

1. One frequently encounters such assessments in histories of the Japanese labor movement, or of modern Japan and the development of capitalism more generally.

The views of Ōkōchi Kazuo, discussed in chapter 2, are typical of many similar interpretations. For example, see Koyama Hirotake, *Nihon rōdō undō shi* (A history of the Japanese labor movement) (Tokyo: Shakai shinpō, 1968), 18: "The frequency with which disputes took the form of rioting can be ascribed to the workers' lack of any leaders, organizational structure such as a union, or any proper method of negotiating. Considering the appalling working conditions, the ubiquitous suppression by authorities of any assertions of democratic rights, and the oppressive nature of status-ridden, semifeudal labor relations, it is only natural that the workers' pent-up energies, denied any other outlet, should have exploded in riotous uprisings."

2. Maruyama Masao, "Patterns of Individuation and the Case of Japan: A Conceptual Scheme," in *Changing Japanese Attitudes toward Modernization*, ed. Marius Jansen (Princeton: Princeton University Press, 1965), 513–14.

3. For example, it is incorrect to speak of "random" recruitment of idle agricultural workers or of "vagrant populations 'voluntarily' flowing into these industries." Place of origin and blood relationships without question played a large part in the recruitment of male workers (chap. 2, app. 1 of the Japanese version of this book has details). Maruyama is also incorrect in maintaining that employers in the 1900s "gave no thought to maintaining stable and continuous labor relations" due to an "almost limitless" pool of workers. Most major employers in fact operated bonus and insurance schemes for their long-term employees, as well as compulsory savings plans. At Ashio, bonuses for long service and insurance programs had been instituted at a fairly early stage.

4. These block quotes are from Maruyama, "Patterns of Individuation," 493–96; Maruyama's emphasis.

5. Ibid., 514.

6. For more on Nagaoka, see Nakatomi Hyōe, *Nagaoka Tsuruzō—Gisei to kenshin no shogai* (Nagaoka Tsuruzō: A life of sacrifice and devotion) (Tokyo: Ochanomizu shobō, 1977). For Nagaoka's work at Ashio, see contemporary accounts in journals of the socialist movement of the time: *Shakaishugi, Shūkan heimin shimbun, Chokugen, Hikari*. Most can be found in NRUS, vol. 2, pp. 175 ff.

7. The role of Christian believers in Japan's early labor and socialist movements was large. Christians have never accounted for more than 1 percent of the Japanese population, but their proportion among labor activists and socialists, especially among the leadership, has been much higher. For example, in addition to Nagaoka, Katayama Sen was a Christian when he met Nagaoka, as was the leader of a famous strike at the Japan Railway company in the 1890s, Ishida Rokujirō, and Suzuki Bunji, in 1912 the founder of the Yūaikai, Japan's longest lived prewar labor union. It is well known that five of the six founding members of Japan's first socialist party, the Social Democratic Party (Shakai minshutō), were Christians.

Why was this the case? Christianity had been forbidden for two centuries in the Tokugawa era (until 1868), and the Emperor of Japan in the new Meiji era was presented to the people as a "living god." Therefore, to become a Christian in this nation ruled by an emperor system with strong religious coloring in many cases meant the believer was subject to persecution and discrimination. One can easily imagine that those who became Christians would develop an acute sense of social injustice. Also, people whose freedom was restricted by the patriarchal family system found in Christianity a powerful spiritual support for criticizing their society. Finally, in Japan at the turn of the twentieth century, the only country that poor people could somehow afford to visit was America, where the social gospel movement was at its peak. This movement offered spiritual and economic support to a number of talented and determined Japanese sojourners to the United States.

At the same time, the prominence of Christians in the early social movements of Japan gave them a problematic tendency toward domination by intellectuals and reliance on translations. For example, the leading publications of the early labor and socialist organizations invariably included an English-language column. This confirms the great curiosity and desire for international exchange among Japan's activists, but such a focus also separated them from the daily concerns of ordinary workers. In this context, Nagaoka was a very unusual Christian socialist. He threw himself into the labor movement with a motto of self-sacrifice, drawing on the overlapping images of Christ on the cross to save humanity from its sins and martyrs who gave their lives to save their comrades in the peasant rebellions of the Tokugawa era.

For more on this topic in English, see Irwin Scheiner, *Christian Converts and Social Protest in Meiji Japan* (Berkeley: University of California Press, 1970).

8. Different versions of the name of this group survive, including Rōdōsha Dōshikai and Nippon Rōdō Dōshikai, but in the journal *Shakaishugi* (Socialism) 8, no. 14 (3 December 1904) there is a copy of the articles of membership that bears the name Dai Nippon Rōdō Dōshikai.

9. "Rōdōsha dōshikai," *Shakaishugi* 8, no. 7 (3 May 1904).

10. Compare the first articles of Nagaoka's bylaws, above, to the following three articles, from p. 140 of Katayama Sen and Nishikawa Mitsujirō, *Nihon no rōdō undō* (1901; reprint Tokyo: Iwanami shoten, 1952):

Article 1: This Association shall work for the establishment of labor unions which will extend the rights of the working people of this country, enrich their lives, eradicate long-standing abuses, and promote mutual aid and solidarity amongst workers in the same industry.
Article 2: The Association will be known as the Association for the Formation of Labor Unions.
Article 3: The Association's offices will be located at Tokyo-shi Nihombashi-ku Hongokuchō 1 chōme 12 banchi.

11. *Shakaishugi* 8, no. 14 (1904): 22 (this publication was the successor to *Rōdō sekai* (Labor world); *Shūkan heimin shimbun* (*Commoners' Weekly*), no. 57 (1904): 4.

12. "Defendant Nagaoka's Deposition," in Nakatomi, *Nagaoka Tsuruzō*, 234.

13. *Chokugen* 2, no. 2 (12 February 1905).

14. *Shimotsuke shimbun,* 3 August 1907.

15. TKS, 602.

16. "Deposition of Yamada Kikuzō," in Nakatomi, *Nagaoka Tsuruzō,* 291.

17. "Ashio kyōtō shūshū jiken sōsa hōkoku sho" (The report on the Ashio riot, section 4), in TKS, 575–76.

18. *Shimotsuke shimbun,* 3 August 1907.

19. The price of 1 shō (1.8 liters) of ordinary white rice at Ashio in the first half of 1906 was 13 sen 5 rin (*Ōkawara Saburō jisshū hōkoku sho* [Ōkawara Saburō's internship report], unpublished manuscript, 9).

20. *Kōfu taigū jirei* (Examples of treatment of miners), reprinted by Kyūshū sangyō shiryō kenkyūkai, 175–76.

21. Nishikawa, "Ashio dōzan yūzei" (Speaking tour to the Ashio mine), *Shūkan heimin shimbun,* no. 57 (12 November 1904).

22. "Hikoku Minami Sukematsu dai go chōsho" (Fifth interrogation of defendant Minami Sukematsu), TKS, 622.

23. Nishikawa, "Ashio dōzan yūzei" (Speaking tour to the Ashio mine).

24. Nagaoka Tsuruzō, "Ashio dōzan" (Ashio copper mine), *Shakaishugi* 8, no. 14 (3 December 1904).

25. Yamamoto Hisashi, "Meiji 39 nen 12 gatsu itsu ka Tsūdō Kaneda za ni okeru rōdō enzetsu kai" (Labor speech at the Tsūdō Kaneda Theater of Meiji 39 [1906], 5 December), and Takeda Tsunagorō, "Meiji 39 nen 12 gatsu itsu ka Shiseikai hakkai shiki rōdō mondai seidan enzetsukai taiyō" (Summary of labor question political speech at the inauguration ceremony of the Shiseikai of 5 December 1906), both in NRUS, vol. 2, pp. 185, 187–88.

26. Nagaoka Tsuruzō's *A Miner's Life* was one of the earliest published worker's autobiographies in Japan. It was published after the Ashio riot as a series of eight articles in nos. 38 (8 March 1908) to 51 (15 January 1909) of *Shakai shimbun* (Socialist newspaper), a publication edited by Katayama Sen, of which Nagaoka himself had become an employee.

27. "He [Yamamoto] spoke of his situation at the time he lost his left hand. The company didn't show any concern or remorse whatsoever. He was still young, but the company's carelessness had made him a cripple, and when he thought of how he wouldn't be able to get married and raise a family, he couldn't help crying bitter tears" ("Rōdō Shiseikai Meeting, 26 December," NRUS, vol. 2, p.190).

28. For the Mining Industry Ordinances and the Mining Industry Supervisory Regulations, see *Shōkō seisaku shi* (A history of industrial policy), vol. 22, *Mining* (part 1), chap. 2, published by the Ministry of International Trade and Industry. Very early on, almost at the time of their enactment, Nagaoka appreciated the significance for the labor movement of the workers' protection legislation provided for by

the Mining Industry Ordinances and the Mining Industry Supervisory Regulations. At the time, he was working at the Innai silver mine, also owned by Furukawa, and together with some fellow workers, formed a study group to examine the Mining Industry Ordinances that, with their reference to the "protection of miners' lives and welfare," made a strong impression on him. Not content merely with studying the contents of the ordinances, he identified the cases in which the Innai mine was falling short of its legal obligations and in February 1893 organized a three-day strike to demand improvements, which succeeded in realizing "70 percent of its aims." Later, at the Asahi mine in Yamagata prefecture, his demands for a doctor to be based at the mine were also grounded in the Mining Industry Ordinances stipulations on "the protection of miners' lives and welfare." Basing their case on the law in this way gave Nagaoka and his colleagues confidence and conviction in the rightness of their cause when dealing with mine owners and the police and enabled them to make demands for miners' rights. This conviction also governed the form their struggles took. Nagaoka made the following revealing comment about the Innai mine strike: "We were not the barbarous rabble rousers they took us for. Our demands were based on the Mining Industry Ordinances and we conducted ourselves in accordance with the law and with good order."

29. Figures for industrial accidents at Ashio for the whole of the year 1905 were recorded in "Tamaki Nigosaku jisshū hōkoku sho" (Internship report by Tamaki Nigosaku) as follows: 28 workers died, 1712 were injured. The main cause of death was cited as "falling down mines" (11 deaths), followed by deaths "handling explosives" and "from falling rocks, falling earth or tunnel cave-ins" (5 deaths each), "contact with moving machinery" (3 deaths), "violent falls" (2 deaths), "truck derailments and collision, electric shock" (1 death each). Of the injuries, 1030 resulted from "falling rocks, falling earth and cave-ins" (p. 168). In the latter half of 1905, 17 workers died from injuries sustained at Ashio, but the mine hospital recorded only 10 "accidental deaths in the course of duties." See "Ōkawara Saburō jisshū hōkoku sho" (Ōkawara Saburō's Internship report), 168. It seems likely that, as Nagaoka often claimed in his criticisms, the company-managed hospital falsified the figures of industrial accidents to make them appear fewer, if only by a small number.

30. On the Ashio pollution incident, see the symposium in *Journal of Japanese Studies* 1, no. 2 (summer 1975).

31. "Meiji 40 nen 1 gatsu 26 nichi rōdō mondai seidan enzetsu taiyō" (26 January 1908 labor problems campaign meeting), NRUS, vol. 2, p. 201.

32. Nishikawa Mitsujirō, "Ashio dōzan yūzei" (Speaking tour to the Ashio mine), *Shūkan heimin shimbun,* no. 57 (11 December 1904).

33. Nagaoka, "Ashio dōzan" (Ashio copper mine).

34. See chap. 3, pp. 290–301, of the Japanese edition of this book.

35. "Kōfu no tomo" (The miner's friend), *Hikari* 1, no. 5 (20 January 1906).

36. "Yamada Kikuzō shirabetori chōshu sho" (The testimony of Yamada Kikuzō), in Nakatomi, *Nagaoka Tsuruzō*, 291.

37. *Shimotsuke shimbun*, 4 August 1907.

38. "Sankō nin Fukuda Fuyo Chōsho" (Witness Fukuda Fuyo's deposition), in Nakatomi, *Nagaoka Tsuruzō*, 284.

39. The sacrifices endured by Nagaoka's family are clearly depicted in a letter Nagaoka wrote to Katayama Sen when he left Yūbari for Ashio:

Thank you very much for the many letters you have written. I am now finally preparing to leave here on the 7th of this month [Dec. 1903]. My business has long been in difficulty; I have had many setbacks and illnesses; I seem to resemble Karl Marx only in the degree of my poverty. But I have resolved to sacrifice myself and my household for the sake of Japan's thousands of miners. . . . I have had to send my family out into the Hokkaidō snows to sell our belongings in order to raise money for my trip. For myself, it is only natural that I should risk my life for the cause. For my family I have decided on the following provision:

1. I will have my four-year-old adopted.

2. The eight-year-old will look after the two-year-old.

3. The ten-year-old will sell sweets after school.

4. The thirteen-year-old will take over cooking the morning and evening meals and will attend school.

5. The fifteen-year-old will work in the machine yard during the day and will sell sweet sake in the evenings.

6. My wife will work as a porter at the station during the day and will sell sweet sake in the evenings. This all began yesterday. I am finally ready to sacrifice myself for the cause in traveling and campaigning throughout the country.

In fact, Nagaoka's family did indeed come close to splitting up altogether. See Nakatomi, *Nagaoka Tsuruzō*.

40. These were two of the four rules for members printed on the back of the Dai Nippon Rōdō Dōshikai membership card. See *Shakaishugi* (Socialism) 8, no. 14 (3 December 1904).

41. Hasunuma Soun, *Ashio dōzan* (Ashio copper mine) (Tokyo: Kōdō shoin, 1903), 72.

42. "Hikokunin Nagaoka Tsuruzō chōsho" (Defendant Nagaoka's deposition), in Nakatomi, *Nagaoka Tsuruzō*, 233. A related article was carried in *Chokugen* 2, no. 17 (28 May 1905).

43. Naikaku kanpō kyoku, ed., *Hōrei zensho* (The complete laws), vol. 25, no. 1.

44. "Hikokunin Nagaoka Tsuruzō chōsho" (Defendant Nagaoka's deposition), in Nakatomi, *Nagaoka Tsuruzō*, 233.

45. Nagaoka Tsuruzō, "Ashio dōzan yori," *Hikari* 1, no. 4 (1 January 1906).

46. "Dai ni kai kōhan bōchō ki" (Second court hearing), *Shimotsuke shimbun*, 3 August 1907.

47. "Ashio dōzan rōdō ka" (The song of the Ashio workman), *Hikari* 1, no. 25 (25 October 1906).

48. "Dai ni kai kōhan bōchō ki" (Second court hearing), *Shimotsuke shimbun*, 3 August 1907.

49. *Ashio kyōtō shūshū jiken sōsa hōkokusho sono ni* (The report on the Ashio riot, section 2) reports Nagaoka as saying to the lodge representatives from Tsūdō's No. 1 lodge: "Your lodge boss was the one who crushed the Dōshikai" (TKS, 560).

50. In his autobiography, Nagaoka writes:

I went on to Innai silver mine in Akita prefecture in the winter of the same year [1886], worked hard until the summer of the following year and made a lot of money, but lost it at gambling as usual and was dirt poor. I couldn't stand it, and so partly out of despair and partly because I liked a good fight, my greatest pleasure was in getting into scrapes with any number of other fellows. Once—I was reading *The Seven Spears of Shizugatake* at the time—a fight broke out amongst a bunch of miners. Fancying myself as the hero of the book, Katō Kiyomasa, and with only three others on my side, I waded into a group of about twenty. We were so strong that they all lost heart, and we won the fight. In those days I used to love throwing others around in a fight and generally making a nuisance of myself, but now I prefer to suffer for others; I like working, spilling my blood, and enduring poverty to help improve their lives. This is what gives me pleasure now. (Nakatomi, *Nagaoka Tsuruzō*, 208)

51. Nagaoka, "Ashio dōzan yori," *Hikari* 1, no. 4 (1 January 1906).

52. "Dai ni kai kōhan bōchō ki" (Second court hearing), *Shimotsuke shimbun*, 3 October 1907.

53. "Kōfu no tomo" (The miners' friend), *Hikari* 1, no. 4 (1 January 1906).

54. *Shimotsuke shimbun*, 4 October 1907.

55. "Meiji 39 nen ju-ni gatsu itsu-ka Tsūdō kaneda-za ni okeru rōdō enzetsu kai kaikyō" (Survey of the workers' rally at Tsūdō's Kaneda theater, 5 December 1906), NRUS, vol. 2, p. 184.

56. Ibid., 188.

57. See chap. 3, pp. 290 ff. of the Japanese edition of this book for more on wage policy.

58. The following was reported in the newspaper *Yorozu chōhō* under the title "The Miners' Case":

To be able to get any white rice or miso paste from the company store, you have to go down the mine, and you can't make ends meet. When you go into debt because rice and miso cost more than you earn, you get money from your reserve fund (a fund made up from deductions of one-fifth of miners' monthly wages); if that's still not enough, you can get money from the guarantors' reserve funds (whereby a group of three debtors team up and pool their reserve money to support each other); if you still then owe more than 8 yen, your food ration booklet is taken away and you can't get any rice or miso. So before you know it you're in debt to the boss. If you can't raise your output, the only thing you can do is get out. When you're sick, no matter what the size of your family, you're never given more than five days' supply of rice—two shō and five gō—so in the end you starve. (cited in TKS, 752)

59. "In the old days you could get 1 to plus 1 shō of rice when you ordered 1 to, and 1 kan plus 100 me of miso for an order of 1 kan [that is, roughly 10 percent extra, a sort of 'bakers dozen'], but these days it's terrible. Recently at Tsūdō, miners ordering 1 to received only 9 shō 3 gō. At Sunokobashi miners drawing 500 me of miso got only 470. I myself ordered 5 gō of sake and got only 4. The company and the officials don't give us anything; they loan us 30 days' pay, and we draw these items against the loan" ("Meiji 40 nen, 1 gatsu, 26 nichi, Rōdō mondai seidan enzetsu taiyō" [Account of the labor problems rally, 26 January 1908], NRUS, vol. 2, p. 199).

60. Natsume Sōseki's novel, *Miner*, was based on the short time spent by a young man working as a mining lodge bookkeeper shortly after the Ashio riot. In the character's notes of what he heard in the lodge, there appears the following: "An old woman came to eat at our place. She couldn't pick up the rice with her chopsticks, because it was too slippery. It wasn't sticky enough. Foreign rice. Like eating bits of plaster. She got a real surprise" (Natsume Sōseki, *Kōfu* [The Miner], in *Sōseki zenshū* (Collected works of Natsume Sōseki), vol. 5 [Tokyo: Kadokawa shoten, 1961], 376).

61. It is known that in 1892 the men had been provided with Japanese rice. See *Asahi shimbun*, 15 February 1907. Also, in a report on the Ashio mines for *Kokumin shimbun* in April 1896, Matsubara Iwagorō noted the poor quality of food provisions at other mines and commented on the "extravagance of the food and drink" at Ashio; he did not mention foreign rice.

62. NRUS, vol. 2, p. 200.

63. Ibid., 185–86.

64. Ibid., 197.

65. Ibid., 185. Hayashi later admitted in court that "xxxx meant strike action" (*Shimotsuke shimbun*, 4 August 1907).

66. "Shakai shugisha enkaku" (The chronicle of socialists; a police report on socialists), vol. 1, cited in *Zoku: Gendai shi shiryō* (More documents of the modern era), vol. 1 (Tokyo: Misuzu shobō, 1984), 33.

67. See "Hikoku Minami Sukematsu dai ni kai chōsho" (The second deposition of defendant Minami Sukematsu), and "Shōnin Uno Tsuruta chōsho" (Deposition of witness Uno Tsuruta), in TKS, 599 and 608.

68. "Ashio kyōtō shūshū jiken sōsa hōkoku: sono ni" (Report into the circumstances of the disorders at Ashio, part 2), in ibid., 560.

69. "One day in mid-November, 27 or 28 lodge bosses (names unknown) from Tsūdō met at Komatsuya [restaurant] with myself, Yamazaki, Imori, Hayashi, and Yamamoto to discuss the setting up of the branch and the previously mentioned four articles which were its objectives. The bosses said that while they couldn't openly agree with it, because the company would dismiss them if they did, they wouldn't oppose it either" ("Hikoku Minami Sukematsu dai ni kai chōsho" [Defendant Minami Sukematsu's second deposition], in TKS, 599).

70. Ibid., 600.

71. In addition, the Honzan brotherhood, in response to the invitation to the Shiseikai inauguration meeting, sent representatives and congratulatory gift money. See "Tantei hōkoku sho" [Detective's report], in ibid., 585.

72. "Tsūdō junshi, Toyama Seiichi, 'hōkokusho'" ("Report" by Constable Toyama Seiichi of Tsūdō constabulary), in NRUS, vol. 2, p. 189.

73. "Tantei 'hōkokusho'" (Detective's "report"), in TKS, 585.

74. "Hikoku Minami Sukematsu dai 4 kai chōsho" (Defendant Minami Sukematsu's 4th deposition), in ibid., 614.

75. "Tantei 'hōkokusho'" (Detective's "report"), in ibid., 586.

76. "Hikoku Minami Sukematsu dai 6 kai chōsho" (Defendant Minami Sukematsu's 6th deposition), in ibid., 633.

77. "Tantei 'hōkokusho'" (Detective's "report"), in ibid., 593–94.

78. At his court hearing, Minami Sukematsu said:

Hayashi Kōtarō had heard from a company office worker that there had been a meeting of top executives at the supply department on the 15th or 16th January [1907]. Director Minami [Teizō] had met with the supply manager Kibe, the pit managers, Kojima, Tazaki (actually Tajima), and Esashi, and with the refinery manager (excluding manager Kawaji). Director Minami had noted that Shiseikai was recruiting members and needed to be eliminated before it did the company any damage. Kibe said that the Shiseikai movement was founded on certain justifiable grievances and that therefore the way to get rid of it would have to be different from methods used previously; they would have to find a way of placating the workers. But Kojima and the Refinery Manager agreed with Director Minami. (TKS, 619)

Probably drawing on the same source, at a public meeting on 1 February, Minami spoke of a secret "anti-Shiseikai company meeting" held on 29 January. At that meeting, Director Minami, pit manager Kojima, Kawaji, and the refinery manager had taken an uncompromisingly hostile position, while Kibe and Esashi were in favor of compromise, and Tajima, the pit manager at Honzan, had said that "step-by-step improvements should be made" (NRUS, vol. 2, p. 206). Because we know that on 29 January Minami Teizō was in Tokyo, Minami Sukematsu's assertion is questionable. But it seems probable that company executives did not agree on the best course of action toward the Shiseikai.

79. Kimura Yoshinosuke, ed., *Kimura Chōshichi jiden* (The autobiography of

Kimura Chōshichi) (Tokyo: privately published, 1938), 313. The actual amount was 1,056,876 yen, to be donated over a five-year period. See *Tokyo asashi shimbun,* 7 December 1906.

80. "Ashio dōzan Ashio machi rōdō shiseikai seidan enzetsukai hōkokusho" (A report of the political meeting held by Shiseikai in Ashio town at Ashio copper mine), in NRUS, vol. 2, p. 192.

81. See *Hara Kei nikki* (The diary of Hara Kei), vol. 3 (Tokyo: Fukumura Publishers, 1965) for 1906: 17 and 30 November, and 1, 4, and 6 December.

82. "Meiji 40 nen 1 gatsu 8 ka rōdō mondai seidan enzetsukai taiyō" (8th January 1907 labor problems campaign meeting), and "Rōdō shiseikai enzetsukai hōkokusho" (Report of Shiseikai public meeting), in NRUS, vol. 2, pp. 195, 197.

83. *Yorozu chōhō,* 7 February 1907, in TKS, 741.

84. *Ashio kyōtō shūshū jiken sōsa hōkokusho sono roku* (Report on the Ashio riot, section 6), and *Sōsa hōkokusho 16* (Criminal investigation report 16), in ibid., 577 and 582.

85. "Tantei hōkokusho" (Detective's report), in ibid., 586.

86. *Kokumin shimbun,* 10 February 1907, in ibid., 723.

87. "Meiji 40 nen 1 gatsu 8 ka rōdō mondai seidan enzetsu taiyō" (8th January 1907 labor problems campaign meeting), and "Shiseikai rōdō mondai seidan enzetsu kai hōkokusho" (Report of the Shiseikai political meeting to discuss labor problems), in NRUS, vol. 2, pp. 196, 203–206.

88. NRUS, vol. 2, p. 196. The record of the decision of the Utsunomiya District Court states that, at the preliminary hearing, Yoneya Ichihei (boss of the No. 8 lodge at Tsūdō) testified that "on 3 January this year all the bosses met to discuss the question of a wage increase and decided to submit a petition on 6 January. In the event of some being forced to quit because of this, it was decided to give them each 500 yen" (TKS, 655).

89. NRUS, vol. 2, pp. 208–209. The end of the document mentions "appending a chart of model daily expenses on a separate sheet." In this were listed details of the apportionment of the 70 sen 8 rin "daily necessities allowance" paid to married workers, which was included in the petition. See p. 321 of the Japanese version of this book.

90. "Jiken sōsa hōkokusho, 6" (Report of the investigations into the incident at Ashio, part 6), in TKS, 577–78.

91. One police investigation report claims that a meeting of the brotherhood was held on 3 January to decide on a petition for a pay increase, with Minami and Nagaoka in attendance (ibid., 557). However, the meeting on the 3rd was in preparation for the next day's assembly, and was attended only by a few assemblymen. Further, it is certain that neither Minami nor Nagaoka attended either meeting. See ibid., 560, 577–78, 690, 695.

92. "Tantei hōkoku sho" (Detective's report), in ibid., 587.

93. "Sōsa hōkoku sho" (Report of the investigation), in ibid., 583.

94. "Tantei hōkoku sho" (Detective's report), in ibid., 594.

95. "Hikokunin Nagaoka Tsuruzō dai ni chōsho" (Defendant Nagaoka Tsuruzō's second deposition), in ibid., 643.

96. "Kōso ikensho" (Statement of appeal), in ibid., 688.

97. "Ashio kyōtō shūshū jiken sōsa hōkoku, 2" (Report of the investigation of the disorders at Ashio, part 2), in ibid, 560–62.

98. "Ashio kyōtō shūshū jiken sōsa hōkoku, 6" (Report of the investigation of the disorders at Ashio, part 6), in ibid., 578.

99. "Meiji 40 nen 1 gatsu 8 ka rōdō seidan enzetsu taikai taiyō" (8 January 1907 labor problems campaign meeting), in NRUS, vol. 2, pp. 194–97.

100. "Hikoku Minami Sukematsu dai yon kai chōsho" (Defendant Minami Suke-matsu's 4th deposition), in TKS, 616.

101. "Ashio kyōtō shūshū jiken sōsa hōkoku, 6" (Report of the investigation of the disorders at Ashio, part 6), in ibid., 578.

102. "Ashio jiken kōhan bōchō ki" (Ashio incident trial report), *Shimotsuke shimbun*, 2 August 1907.

103. "Ashio bōdō jiken Utsunomiya saibanjo hanketsu" (Utsunomiya District Court judgments in the Ashio riot incident case), in NRUS, vol. 2, p. 233.

104. "Ashio kyōtō shūshū jiken sōsa hōkoku" (Report of the investigation of the disorders at Ashio), in TKS, 565.

105. "Ashio kyōtō shūshū jiken sōsa hōkoku, 1" (Report of the investigation of the disorders at Ashio, part 1), and "Hikokunin Minami Sukematsu dai go kai chōsho" (Defendant Minami Sukematsu's 5th deposition), in ibid., 558, 618.

106. "Hikokunin Minami Sukematsu dai go chōsho" (Defendant Minami Suke-matsu's 5th deposition), in ibid., 618.

107. While scholars of labor history have usually described this law of 1900 as a tool to suppress labor organizing and social activism more generally (which in large measure it was), the law in fact treated workers and managers in symmetrical fashion, reflecting the classical liberal European tradition from which it derived. It forbade "violence, threats, public defamation, agitation, or solicitation directed at others" for any of several purposes, including encouraging *or obstructing* entry into an organization intended to take joint actions concerning labor conditions or pay. In theory it thus limited managerial coercion to the same extent that it constrained workers and unions. Nagaoka's behavior offers important evidence that some labor activists understood the law quite well and sought to take advantage of it.

108. "Ashio kyōtō shūshū jiken sōsa hōkoku, 22" (Report of the investigation of the disorders at Ashio, part 22), in TKS, 591–92.

109. "Ishida Kishirō kōhantei chinjutsu" (Ishida Kishirō's statement in court), *Shimotsuke shimbun*, 22 August 1907.

110. "Kōsō iken sho" (Statement of appeal), in TKS, 688.

111. "Meiji 40 nen 1 gatsu 26 nichi rōdō mondai seidan enzetsukai taiyo" (26th January 1907 labor problems campaign meeting), in NRUS, vol. 2, p. 200.

112. Ibid., 202.

113. "Ashio bōdō jiken Utsunomiya saibansho hanketsu" (Utsunomiya District Court judgments in the Ashio riot incident case), in ibid., 233.

114. For details of the lodge charge, see "Kōsō ikensho" (Statement of appeal), in TKS, 682–84.

115. The first trial judgment after the riot notes that in his deposition, Ishida Kishirō stated:

> On the 28th January the box was returned to the assemblymen. Assembly expenses were to be paid out of the lodge charge, but if the assemblymen had demanded that they be paid all the costs of their activities, the 1 yen 50 sen charge wouldn't have covered the cost, so I proposed that the assembly costs and the bathing fee be borne by the miners, and that I would deduct the 18 sen [paid by each man toward] assembly expenses and the 12 sen bathing fee from the 1 yen 50 sen (so the men would pay 1 yen 20 sen). At that point I was invited to a meeting at the lodge on 29 January and asked to accept 80 sen (rather than 1 yen 20 sen). I said I couldn't possibly afford that and told them I would rather they dealt with the matter themselves, I'd had enough, and that afternoon my *hanba* became the only one without a lodge charge system, because I abolished the charge altogether. Ōnishi Saichi was the miners' representative who pressed me to accept the 80 sen level. (NRUS, vol. 2, p. 234)

What emerges from this testimony is that the miners demanded a reduction in the lodge charge, and Ishida responded by abolishing the system itself.

116. Kamata Nobutarō had been a miner from lodge No. 1 at Tsūdō and had a relationship with Ōnishi Saichi that was "by no means shallow." See "Ashio kyōtō shūshū jiken sōsa hōkokusho" (Report of the investigation of the disorders at Ashio, part 24), in TKS, 595.

117. "Kōsō ikensho" (Statement of appeal) in ibid., 681–82.

118. This account and quotations describing the 1 February meeting are taken from "Tantei hōkoku sho" (Detective's report), in ibid., 588–89.

119. See "Ashio kyōtō shūshū jiken sōsa hōkokusho, 1" (Report of the investigation of the disorders at Ashio, part 1), submitted by Police Officer Tamura Kan'noshin to District Attorney Kakihara Takurō, in ibid., 559.

120. The main sources used for the description of the course and the result of the riot are "Dai isshin hanketsu" (First trial judgment), "Kōsō iken sho" (Statement of appeal), and the Ashio mine office document "Ashio dōzan bōdō gaiki" (Outline of the Ashio copper mine riot). This last document includes some very interesting material in that it is, after all, a record of the event seen from the "victim's" point of view. Many newspaper reports of the riot are unreliable. They are mostly based on

hearsay and conjecture rather than on direct reporting, a case in point being reports of events prior to 2 A.M. on 7 February. Many such reports were copied from other newspapers and simply rewritten.

121. See Inspector Kawashima Hyōzaburō, "Dai 4 kai hōkokusho" (Fourth report) to Tochigi Prefecture Police Chief Superintendent Uematsu Kaneaki, in TKS, 575. Regarding Minami's reported use of the phrase "the crimes you have committed," we should remember that this record comes from a police report.

122. "Ashio dōzan bōdō gaiki" (Outline of the Ashio copper mine riot), in NRUS, vol. 2, p. 211.

123. "Shōnin Minami Teizō chōsho" (Testimony of Minami Teizō), in TKS, 551–52.

124. Yasumaru Yoshio, Nihon no kindaika to minshū shisō (The modernization of Japan and popular thought) (Tokyo: Aoki Shoten, 1974), 238–48.

125. "Kanteinin Shinozaki Kōjirō chōsho" (Expert opinion of Shinozaki Kōjirō), in TKS, 555.

126. "Ashio dōzan bōdō gaiki" (Outline of the Ashio copper mine riot) in NRUS, vol. 2, p. 217, and Kokumin shimbun, 6 February 1907, in TKS, 707.

127. Correspondent Nishikawa, "Ashio bōdō shōhō, 6" (Full report of the Ashio disturbances, part 6), in Nikkan heimin shimbun, 9 February 1907.

128. "Keibu, Kawashima Heisaburō yori Tochigi ken dai yon buchō, Uematsu Kaneaki ate, 'Ashio dōzan kyōtō shūshū hikoku jiken sōsa tenmatsu, dai ichi hōkoku'" (Inspector Kawashima Hyōzaburō's "First report into the circumstances of the disturbances at the Ashio copper mine" for Tochigi Prefecture Police Chief Superintendent Uematsu Kaneaki) in TKS, 569.

129. "Tochigi ken dai yon buchō, Uematsu Kaneaki dan" (Interview with Chief Superintendent Uematsu Kaneaki, police division, Tochigi prefecture), in Kokumin shimbun, 10 February 1907, in TKS, 718.

130. Among the "Ashio sōdō jiken ni kan suru kimitsu shorui" (Confidential documents relating to the Ashio disturbances) in the archive of the Utsunomiya district attorney's office is a report addressed to Attorney Mukai Iwao of that office from Uematsu Kaneaki, chief superintendent of police division, Tochigi prefecture, titled "Ashio dōzan rōdōsha no kōdō" (The activities of Ashio copper mine workers). The section marked "Secret—No. 127/1" begins, "As has previously been reported, Minami Sukematsu, founder of Shiseikai," indicating that such reports were continuous and surveillance constant.

131. Ashio Police Chief Fujiyama Sainosuke to Utsunomiya District Attorney Yoshida Keiichi, "Hōkokusho" (Report documents), in TKS, 542.

132. "Ashio sōjō jiken ni kansuru himitsu shorui" (Confidential documents relating to the Ashio disturbances), held in the archive of the Utsunomiya district attorney's office.

133. Nishikawa, "Minami, Nagaoka nado no kōin" (Minami, Nagaoka, and others arrested), *Heimin shimbun*, 9 February 1907. See also telegrams from District Attorney Mukai to the justice minister, the attorney general, and to other district attorneys in "Ashio sōjō jiken ni kansuru kimitsu shorui" (Confidential documents relating to the Ashio disturbances), held in Utsunomiya district attorney's archives.

134. "Kimitsu shorui" (Confidential documents), in ibid.

135. "Ashio dōzan bōdō gaiki" (Outline of the Ashio copper mine riot), in NRUS, vol. 2, p. 215.

136. Ibid.

137. On 6 February the governor of Tochigi prefecture had given the order "to keep swords sheathed at all times" to Police Chief Superintendent Uematsu, who had been sent to Ashio. See *Kokumin shimbun*, 10 February 1907, cited in TKS, 719.

138. "Kimitsu shorui" (Confidential documents relating to the Ashio riot incident), Utsunomiya district attorney's office archive.

139. See ibid. Minami, Nagaoka, and the others had already left Ashio after 1 P.M. on 6 February when they were taken, via Nikkō, to Utsunomiya and remanded in custody some time after 9 P.M. the same day.

140. "Uematsu dai yon buchō no danwa" (Interview with Police Chief Superintendent Uematsu), *Kokumin shimbun*, 9 February 1907, in TKS, 749.

141. "Shihōkan no tonsō" (The flight of the judges), *Kokumin shimbun*, 8 February 1907, in ibid., 711.

142. "Kisha no yukue fumei" (Reporters' whereabouts unknown), *Kokumin shimbun*, 9 February 1907, in ibid., 715.

143. "1896 Tochigi ken keisatsu tōkei" (1896 Tochigi prefectural police statistics) in ibid., 455–56.

144. "Minemura keibu yori Mukai kenjisei ate denwa" (Telephone message from Inspector Minemura to Attorney Mukai), in "Kimitsu shorui" (Confidential documents), in Utsunomi district attorney archives.

145. *Hara Kei nikki* (The diaries of Hara Kei) (Tokyo: Fukumura Publishers, 1965), vol. 3, p. 225 (entry for 7 February 1907).

146. *Yorozu chōhō*, 8 February 1907, in TKS, 742.

147. "Ashio dōzan bōdō gaiki" (Outline of the Ashio Copper Mine riot), in NRUS, vol. 2, p. 218.

148. "Uematsu dai yon buchō no danwa" (Interview with Police Chief Uematsu), *Kokumin shimbun*, 9 February 1907, in TKS, 749.

149. See "Kimitsu shorui" (Confidential documents), dated 27 February 1907, in the Utsunomiya district attorney's office archive.

150. "Kensho chōsho" (Inspection report), in TKS, 544–51.

151. "Ashio dōzan bōdō gaiki" (Outline of the Ashio Copper Mine riot), in NRUS, vol. 2, p. 216.

152. "Ashio dōzan no songai daka" (The cost of damages at Ashio copper mine), *Yorozu chōhō*, 12 February 1907, in TKS, 761. The total cited was 283,062 yen.

153. The tactic of firing the entire workforce and then selectively rehiring those who reapplied was probably picked up by the Ashio management following its first use after a dispute at the Akazawa (Hitachi) copper mine in May 1905. See *Nihon rōmu kanri nenshi* (The Japan labor management chronicle), vol. 2, p. 35.

154. "Ashio dōzan bōdō gaiki" (Outline of the Ashio Copper Mine riot), in NRUS, vol. 2, p. 220.

155. "Ashio dōzan bōdō hōkoku" (Report on the Ashio copper mine riot), "Ashio dōzan bōdō jōkyō" (The circumstances of the Ashio copper mine riot), and "Ashio dōzan sōjō jōkyō" (The circumstances of the disturbances at the Ashio copper mine), in "Kimitsu shorui" (Confidential documents), Utsunomiya district attorney's office archives.

156. "Kōfu no tōta" (Miners weeded out), *Yorozu chōhō*, 14 February 1907, cited in TKS 2, p. 762.

157. "Meiji 40 nen 2 gatsu 12 nichi, hi dai 177 gō, Ashio dōzan bōdō jōkyō" (12 February 1907, secret, no. 177: The situation of the Ashio copper mine riot), in "Kimitsu shorui" (Confidential documents), in Utsunomiya district attorney's office archives.

158. "Meiji 40 nen 2 gatsu 13 nichi, hi dai 177 gō, Ashio dōzan bōdō jōkyō" (13 February 1907, secret, no. 179: The situation of the Ashio copper mine riot) in ibid.

159. Ashio dōzan bōdō gaiki" (Outline of the Ashio copper mine riot), in NRUS, vol. 2, p. 221.

160. "Hi dai 269 gō, Ashio Dōzan bōdō jōkyō" (Secret, no. 269: The situation of the Ashio copper mine riot), and "Hi dai 273 gō, Ashio Dōzan bōdō jōkyō" (Secret, no. 273: The situation of the Ashio copper mine riot), in "Kimitsu shorui" (Confidential documents), in Utsunomiya district attorney's office archives.

161. "Ashio dōzan bōdō gaiki" (Outline of the Ashio copper mine riot), in NRUS, vol. 2, p. 222.

162. "Hi dai 285 gō, Ashio Dōzan bōdō jōkyō" (Secret, no. 285: The situation of the Ashio copper mine riot), in "Kimitsu shorui" (Confidential documents), in Utsunomiya district attorney's office archives.

163. NRUS, vol. 2, p. 228.

164. Nishikawa [Mitsujirō], "Report on the Ashio Riot," *Heimin shimbun*, no. 19 (8 February 1907).

165. "Ashio dōzan no bōdō, dai 10 ho" (The Ashio copper mine riot, 10th report), *Kokumin shimbun*, 7 February 1907, in TKS, 709.

166. See "Shōnin Umatani Shinkichi dai ikkai chōsho" (First protocol of witness Umatani Shinkichi), cited in *Kōsō iken sho* (Statement of appeal), in ibid., 679.

167. One Shiseikai member spoke of how officials had used contemptuous language toward miners:

When I was a miner I was told by clerks that I should regard them as my bosses. . . . when I had finished work one day I went to the pithead cabin to collect my card. There were so many other miners there, it was like trying to buy a ticket at the station. I was very tired and had to wait in the cold which froze my hands and feet, so I got impatient and told the clerk to hurry up with my card. He got really angry and told me to take my headgear off when I spoke to him. He told me I was rude and had no manners. Certainly on that occasion there was something in what he said, but you can understand from this example the kind of high-handed and cold-hearted manner in which officials spoke to us miners. ("Shiseikai rōdō mondai seidan enzetsu kai hōkokusho" [Report of the Shiseikai labor problems campaign meeting], in NRUS, vol. 2, p. 203)

168. "Ashio bōdō jiken Utsunomiya saibansho hanketsu" (Verdict of the Utsunomiya District Court in the Ashio riot incident), in ibid., vol. 2, p. 234.

169. Ibid.

170. Ibid., 228.

171. See "Kōsō iken sho" (Statement of appeal), in TKS, 668–704. For the company view, see "Ashio dōzan bōdō gaiki" (Outline of the Ashio copper mine riot), in ibid., 211.

172. Suge Yoshirō, "Yokka kōnai bōkō no sai kōba fukin jōkyō hōkoku" (Report of the situation in the pithead areas on the Feb. 4 violence in the mines), in "Kōsō ikensho" (Statement of appeal), in ibid., 564, 702.

173. "Rōdō shiseikai enzetsukai hōkokusho" (Report of a Shiseikai public meeting), and "Shiseikai rōdō mondai seidan enzetsukai hōkoku sho" (Report of a Shiseikai labor issues campaign meeting), in NRUS, vol. 2, pp. 198, 204.

174. "Ashio jiken kōhan bōchō ki" (Ashio incident, trial report), *Shimotsuke shimbun,* 4 August 1907.

175. "Ashio jiken kōhan bōchō ki" (Ashio incident, Trial report), *Shimotsuke shimbun,* 13 August 1907, and 16 August 1907.

176. This issue will be dealt with more fully in chap. 2.

177. Inspector Tamura Kan'noshin, "Ashio kyōtō shūshū jiken sōsa hōkoku" (Investigative report into the circumstances of the Ashio riot), in TKS, 565–66.

178. Suge Yoshirō, "Yokka kōnai bōkō no sai kōba fukin jōkyō hōkoku" (Report of the situation in the pithead areas during the violence in the mines on Feb. 4th), in ibid., 564.

179. "Kōsō ikensho" (Statement of appeal), in ibid., 681–86.

180. These details are in the Japanese version of this book, p. 97.

181. "Daisan kai Ashio kōhan" (The third Ashio trial), *Shimotsuke shimbun,* 4 August 1907.

182. "Kōsō ikensho" (Statement of appeal), and "Dai isshin hanketsu" (First trial verdict), in TKS, 685, 657.

183. Inspector Tamura Kan'noshin, "Ashio kyōtō shūshū jiken sōsa hōkoku" (Investigative report into the circumstances of the Ashio riot), in ibid., 565.

184. *Yorozu chōhō,* 9 February 1907, in ibid., 750–51.

185. "Rōdō shiseikai enzetsukai hōkoku sho" (Report of a Rōdō Shiseikai public meeting), in NRUS, vol. 2, p. 197.

186. "Shiseikai rōdō mondai seidan enzetsu kai hōkoku sho" (Report of a Shiseikai labor problems campaign meeting), in ibid., 204–5.

187. "Ashio dōzan no daigi seido" (The representative system at the Ashio copper mine, part 2), *Yorozu chōhō,* 18 February 1907, cited in TKS, 764.

188. Ibid., 765.

189. Takahashi Yūji, *Saikōhō chōsa hōbun* (Survey report on methods of extraction, part 2) (Tokyo: n.p., 1907) 84–85. The average was 56.25 kg. per man, the majority of miners (1442 men out of a total workforce of 10,672) extracting 30 kg.

190. Ibid., 77.

191. An easily accessible account of the wage system in use at Ashio at the time can be found in "Kōsō ikensho" (Statement of appeal), in TKS, 677–79. The description here is based on observation study reports made by two graduating students of Tokyo University's Faculty of Engineering held in the faculty's archive, "Hosoya Genshirō jisshū hōkokusho" (Hosoya Genshirō internship report) (1905) and "Tamaki Nigosaku jisshū hōkokusho" (Tamaki Nigosaku's internship report) (1907), as well as the above-cited Takahashi, *Saikōhō chōsa hōbun* (Survey report on methods of extraction, part 2), 77–93.

192. That is, the height was 6 *shaku,* while the width varied from 1 *shaku* 5 *sun* to 12 *shaku.*

193. It was, of course, possible in theory to pay a different price for the ore from each face, but this would have been extremely complicated to administer, and there were many cases of miners working other men's places or stealing other men's ore. Some miners would gang together and divert ore from low-rated faces to high-rated ones to get a higher price for it.

194. "Kōsō ikensho" (Statement of appeal), in TKS, 677.

195. *Niroku shinpō,* 15 February 1907, in ibid., 768.

196. "Since coming to Honzan, I've heard a lot of talk of bribery, but at Kodaki, there was none" (Court testimony of Yonezawa Yasaburō, *Shimotsuke shimbun,* 6 August 1907).

197. According to the "Bonus and Penalty Regulations for Miners," a year was divided into three periods. If a man was absent for fewer than seven days in any one period (not including public holidays), he received the equivalent of five days' wages. If absent for fewer than ten days, he received the equivalent of three days' wages.

Those who earned such bonuses in each of the three periods were paid a further bonus at the end of the year. There was, however, one condition. The bonus was to be paid to those "who have worked for a designated period without incurring any penalties and who have been earning the daily average amount of pay due to one worker." Penalties for lateness were levied at one-tenth of the daily wage.

198. "Ashio dōzan no daisōdō" (Major riot at Ashio copper mine), *Kokumin shimbun*, 10 February 1907, in TKS, 752.

199. "Sōdō no gen'in, sono 2" (The causes of the riot, part 2), *Kokumin shimbun*, 10 February 1907, in ibid., 720.

200. Tsuru Mineo, "Bōdō shokan (2)," (A view of the riot, part 2), *Niroku shinpō*, 15 February 1907, in ibid., 768.

201. "Ashio bōdō jiken Utsunomiya saibansho hanketsu" (The verdict of the Utsunomiya District Court in the Ashio riot incident), in NRUS, vol. 2, pp. 231–32.

202. These regulations were all laid down in the "Bonus and Penalty Regulations for Miners." The regulations provide for bonuses to be paid only to miners with records of good attendance and long service. Penalties, on the other hand, are dealt with in nine articles and thirty-four clauses, which included penalties for unreported lateness or absence as well as penalizing both those who asked their colleagues to report their absence and the colleagues who did so.

203. The "Miners' Service Regulations" introduced under Minami reduced the number of holidays from the previous twenty-seven days a year (three days each in January, July, and December, and two days in the other months) to just seven days a year: New Year's Day, National Founding Day, the mine guardian shrine festival days (11–12 May), the summer Obon festival, the emperor's birthday, and New Year's Eve. The other twenty days were put on a rotation system.

204. Furukawa Toranosuke biography editorial committee, ed., *Furukawa Toranosuke kun den* (A biography of Furukawa Toranosuke) (Tokyo: Furukawa Mine Co., 1953), 103. An article in *Tokyo asahi shimbun* of 19 February 1907 contains a similar assessment of Minami's character: "Three years ago Minami Teizō replaced Kondo as the mine director. Former bureaucrat that he was, he insisted on strict adherence to regulations. The officials who had been working with the miners now began to behave like bureaucrats and to treat the miners with severity. A violently authoritarian wind from another world began to blow through the mine, which caused anger and resentment among the miners. The riot was not simply over wage increases; the single main cause was the outburst of pent-up fury against the officials' behavior."

205. Furukawa Company, Ashio Copper Mine Mine Workers' Service Regulations, Article 13: "The working day for mine workers shall be 8 hours or 12 hours, although the circumstances of the mine may also require temporary periods of 6 hours to be worked" (*Ashio dōzan zue* [Ashio copper mine pictorial], July 1901).

206. NRUS, vol. 2, pp. 196, 198, 201, 205.

207. David Montgomery, "Spontaneity and Organization: Some Comments," *Radical America* 7, no. 6 (December 1973): 74.

208. Western scholars have pointed out that migrants to the cities, newly arrived from rural areas, did not quickly become involved in riots and other criminal activities. Such behavior occurred only after some time had elapsed, and only after they had moved beyond the small circles of their immediate family and friends. See Charles Tilly, "Collective Violence in European Perspective," in *The History of Violence in America: Historical and Comparative Perspective*, ed. H. D. Graham and T. R. Gurr (New York: Bantam Books, 1969), 9.

209. Nagaoka Tsuruzō, "Kōfu no shōgai" (A miner's life), in Nakatomi, *Nagaoka Tsuruzō den* (Biography of Nagaoka Tsuruzō).

210. For my own view of the character of prewar Japanese trade unionism, see "Kigyō betsu kumiai no rekishiteki haikei" (The background of enterprise-based unions), Hosei University, Ōhara Institute for Social Research, *Kenkyū shiryō geppo* (Monthly research digest), no. 305 (March 1984), and "Nihon rōshi kankei no rekishiteki tokushitsu" (Some historical characteristics of Japanese industrial relations), in *Shakai seisaku gakki nenpō, 31: Nihon no rōshi kankei no tokushitsu* (Bulletin of the Society for the Study of Social Policy, no. 31, The characteristics of Japanese industrial relations) (Tokyo: Ochanomizu Shobō, 1987).

211. My object here is not to present a critique of Maruyama Masao's paradigm itself. But I should nonetheless point out that as an explanation of the characteristics of change in any one society, it is rather too simplistic. Maruyama drew on the work of Abbot Lawrence Lowell, *Public Opinion in War and Peace* (London, 1923), who identified four individual modes of thought or attitude as comprising the range of attitudes in any one society: liberal, conservative, reactionary, and radical. These four modes of thought were based on the two criteria of (1) whether or not people were basically satisfied with the status quo, and (2) whether or not they were optimistic that society could be changed for the better. In response to Lowell's ideas, Maruyama posited that the liberating influence of the process of "modernization" on those living in "traditional" societies produced a variety of "individual attitudes" in reaction, and he attempted to describe all social characteristics in terms of that variety of attitudes. The extent of the effects of modernization is, of course, modified by the individual's occupation and social class. Some individuals remain hardly touched by the modernization process. Maruyama maintains that in early-twentieth-century Japan the pattern of the "atomized individual" was dominant, yet workers in the manufacturing and mining industries accounted for only 5 percent of the total population at the time. His characterization of Japanese society can therefore hardly be said to fit the facts.

212. Philip Taft and Philip Ross, "American Labor Violence: Its Causes, Character and Outcome," in *The History of Violence in America*, Graham and Gurr, 380.

213. Slason Thompson, "Violence in Labor Disputes," *World's Work* (December 1904), cited in ibid.

214. David Brody, "The Expansion of the American Labor Movement: Institutional Sources of Stimulus and Restraint," in *The American Labor Movement*, ed. David Brody (New York: Harper and Row, 1971).

215. Philip S. Foner, *History of the Labor Movement in the United States* (New York: International Publishers, 1964), vol. 3, p. 60.

216. Tomono Sotokichi, *Horonai tanzan bōdō shimatsu* (The Horonai Coal Mine riot) (Tokyo: Miyama shobō, 1975).

217. NRUS, vol. 2, pp. 162–65.

218. Ibid., 127–34.

219. "Himitsu 189 gō: 2/14/1907, Ashio dōzan sōjō jōkyō" (Confidential item 189: 14 February 1907, The current situation in the disturbances at the Ashio copper mine), in "Kimitsu shorui" (Confidential documents), Utsunomiya district attorney's office archive.

220. "Himitsu 206 gō: 2/19/1907, Ashio dōzan sōjō jōkyō" (Confidential item 206: 19 February 1907, The current situation in the disturbances at the Ashio copper mine), in ibid.

221. "Himitsu 300 gō: 3/5/1907, Ashio dōzan sōjō jōkyō" (Confidential item 300: 5 March 1907, The current situation in the disturbances at the Ashio copper mine), in ibid.

222. "9/16/1907, Ashio keisatsu shochō Tadokoro yori Utsunomiya chihō saibansho kenjisei Mukai Iwao ate" (16 September 1907, Report from Ashio Police Chief Tadokoro to Utsunomiya District Court Prosecutor Mukai Iwao), in ibid.

223. That the assemblyman system was abolished at Kodaki by February 1908 at the latest would seem to be indicated by clauses relating to miners' affairs which were appended to the Regulations of the Miners' Hanba Union at Kodaki in that month. See Rōmu kanri shiryō hensan kai, ed., *Nihon rōmu kanri nenshi* (Japan personnel management chronicle, vol. 2) (Tokyo, 1964), 222–26.

224. Nimura Kazuo, "Zenkoku kōfu kumiai no soshiki to katsudō" (The organization and activity of the national miners' union), pts. 1–3, Hosei University, Ōhara Institute for Social Research, *Shiryō shitsu hō* (Resource digest), nos. 109, 168, 185.

225. The boarding fee accounted for three meals a day and two futon quilts.

226. Ōyama Shikitarō, *Kōgyō rōdō to oyakata seido* (Mine workers and the Oyakata system) (Tokyo: Yūhikaku, 1964), 180. I have supplemented this quotation by drawing from *Nihon rōmu kanri nenshi* (Japan personnel management chronicle, vol. 2), 52.

227. Ōyama, *Kōgyō rōdō to oyakata seido* (Mine workers and the Oyakata system), 179.

228. The Ashio management's decision that the company should train new miners was also to be of great significance for the brotherhood, since technical training within the bonds of a master-pupil (*oyabun-kobun*) relationship had been the major

function of the brotherhood. The company's assumption of the training role inevitably led to the decline and ultimate extinction of the brotherhood.

NOTES TO CHAPTER 2

1. The study on which this chapter was based was originally published in 1959.

2. Ōkōchi Kazuo has published a great many books and papers on the migrant labor theory, among which the major ones are: "Chin rōdō ni okeru hokenteki naru mono" (The feudalistic aspects of [Japanese] wage labor), and "'Genshiteki rōdō kankei' ni okeru seiyō to tōyō" ("Primitive labor relations" in East and West), in *Shakai seisaku no keizai riron* (Economic theory of social policy) (Tokyo: Nihon Hyōron Shinsha, 1952); *Reimeiki no Nihon no rōdō undō* (The dawn of the Japanese labor movement) (Tokyo: Iwanami Shinsho, 1952); *Sengo Nihon no rōdō undō* (The postwar Japanese labor movement) (Tokyo: Iwanami Shinsho, 1955); "Rōdōsha no ishiki" (Workers' attitudes), in *Nihon no rōdōsha kaikyū* (The Japanese working class), ed. Ōkōchi Kazuo and Sumiya Mikio (Tokyo: Tōyō Keizai Shinpōsha, 1955); "Rōdō kumiai ni okeru Nihon gata ni tsuite" (On Japanese-style labor unions), *Keizai kenkyū* (Economic studies), 2, no. 4 (October 1951).

3. Ōkōchi, "Chin rōdō ni okeru hokenteki naru mono" (The feudalistic aspects of [Japanese] wage labor), 212.

4. Ōkōchi, *Reimeiki no Nihon rōdō undō* (The dawn of the Japanese labor movement), 3.

5. Ōtomo Yoshio, "Soshiki" (Organization), in *Tōitsu-teki rōdō undō no tenbō* (Prospects for a unified labor movement), ed. Endō Shōkichi, Funahashi Naomichi, Fujita Wakao, and Ōshima Kiyoshi (Tokyo: Rōdō Hōritsu Junpōsha, 1952), 73–74.

6. Funahashi Naomichi, "Rōdō kumiai soshiki no tokushitsu" (The characteristics of labor union organization), in *Nihon no rōdō kumiai* (Japanese labor unions), ed. Ōkōchi Kazuo (Tokyo: Tōyō Keizai Shinpōsha, 1954).

7. Ōkōchi, "Chin rōdō ni okeru hokenteki naru mono" (The feudalistic aspects of [Japanese] wage labor), 216–22, and *Reimeiki no Nihon rōdō undō* (The dawn of the Japanese labor movement), 4.

8. For a recent English-language study arguing that female textile workers of rural origin were not temporary migrants, but tended to settle in cities after leaving their initial employers, see Barbara Molony, "Activism among Women in the Taisho Cotton Textile Industry," in *Recreating Japanese Women, 1600–1945,* ed. Gail Bernstein (Berkeley: University of California Press, 1991).

9. Namiki Shōkichi, "Nōka jinkō no ryūshutsu keitai" (The pattern of rural out-migration), *Nōgyō sōgō kenkyū* (General agricultural studies) 10, no. 3 (July 1956), and "Nōka jinkō no sengo jū nen" (The postwar rural population 1945–55), *Nōgyō sōgō kenkyū* (General agricultural studies) 9, no. 4 (October 1955).

10. Ōkōchi, *Reimieiki no Nihon Rōdō undō* (The dawn of the Japanese labor movement), 153–54, 207–8, 214.

11. The spontaneity theory has already been addressed in chapter 1 of this book. The question of working conditions is taken up in chapter 3 of the Japanese version (not included in this translation). I should point out that the assertion that wages were held down during the Russo-Japanese War is incorrect. Wages rose in the metalworking and engineering industries and especially in military arsenals, although only in return for longer working hours (see Nimura, "Rōdōsha kaikyū no jōtai to rōdō undō" [The labor movement and the economic circumstances of the working class], in *Iwanami kōza: Nihon rekishi* [The history of Japan] [Tokyo: Iwanami shoten, 1975], vol. 18).

12. According to Ōkōchi, the term *primitive labor relations* "refers to a particular phase in the early development of capitalism soon after the industrial revolution when many wage laborers, especially women, children and adolescents were forced to work in factories without any legal protection or any permissible means of autonomous resistance. It was a phase in which labor relations were characterized by low wages, long working hours and, as a rule, authoritarian control allied to status-bound relationships between superiors and subordinates at all levels" (" 'Genshiteki rōdō kankei' ni okeru seiyō to tōyō" ["Primitive labor relations" in East and West], in *Shakai seisaku no keizai riron* [Economic theory of social policy], 184). "This is the period during or just after the industrial revolution, before factory legislation and measures to protect workers' rights enabled the workers to play any part in the determination of labor relations or working conditions," "a category or historical phase of labor relations different from those obtaining prior to the industrial revolution" ("Shohyō: Nihon chinrōdō shiron" [Book review of "The history of Japanese wage labor"], *Keizaigaku ronshū* [Essays in economics] 24, no. 2 [February 1955]). In short, Ōkōchi conceives of three developmental phases in labor relations: (1) the "immature" period of wage labor, when a regime of low wages and long working hours is maintained through noneconomic means; (2) a period when low wages and long hours are maintained through a laissez-faire economic policy made possible by an abundance of wage labor and the introduction of machinery; and (3) a period when low wages and long hours are regulated by factory and industrial legislation. The phase of primitive labor relations corresponds to the second of these three.

13. *Dormitory* would be another possible translation for *hanba*, but because of the centrality of dining in the word itself and in the functions of the system, I feel *lodge* better conveys the sense of the Japanese term.

14. Nōshōmu shō, kōzan kyoku (Ministry of Agriculture and Commerce, Mining Bureau), "Kōfu taigū jirei" (Mine workers' working conditions), reissued by Kyushu sangyō shika kenkyū kai (Kyushu Industrial History Research Group), 1957, 213.

15. The violent manner in which the lodge bosses controlled their men was exemplified in the Takashima coal mine incident, a famous case in which the abusive

treatment of miners was exposed to the public, often cited to illustrate the "slavery" of the lodge system. However, there is reason to believe that this charge of violent, coercive control has been exaggerated. Even under the lodge system, miners moved around frequently. According to the "Mine Workers' Working Conditions," those attached to a lodge boss moved more often than those who were under the company's direct supervision, as the following chart illustrates.

Mines	Mobility of mine workers directly employed by the company		Mobility of lodge mine workers	
	Hired	Left	Hired	Left
Metal mines	60.0%	57.6%	92.4%	85.2%
Coal mines	120.0%	112.8%	148.8%	152.4%
Average	98.4%	90.0%	120.0%	116.4%

Source: "Kōfu taigū jirei" (Mine workers' working conditions), 12. The mobility percentages result from dividing the number of workers moving by the total number of workers registered. In the original document, monthly averages were listed, but those shown above have been revised to show the annual average.

16. Takahashi, *Saikōhō chōsa hōbun.*

17. "Kōfu taigū jirei" (Mine workers' working conditions), 216–24.

18. Kobata Atsushi, *Kōzan no rekishi* (The history of mining) (Tokyo: Shibundō, 1956), 132–77.

19. Itsuka Kai, ed., *Furukawa Ichibei ō den* (The life of Furukawa Ichibei) (Tokyo: Itsukakai, 1926), 108.

20. Ibid., 119.

21. Shigeno Kichinosuke, *Kimura Chōbei den* (The life of Kimura Chōbei) (Shikaban, 1937), 27.

22. Itsuka, *Furukawa Ichibei ō den* (The life of Furukawa Ichibei), 117–18, 119–20.

23. Shigeno, *Kimura Chōbei den* (The life of Kimura Chōbei), 49.

24. Ibid., 53–54.

25. *Kōbu shō enkaku hōkoku* (Report on the development of the Mines Bureau), in *Meiji zenki zaisei keizai shiryō shūsei* (Financial and economic history documents of the early Meiji period), ed. Ōuchi Hyōe and Tsuchiya Takao, vol. 17 (Tokyo: Kaizō sha, 1931), 127–32. With the purchase of these new mines, Furukawa was able not only to procure the latest technology and equipment such as drilling machines and electric pumps, but also to gain the services of the university-educated technicians employed there. Such men were very scarce at the time. The agreement mentioned

here was a commitment to buy all the copper Furukawa was able to produce over a twenty-nine-month period from August 1888 to December 1890. At first negotiations were entered into with a French copper syndicate that was seeking to corner the copper market, but Furukawa drew back from a direct contract with the syndicate and instead signed a contract with the British trading company, Jardine Matheson, which acted as intermediary. The agreement was thus protected when the syndicate collapsed in 1889, and with a stable market and high prices for his copper, Furukawa was able to carry out a rapid modernization of the Ashio mine.

26. Takahashi, *Saikōhō chōsa hōbun.*

27. "Kōfu taigū jirei" (Mine workers' working conditions), 217.

28. Ibid., 206.

29. Ōkōchi, "Chin rōdō ni okeru hokenteki naru mono" (The feudalistic aspects of [Japanese] wage labor), 212, 218.

30. Ōkōchi, *Reimeiki no Nihon rōdō undō* (The dawn of the Japanese labor movement), 12.

31. Ōkōchi emphasizes the lack of a unified labor market, but in fact there was a horizontal labor market for mine workers, and especially for miners, in existence at that time, a point that is discussed further in an appendix to the Japanese version of this book. Ōkōchi argues that a low level of labor stability = high labor mobility, and that both were a product of the migrant labor pattern of labor (*Reimeiki no Nihon rōdō undō* [The dawn of the Japanese labor movement], 13), but there is of necessity a high degree of mobility in a horizontal labor market, and workers tend not to remain with a single company. Ōkōchi's argument is thus questionable on both historical and logical grounds. The factors that, in the mining industry, made necessary a method of labor supply like the lodge system were (1) the extreme deprivation and danger of the working environment compared with those of other industries, (2) the consequent high rate of exhaustion of the workforce and the inevitable high mobility, (3) the difficulty of maintaining a stable workforce in remote mountainous regions, and (4) the need for rapid increases in labor supply to keep pace with an equally rapid expansion of production capacity.

32. Chapter 3 of the Japanese version of this book has a full description of the mechanization and modernization of the ore-dressing and refining operations.

33. The power drills used at Ani and Ashio are discussed in chapter 3 of the Japanese version.

34. "Ashio dōzan kiji" (Report from the Ashio copper mine), *Nihon kōgyō kaishi* (Bulletin of the Japanese Mining Industry Association), no. 25 (August 1885).

35. Karl Marx, *Capital,* trans. Hasebe Fumio (Tokyo: Aoki shoten edition, 1952), vol. 1, p. 865.

36. Ibid.

37. Ibid.

38. One of Furukawa's first moves after purchasing the Ani copper mine from the state was to drop overhand stoping in favor of raccoon digging to boost profits. Concerning this matter, Kimura Chōbei wrote:

The so-called overhand stoping method was in use at the mine at that time. Entire areas of ore-bearing rock were dug whether they were good or not. Both ore and rock were thus carried to the ore-dressing station and sorted mostly by hand, the small lumps being placed on a jigger belt. After I had completed an inspection and returned to the office, I conveyed to Messrs. Kondo and Kozaki, who had accompanied me, my opinion that the method of extraction then being employed was not beneficial, because all the products of extraction were mixed up and sent off to the dressing station, the efficiency of which suffered accordingly. I suggested that good lumps of ore be sorted at the face, placed immediately into sacks and sent off for refining, while the rest could go to the dressing station, thus improving the efficiency of the ore-dressing operation. The two gentlemen thought my idea most interesting. It had not been used thus far, but they considered it to offer such benefit as to warrant immediate implementation, which took place soon after our conversation. (Shigeno, *Kimura Chōbei den* [The life of Kimura Chōbei], 193–94)

39. Itsuka Kai, ed., *Furukawa Junkichi kun den* (The life of Furukawa Junkichi) (Tokyo: Itsukakai, 1926), 78.

40. According to the Furukawa kōgyō kaisha Ashio kōgyōsho (The Furukawa Mining Company Ashio Mine Office), *Saikō geppō* (Mining monthly report).

41. Hiratsuka Masatoshi, ed., *Besshi kaikō 250 nenshi* (250 years of the Besshi mine) (Tokyo: Kabushiki kaishi Sumitomo honsha, 1941), 416–17.

42. Nihon kōgaku kai (The Japan Society of Engineers), ed., *Meiji kōgyō shi: Kōgyō hen* (History of engineering in the Meiji period: Mining) (Tokyo: Nihon Kōgaku Kai, 1930), 183–84.

43. *Kōfu taigū jirei* (Mine workers' working conditions), 213.

44. Karl Marx, *The Communist Manifesto*, in *The Marx-Engels Reader*, ed. Robert C. Tucker (New York: Norton, 1972), 338.

NOTES TO CONCLUSIONS

1. The mining industry employed 214,435 workers in 1907, an increase of 59,460 over 1905 and 26,513 over 1906 (Nimura Kazuo, "Genchikuki ni okeru kōzan rōdōsha sū, 1" (The number of mine workers in the early period of Japanese industrialization, part 1), *Kenkyū shiryō geppō* (Monthly research bulletin), no. 289 (September 1982). I first drew attention to the fallacy of the often-asserted connection between the 1907 recession and the strikes of that year in the 1959 essay that is the basis for chapter 2 of this book. The reason for the persistence of this erroneous view is

probably due to the preconception that disputes and riots are the inevitable result of poverty caused by inferior working conditions. It has simply been assumed, without investigation, that because the strikes and the recession occurred in the same year, they must have been connected.

2. This survey is contained in Sumiya Mikio, ed., *Shokkō oyobi kōfu chōsa* (A survey of industrial workers and miners) (Tokyo: Kōseikan, 1970).

3. This table has been compiled from several different sources, and includes a number of entries of dubious veracity. For example, the dispute at Miike coal mine on 6 February did not actually take place. The Japanese version of this book includes a long discussion, here omitted, of how such a false report found its way into the newspaper. Although one finds such false reports, there are also surely incidents for which documents have not yet been uncovered, or which were never recorded in any surviving documentary source in the first place. In the report on "Mining Industry Trends in 1907," five strikes are listed for which no corroborating information can be found. Table C.1 also shows a number of strikes that did indeed occur, but that do not appear in the surveys carried out by the Ministry of Agriculture and Commerce.

4. *Fūzoku gahō* (The illustrated news) put out a special issue on "The Ashio Riot in Pictures," just as it had done with the Hibiya anti-treaty riot in 1905. The Kansai Moving Pictures Association showed a newsreel about the riot at the Bentenza Theater in Osaka on 4 April 1907 titled "The Ashio Riot from Its Beginnings to the Arrests of the Rioters." See *Osaka asahi shimbun*, 22 April 1907.

5. For an overview of the trial, see Odanaka Satoki, "Ashio bōdō jiken" (The Ashio riot), in *Nihon no seiji saiban shiroku: Meiji (II)* (A historical record of political trials in Japan: The Meiji period, part 2), ed. Wagatsumu Sakae, Hayashi Shigeru, Tsuji Kiyoaki, and Dandō Shigemitsu (Tokyo: Daiichi hōki shuppan, 1969).

6. The low profile of the former Shiseikai activists after their release from jail can be inferred from articles and reports in socialist newspapers such as *Shakai shimbun* and other left-wing publications. Nagaoka evidently found his place working with Katayama Sen, while Minami Sukematsu remained close to the anarchist group.

7. For the National Miners' Union, see Nimura Kazuo, "Zenkoku kōfu kumiai no soshiki to katsudō" (The organization and activity of the National Miners' Union, 1–3), *Hōsei daigaku Ōhara shakai mondai kenkyūjo shiryō geppō* (Hōsei University, Ōhara Institute for Social Research archival report), nos. 159, 168, 185 (February 1970, January 1971, August 1972).

8. On the Nankatsu Labor Association, see Andrew Gordon, *Labor and Imperial Democracy in Prewar Japan* (Berkeley: University of California Press, 1991), 152, 178, 181, 199.

9. *Rōdō shimpō* (Labor news), no. 47 (20 August 1920).

10. Kasumi Sei, "Tero to ka shita Ashio dōzan kaisōroku" (Memoirs of terror at Ashio Copper Mine in 1907), *Kōzan rōdōsha* (Mine worker) 3, no. 11; 4, nos. 1, 2

(December 1922–February 1923). Kasumi Sei is thought to be a pen name for Ishida Yukimasa, former general secretary of the Ashio branch of the Yūikai.

11. *Rōdō* (Labor), no. 163 (5 February 1925).

12. "Nihon Shakaitō kōhō" (Bulletin of the Japan Socialist Party) *Hikari* (Light), no. 22 (25 September 1906).

13. *Heimin shimbun,* no. 28 (19 February 1907). The powerful impression made upon Kōtoku Shūsui by the news of the Ashio riot was recorded by Yoshikawa Morikuni: "When Kōtoku heard the news he was so excited he couldn't control himself; he was constantly in and out of the office, his face quite flushed." See Yoshikawa Morikuni, *Keigyakusei sōshi* (The bleak rebellious years) (Tokyo: Aoki shoten, 1957), 125.

14. The efforts of Nagaoka and the other activists to stop the riot had already been reported in the *Heimin shimbun,* no. 19 (8 February 1907) by the paper's special correspondent Nishikawa Mitsujirō, but Kōtoku merely praised the riot itself.

15. On the streetcar and treaty riots, see Gordon, *Labor and Imperial Democracy,* chap. 2.

16. NRUS, vol. 2, pp. 222–23.

17. On the meaning and significance of this term in this era, which could also be translated "individual dignity" or "personality," see Thomas C. Smith, "The Right to Benevolence: Dignity and Japanese Workers, 1890–1920," in *Native Sources of Japanese Industrialization* (Berkeley: University of California Press, 1988), 261–63.

18. Most issues of *Ashio dōzan kōfu no tomo,* from the first through no. 107 (January 1926), can be found in the archive of Meiji period newspapers and magazines of the Faculty of Law, Tokyo University.

19. *Hara Kei nikki* (The diaries of Hara Kei) (Tokyo: Fukumura Shuppan, 1965), entries for 7 February 1907, 12 June 1907. The head of the Sumitomo family, Sumitomo Tomoito, was the younger brother of the prime minister, Saionji Kimmochi.

20. There were some at that time who felt that new legislation was needed to provide for a complete remodeling of labor-management relations, but how much weight their views carried is unclear. "The cause of the current spate of mine riots seems to be (the demand for) higher wages which results naturally from price inflation. As industrial circles have expressed considerable concern for the future, the Ministry of Agriculture and Commerce is considering ways of ensuring long-term harmony between laborers and employers based on the need for a fundamental reconciliation of the interests of both parties, and is currently investigating the possibility of drawing up legislation which would provide for binding contractual agreements between both parties" (*Osaka asahi shimbun,* 13 June 1907).

21. In this case, "the authorities" in question were not the Ministry of Agriculture and Commerce, which normally supervised mining affairs, but the officials of the Police Bureau of the Home Ministry (*Shakai shimbun,* no. 4 [23 June 1907]).

22. *Osaka asahi shimbun,* 4 July 1907.

23. The cost of maintaining such special constables was borne by private individuals or organizations. They were patrolmen whose duties were specified in the official request made to the authorities. The system is explained in more detail in Naimushō, Keiho kyoku (Home Ministry, Police Bureau), ed., *Keisatsu kyōkasho: keimu hen* (Police manual: Police duties section) (Tokyo: Naimushō, 1938), 35–36. It describes a system whereby "officers are dispatched in response to requests made by banks, companies or private individuals and the costs of the dispatch are borne by those making the request ('Deployment of officers dispatched in response to requests from banks, companies, or individuals, April 1881, Ministry of the Home Directive no. 22'). The response to a request for a dispatch is at the discretion of the police department. The method of deployment of officers to meet the requirements of the request is determined by the police department, and officers remain at all times under the sole direction of the police authorities."

24. Aoki Masahisa, "Nittetsu kikankata sōgi no kenkyū" (Studies of the Japan Railways strike), in *Reimei ki Nihon rōdō undō no saikentō* (The early years of the Japanese labor movement: A reassessment) (Tokyo: Rōdō Junpōsha, 1979), 16.

25. NRUS, vol. 2, pp. 90–91.

26. Suzuki Masayuki, *Kindai tennō sei no shihai chitsujo* (The emperor system and the modern power structure) (Tokyo: Azekura Shobō, 1986).

27. International comparisons help to clarify not only the differences but also the similarities in labor movements. Common features of the production process, for example, led to similarities in labor-management relations and labor movement activity. I indicated in chapter 1 how workplace injuries and problems of safety and health were significant factors in the emergence of outstanding labor leaders. Nagaoka Tsuruzō and Yamamoto Riichirō both joined the Ashio movement prompted by feelings of indignation at the behavior of mine owners whose pursuit of profits ruled out expenditure on safety measures and constantly endangered workers' lives. This situation was surely not unique to Japan, and no doubt accounts for much of the militance of miners, who are particularly exposed to danger on a daily basis, but comparative, cross-national research is needed to substantiate this point.

28. John Rowe, *The Hard-Rock Men* (Liverpool: Liverpool University Press, 1974); Richard E. Lingenfelter, *The Hardrock Miners* (Berkeley: University of California Press, 1974).

29. "Fukoku kyōhei," the slogan of the modernizers of the Meiji era.

30. Suzuki, *Kindai tennō sei* (The emperor system).

31. Mizubayashi Takeshi, "Kinsei no hō to kokusei kenkyū josetsu (1)–(6)" (An introduction to studies of early modern law and the state system, 1–6), *Kokka gakkai zasshi* (Journal of the Academy of the State) 90, nos. 1–2 (1977), and 95, nos. 1–2 (1982).

32. For example, William H. Sewell Jr., *Work and Revolution in France* (Cambridge:

Cambridge University Press, 1980); E. P. Thompson, *The Making of the English Working Class* (London: V. Gollancz, 1963); Herbert Gutman, *Work, Culture and Society in Industrializing America* (New York: Knopf, 1976).

33. Nishi Kazuo, "Kinsei daiku to sono soshiki" (Edo period carpenters and their organization), in *Kōza: Nihon gijutsu no shakai shi: 7* (A social history of Japanese technology), ed. Nagahara Keiji and Yamaguchi Keiji (Tokyo: Nihon Hyōronsha, 1983).

34. Criticism of the brotherhoods was not entirely lacking among mine owners and managers. In the June 1891 issue of *The Bulletin of the Japanese Mining Industry Association,* an essay by Naoi Komakichi of Kuromori mine appeared with the title "Mine Owners Please Read!" It included the following comment: "Among the many workers employed by mine owners, those most likely to form combinations in order to foment trouble are the miners." The writer went on to call for owners to create blacklists, claiming that miners bound by patron-client ties "always easily join forces since they are under an obligation to unite in solidarity with their fellows."

35. Lingenfelter, *The Hardrock Miners,* 83–84.

36. A general discussion of this subject can be found in Nimura Kazuo, "Nihon rōshi kankei no rekishiteki tokushitsu" (Distinctive historical characteristics of Japanese labor-management relations), in *Nihon no rōshi kankei no tokushitsu, shakai seisaku gakki nempō dai 31 shū* (Characteristics of Japanese labor management, annual bulletin of the Association for Social Policy Studies, vol. 31) (Tokyo: Ochanomizu shobō, 1987). For the significance of resentment against discrimination in the history of the Japanese labor movement, see Nimura Kazuo, "Kigyō betsu kumiai no rekishiteki haikei" (The historical background of the enterprise union), in *Ōhara shakai mondai kenkyūjo shiryō geppō* (Hōsei University, Ōhara Institute for Social Research archival report), no. 305 (March 1984).

NOTES TO EPILOGUE

1. Nimura Kazuo, "Japan," in *The Formation of Labour Movements, 1870–1914: An International Perspective,* ed. Marcel van der Linden and Jürgen Rojahn (Leiden: Brill, 1990), vol. 2, p. 678.

2. Clark Kerr and Abraham Siegel, "The Industry Propensity to Strike: An International Comparison," in *Industrial Conflict,* ed. A. Kornhauser, R. Dubin, and A. M. Ross (New York: McGraw-Hill, 1954), 189–212. However, due to limitations in the statistical data, the article did not touch on the turn-of-the-century struggles taken up in this book.

3. Ibid., 191–93.

4. Ibid., 195.

5. Ibid., 196.

6. P. K. Edwards, "A Critique of the Kerr-Siegel Hypothesis of Strikes and the Isolated Mass: A Study of the Falsification of Sociological Knowledge," *Sociological Review* 25, no. 3 (August 1977).

7. Papers submitted in 1989 to the Second International Mining History Congress held in Germany included many with direct and indirect criticisms of the "isolated mass" thesis. See Klaus Tenfelde, ed., *Towards a Social History of Mining in the Nineteenth and Twentieth Centuries: Papers Presented to the International Mining History Congress, Bochum, Federal Republic of Germany, September 3rd–7th, 1989* (Munich: Verlag C. H. Beck, 1992).

8. Alan B. Campbell, *The Lanarkshire Miners: A Social History of Their Trade Unions, 1775–1974* (Edinburgh: J. Donald, 1979), chap. 6, 145–177. Campbell also addresses the issue in an essay in Roydon Harrison, ed., *Independent Collier: The Coal Miner as Archetypal Proletarian Reconsidered* (Hassocks, Sussex: Harvester Press, 1978).

9. G. V. Rimlinger, "International Differences in Strike Propensity of Coal Miners: Experience in Four Countries," *Industrial and Labor Relations Review* 12 (1959): 389–405.

10. Ibid., 400. The well-known American mining labor movement leader Bill Haywood lost his arm in an accident. See Joseph R. Conlin, *Big Bill Haywood and the Radical Union Movement* (Syracuse: Syracuse University Press, 1969).

11. This is a point emphasized by Kerr and Siegel: that the holding of a common grievance against the same opponent, at the same time, in the same place, is a crucial factor in conflict.

12. For the example of American coal mining, see David Brody, "Market Unionism in America: The Case of Coal," in *Labor's Cause: Main Themes on the History of the American Worker*, ed. David Brody (New York: Oxford University Press, 1993), 131–74.

13. Other systems were used, for example in the United States, where there was organized labor resistance to piecework pay or when that system seemed inadequate to provide financial stimulation.

14. For details, see chapter 1, "Problems Posed by the Riot."

15. David Montgomery, *The Fall of the House of Labour: The Workplace, the State, and American Labor Activism, 1865–1925* (London: Cambridge University Press, 1987), 333.

16. Campbell, *The Lanarkshire Miners*, 153.

17. Price V. Fishback, "An Alternative View of Violence in Labor Disputes in the Early 1900s: The Bituminous Coal Industry, 1890–1930," *Labor History* 37, no. 3 (summer 1995).

18. English mine violence frequently took the form of attacks on local shopkeepers, markets, food warehouses, and port food storage, rather than "labor disputes." This

is probably because, unlike in the United States where most mines were in newly developed "frontier" areas, English mines had a long history and were located near villages and towns. Crew has called for mining labor history to distinguish between "frontier" and "nonfrontier" mining regions, a distinction I think is quite important. See David F. Crew, "Rapport: Comparative History of Mining Community," in *Towards a Social History of Mining*, ed. Klaus Tenfelde (Munich: Verlag C. H. Beck, 1992), 55.

19. Fishback, "An Alternative View of Violence in Labor Disputes," 429.

20. Melvyn Dubofsky, *We Shall Be All: A History of the Industrial Workers of the World*, 2d ed. (Urbana: University of Illinois Press: 1988), 37.

21. Fishback, "An Alternative View of Violence in Labor Disputes," appendix A: Chronology of Major Violent Episodes in the Bituminous Coal Industry, 446–56.

22. Jack Barbash, *The Elements of Industrial Relations* (Madison: University of Wisconsin Press, 1984).

23. For an interesting recent elaboration of this position, see Daniel H. Foote, "Judicial Creation of Norms in Japanese Labor Law: Activism in the Service of—Stability?" *UCLA Law Review* 43, no. 3 (February 1996): 635–709.

24. Nimura Kazuo, "Kigyō betsu kumiai no rekishiteki haikei" (The historical background of individual company unions), *Kenkyū shiryō geppō* (Research and documents monthly), Hōsei daigaku Ōhara shakai mondai kenkyūjo (Hōsei University, Ōhara Social Problems Research Institute), no. 305 (March 1984).

25. George Orwell, *The Road to Wigan Pier* (London: V. Gollancz, 1937).

26. Andrew Gordon has aptly stated this demand as "the continued desire for *human* treatment and fuller membership in both society and the enterprise" (emphasis added). See Andrew Gordon, *The Evolution of Labor Relations in Japan: Heavy Industry, 1853–1955* (Cambridge: Harvard Council on East Asian Studies Monographs, 1985), 423.

27. The Taishō era was 1912 to 1926, but the political demarcation "Taishō Democracy" usually indicates the 1918–1932 period.

28. However, these seemingly unified promotion principles are in name only. In actual practice a barrier remains in effect.

29. David Montgomery, *Workers' Control in America* (London: Cambridge University Press, 1979), 12.

30. Campbell, *The Lanarkshire Miners*, 57.

Index

NIMURA KAZUO, a well-known labor historian in Japan, is Professor of Labor History at Hosei University in Tokyo and former director of the Ohara Institute for Social Research at Hosei. He has published extensively in Japanese. This is his first book-length work to appear in English. The Japanese version of this book won the Annual Award for Research Monographs on Labor from the Japan Institute of Labor.

TERRY BOARDMAN has an honours degree in history (1973) from Manchester University, UK, has lived in Japan for ten years, and currently resides in the UK, where he works as a translator, language teacher, and writer.

ANDREW GORDON is Professor of History at Harvard University and an expert in the history of labor in Japan. He is the author of *The Evolution of Labor Relations in Japan* and *Labor and Imperial Democracy in Japan*. He is editor of *Postwar Japan as History* and has recently edited a translation of Kumazawa Makoto's *Portraits of the Japanese Workplace*.

Library of Congress Cataloging-in-Publication Data

Nimura, Kazuo.

[Ashio Bōdō no shiteki bunseki. English]

The Ashio riot of 1907 : a social history of mining in Japan / Nimura Kazuo ; edited by
Andrew Gordon ; translated by Terry Boardman and Andrew Gordon.

p.   cm.

Includes index.

ISBN 0-8223-2008-8 (cloth : alk. paper). — ISBN 0-8223-2018-5 (paper : alk. paper)

1. Copper miners—Japan—Ashio-machi—Political activity—History.   2. Labor
disputes—Japan—Ashio-machi—History.   3. Wages—Copper miners—Japan—Ashio-
machi—History.   4. Quality of work life—Japan—Ashio-machi—History.   5. Ashio-
machi (Japan)—History.   I. Gordon, Andrew.   II. Title.

HD8039.M72J3513   1998

322.4'4'0952132—dc21   97-24268